Tom Murphy
Plays: One

Famine, The Patriot Game, The Blue Macushla

'The most distinctive, the most restless, the most obsessive imagination at work in the Irish theatre today is Murphy's.' Brian Friel

'The excellence of Mr Murphy's play does not, of course, derive from the fact that it expresses deeply humanitarian feelings ... The distinctive feature of *Famine* is that it does not preach at all. It is an almost perfect parable that can speak for itself.' *The Sunday Press*

The Patriot Game is concerned with the Easter Rising of 1916 in Dublin and *The Blue Macushla* uses the gangster movie genre as a metaphor for a play about Ireland in the 1970s.

Tom Murphy's work includes the internationally acclaimed *A Whistle in the Dark* (Theatre Royal, Stratford East, 1961, Long Wharf Theatre, New Haven, Connecticut and New York; Royal Court, London 1989), *Famine* (Peacock Theatre, Dublin, 1968, Royal Court, London 1969), *Bailegangaire* (Druid Theatre Company, Galway, 1985, Donmar Warehouse, London 1986, BBC Radio 1987) winner of the Harvey's Best Play Award and the Sunday Tribune Theatre Award 1985–6, *Too Late for Logic* (Abbey Theatre, Dublin, 1989), *The Patriot Game* (Peacock Theatre, Dublin, 1991), and *The Gigli Concert* (Abbey Theatre, Dublin 1983 and 1991 and Almeida Theatre, London, 1992). He was born in Tuam, County Galway. During the sixties he lived in London and now lives in Dublin. He is a member of Aosdána and the Irish Academy of Letters.

TOM MURPHY

Plays: One

Famine
The Patriot Game
The Blue Macushla

with an introduction by the author

Methuen Drama

METHUEN WORLD CLASSICS

This edition first published in Great Britain 1992
by Methuen Drama
an imprint of Reed Consumer Books Ltd
Michelin House, 81 Fulham Road, London SW3 6RB
and Auckland, Melbourne, Singapore and Toronto
and distributed in the United States of America
by Heinemann, a division of Reed Publishing (USA) Inc
361 Hanover Street, Portsmouth, New Hampshire. NH 03801 3959

Reissued with a new cover design 1993

ISBN 0–413–66570–4

A CIP catalogue record for this book is available from the British Library

The front cover shows *Head of a Boy* (1970) 16″ × 20″ oil on canvas by
Louis le Brocquy (Private collection).

Photoset by Wilmaset Ltd, Wirral
Printed and bound in Great Britain
by Cox & Wyman Ltd, Reading, Berkshire

Contents

Tom Murphy:
A Chronology

Introduction

The three plays contained here come together because of a political-historical factor. It does not follow necessarily, however, that what gives cohesion to a volume gives it its content. Plays suffer because of labels.

I am perhaps labouring the point but, in relation to these and other plays of mine, I have had to declare on several occasions that I have no politics whatsoever, good, bad, indifferent. A lie, of course. There is no such thing as an apolitical person. But I have had to protect myself from tedious, linear discussion and, hopefully, the plays from abstractionist logicians who would, given the whiff of an ism, reduce a tapestry to a single thread.

In writing a play I attempt to create or recreate the *feeling* of life; *ideas* follow and are developed as appropriate: this is a bonus. Why I should want first and foremost to create or recreate the feeling of life is a good question. I am tired of being victim to feeling and would through my characters wrest autonomy for myself, create a new power? I don't know. Perhaps I simply resent waking in the morning to the whim of existence that has already decided I am in good mood/I am in bad mood/I am in-between and, though I cannot do a blessed thing about whatever the allotted state, I can retaliate, declare to whimsical existence, 'Look, I can do it too!'

There are three broad approaches from which one can look at *Famine* and its genesis. It is historical and, I believe, accurate in the historical facts that it presents to the degree of my ability and my judgement in writing a play of this kind. It is autobiographical, the subject offering me the opportunity to write about myself, my private world and my times. It has, as a play, a life of its own and, tired of history, tired of me, it continues its own process of discovery to its own conclusions, now with me, the author, not in the ascendancy but in pursuit.

The Famine in Ireland in the 1840s was and is the greatest punctuation mark in Irish history. It stopped the Irish race in its tracks. Nature, politics and the victims themselves joined in a conspiracy to ensure its magnitude. Exact records were not kept, were not possible, but it is estimated that there was a loss of two and a half million people. (A million and a half died of hunger, its attendant diseases and fever; a million emigrated. The census population in 1841 was 8,175,124. Though, 'officers engaged in relief work put the population as much as 25 per cent higher'. [*The Great Hunger.*] The population is usually given as circa nine million.)

I first read the facts of the Irish Famine in Cecil Woodham Smith's book, *The Great Hunger*. I was living in London at the time and I believe that that geographical distancing from my roots both objectified and personalised what might otherwise have been a purely emotional, racial response.

The Great Hunger was a major event in the publishing world (1962) and I expected it to inspire a half-dozen plays on the subject of the Irish Famine. I'm still surprised that they did not materialise. In the next couple of years, for my part, the only thing that happened was a call from an out-of-work actor friend who was prolific in ideas for projects for Broadway and whose present one was that he had found a brilliant young musician who would, if I did the libretto, write the music for a big musical to be called *The Great Hunger*.

Another couple of years on, I started to research the Irish Famine: histories, memoirs, accounts. In fiction I read William Carleton. Carleton, 'the first Irish peasant writer' had set one of his novels, *The Black Prophet*, in earlier famine times and, as well as being a great read, his *Traits & Stories of the Irish Peasantry* is a mine of social history.

Research tends to perpetuate itself and postpone the writing and, to achieve balance I told myself, I went further afield, to Europe. By no means was Ireland the only place stricken by famine in the mid-nineteenth century. Among other things, I found a book translated from the French, a moving account of famine among the Eskimos in the 1840s; its title, too, was *The Great Hunger*. (The Irish, in the Gaelic, referred to the Famine as 'an t-ocras mór', the big or great hunger; the Eskimos used the same phrase in their language.)

I bought newspapers and magazines for the contemporary scenes of starvation. I read about a famine that was said to be, for three years, raging in Bihar. In one of the Sunday newspapers, a cross Mrs Ghandi was declaring that, contrary to what was believed and much as it might disappoint people, there was no famine in Bihar. Her story was, perhaps, the correct one. But now, as was pointed out, the astonishing thing was not the existence or non-existence of famine in Bihar but that there should be any doubt in the matter. Another interesting one, again involving India, was when the USA offered to ship its vast surplus of grain to India: then it was discovered that no system of transport could be devised to distribute it. (And how India or Pakistan could mobilise overnight if one declared war on the other! How things are done today in the Gulf!)

And the medieval 'Anti Christ' re-emerged in Northern Ireland.

This research, and more, has found resonance in *Famine*.

Perhaps simultaneous with the research but more than likely when the actual writing started, consciously or unconsciously, the thought was emerging that the absence of food, the cause of famine, is only one aspect of famine. What about the other 'poverties' that attend famine? A hungry and demoralised people becomes silent. People emigrate in great numbers and leave spaces that cannot be filled. Intelligence becomes cunning. There is a poverty of thought and expression. Womanhood becomes harsh. Love, tenderness, loyalty, generosity go out the door in the struggle for survival. Men fester in vicarious dreams of destruction. The natural exuberance and extravagance of youth is repressed . . . The dream of food can become a reality – as it did in the Irish experience – and people's bodies are nourished back to health. What can similarly restore mentalities that have become distorted, spirits that have become mean and broken? Or, what price survival?

Even assuming it to be true, it would be foolish to suggest that the moodiness of the Irish personality that is commented on – we blow hot, we blow cold, swing from light to black, black to jet black – stems solely from the Famine, as it would be foolish to suggest that the Irish race was a singularly warm, wild and happy one in pre-Famine times. But Famine is a racial memory, it provides a debilitating history and that it has left its mark I have no doubt. And, consciously or unconsciously, rightly or wrongly, another thought/ feeling was emerging: Was I, in what I shall call my times, the mid-twentieth century, a student or a victim of the Famine? It was that thought/feeling, I believe, that made me want to write the play, the need to write about the moody self and my times.

Though I can boast grand moments of under-privilege in my childhood and upbringing, I was fed and, so, I cannot boast that I was altogether blighted. I was respectable. The people in my times were not mean, they were respectable. We were unnaturally docile and obedient. Only the bank-manager and the three-card-trick man wore a moustache or suede shoes. The powers that ruled over us – the institutions, offices and officers – didn't want trouble and neither did we. We called them, then as now, 'The Authorities'. We were a suspicious and secretive people, shameful of the universal conditions that apply to humankind. Everyone had a sense of inferiority. We were smug about Catholicism, the one true Church. There were occasions when undefined, ingrowing resentment festered into rage and erupted in violence but it was mindless stuff ultimately, more self-destructive than destructive. Breaking from the norm too, occasions when words and the mouths that said them became distorted, sounded and looked ugly, as if at war with their messages, counsel to meekness, obedience, self-control. And though the Blessed Virgin had the right ear of God, still, the greatest moral law of all was sometimes broken when a boy and girl stayed out all night together – in the race course in my hometown. The Church authorities did their damnedest about that kind of thing but, in that kind of thing, contrary to exaggerated reports, their job was not so all-consuming or demanding: staying out all night in a race course is exceptional behaviour, as can be imagined. Undoubtedly, the Irish Catholic Church was and is very hot on sex but I do not leave the Irish, sexual preoccupational malady entirely on its doorstep, or the enigma of the great many bachelors about in my times who appeared to be sexless rather than being sexually repressed by any church or institution.

Eamon de Valera, an Taoiseach (Prime Minister), in a famous, much-commented on speech, saw us as a happy people, enjoying frugal comforts, with comely maidens dancing at the crossroads. Actually, the comforts were often better than frugal and the comely maidens, though dancers, wouldn't be seen – as some of their great-grandmothers had been seen? – dead at the crossroads. We danced in ballrooms and, depending on the answer to 'What do you do?' we fell in love.

We didn't complain; we conformed. Nobody wanted 'to go getting their names up'. 'Be wise' could be said to be the slogan of the times. A boy aged twelve – maybe a little more – stole a shilling from the chemist shop where he worked as a messenger-boy. He was interrogated by 'The Authorities' and further interrogations were forthcoming. He stole a tin of rat-poison out of the same chemist shop, ate it, and died. Only one person in a town of 5,000 people, a woman, complained to 'The Authorities' about it. The system appeared to be working.

The system worked. Emigration was happening on a grand scale.

Most families were touched by it; some were decimated, as was mine. (The census population for the Republic in 1951 was 2,960,593, in 1961 it was 2,818,341.) Consciousness of disease was intense. TB was the dreaded one. In retrospect it is amusing. I was into manhood when I discovered one day that momentary alarm had overtaken me at what I was reading. Germs can issue from a mouth at 20,000 miles per second – or some such incredible speed said *The Reader's Digest*. It was chance, mere luck that had saved me from such determined velocity, not the cunning strategems I had employed. Oh, the need to write about the self – and to conceal the privacies!

There was consciousness of education too and it could be had free if the money wasn't there to pay for it. The teachers, mainly clerics, celibates, so understanding in their willingness to waive fees but so starved of affection in their own lives behaved, with few exceptions, in a brutal manner to the children in their care.

There was another mythology – not de Valera's. Well, maybe it was – about the Travelling People ('Tinkers') who lived in makeshift tents on the roadside. They never used bad language, they were strictly monogamous, and so on. School friends from outlying areas used to talk about passing these tents. I heard a school friend one morning say that he had seen an infant's legs covered with hoar and frost sticking out from under a monogamous tent. Later in life, a man of the Travelling People told me that they had a phrase, 'Fuck or freeze'.

As children, when our street-games went wrong, better than four-letter words of insult to one another was 'Pauper'. Or 'Tinker'.

Pause for a moment for relief. I should have said at the start that of course there were good times. My eldest brother once told me that I've got it wrong, that I exaggerate. I asked him did he ever dance with a comely maiden at a crossroads. He said he did, often. He was seventeen years older than me; he emigrated in 1939; his first visit home was twenty years later; his equivalent to my times would have been the 1930s. I don't know about the 1930s, so, maybe he did. I hope he did, often.

But I'm talking about famine. My father was a quiet man, fond of hunting, shooting and fishing. He was a very resourceful man. He kept a great vegetable garden. He was a carpenter by trade. A dominant memory of him, prior to his emigrating, is of a man making coffins in his workshop. Sometimes he had to make one of a Sunday – an emergency, I suppose, or a work of mercy; sometimes the coffins were for children. I understand, but I'm surprised that he did not emigrate earlier. I used to play with the shavings and I loved the smell of pine.

Almost up to manhood I used to visit an uncle who lived alone on his farm in the country. Though he had cutlery and a dresser filled with shining delph, he used his thumbnail to peel a potato – one hand, expert as a sculptor. I was ashamed of that. I used to accompany him to the post-office-cum-pub to collect his pension and meet his pensioner friends. They too had thumbnails and – or so it appeared to me – were bachelors. It was a great supplementary education but I was mostly bored to death, no matter what the perks. They enjoyed these soirées, joking about diverse subjects, from cutting turf to India to handball to their confusion as to whether they were dreaming or not when people they knew gathered round the bed at night, which was 'comical'. Some of them, like my uncle, taciturn, monosyllabic grunts; others, babbling and piping, perhaps in incipient senility.

A few years after my mother was widowed and living alone, I asked her to come and live with me and my family in London, or, to take her pick, live with one or another of her children. Her reply was quiet, she could have been reflecting aloud to herself, and was perhaps made strange by the fact that the conversation was happening in the small hours of the morning: 'I was born here, I'll die here and I'll rot here.' It gave me a shiver; simultaneously, it excited me and I felt an immense pride in her.

John Connor and Mother in *Famine* are not my mother and father but the influence will be obvious. Consciously and unconsciously, in the writing of the play, while aware of the public event that was the Irish Famine in the 1840s, I was drawing on the private well and recreating moods and events, apprehensions of myself and my own times.

And, incidentally, in terms of the dialogue, my problems were no more, no less than in writing plays set in modern times.

The main characters are as rounded as I could make them; they are each given further individuality by having a dominant line to follow in their attempts to survive. Mother tries to live by facing the reality of what is happening; Mickeleen, literally, by spite (until, unfortunately for himself he becomes interested in John Connor's so-called 'moral right'); Liam, the most reasonable of them all, by his natural intelligence; Dan, by conversation – he is alive as long as he can hear himself talking; and so on. It was difficult in the usual way of writing to bring this along, but nothing so difficult as John Connor.

The main thrust of the emerging story was beginning to hang on John Connor and I didn't know that I wanted that; as a lifeline he was choosing a form of pacifism: I didn't know that I wanted that either. Considering the scale of the calamity, I suppose I did not think him grand enough for special attention; and I suppose, too, that my personal sense of outrage was not what I thought it to be – controlled – and he was not sufficient to it. I resisted him; the play went on insisting: I looked elsewhere for an alternative, to characters who did not make the end of a draft and, for instance, to the violent (and psychopathic?) Malachy. (In one draft I promised Maeve to Malachy – as a sort of reward, I suppose, for his violent retaliatory course of action.) The play – and Malachy – refused.

My problem with John Connor, I now consider, was that he appeared to be too *ordinary*. He is not stupid, but Liam, Mother and Mickeleen are all more intelligent. He is a reluctant leader; leadership embarrasses him, impels him into outbursts of unreasonable resentment and into retreats of moody introspection. He is a physical force man, one of the 'mad and vicious Connors' who would, if it came to a confrontation (it nearly does at one point) be more than a match for Malachy. He is expected to come up with a 'brave' plan, instead of which he espouses a pacifist line. (Yes, good drama: he is now 'at war' with the crisis and also with his own nature.) But he is *not* a moral man. Or moral in the sense that we know it. He espouses a pacifist line *for himself*. Increasingly he is now declaring he must do only 'what's right', inures himself in this abstract which, at best, he only half-comprehends, gobbledygooks and blusters about it to compel himself to swallow it. All the while, Mother, his wife, can only look reality in the face, use her practical resources, which include stealing, to protect him and her family. He appears to be blind to that, even refusing to acknowledge the ruin that literally gathers around him. Instead, he begins to affect a drunken regality and presents himself as a man invested in some greater truth.

I didn't understand him. And plays I had seen and read – epic plays – appeared to be unrelentingly consistent and grand in movement and main character. John Connor in my play, by comparison, appeared to be contradictory, selfish, dishonest, questionable rather than questioning – ordinary. Still, I didn't like those other plays I had seen and read!

It is easy for a writer to become a snob, feel superior to his material. Had I thought of going back to my own times – or to anybody's times

– I *might* have found a solution. I might, for instance, have thought of demonstrators protesting, marching for their rights without *necessarily* knowing *what rights*; yes, having a day out as well, but *marching*; people marching in Corpus Christi processions without necessarily believing in Christ, his Body or his Bride, the Church: but, nevertheless, *marching – for something*. Or I might have remembered gathering with others as spectators to see the 'Tinkers' seemingly mindlessly and, yes, drunkenly, beating up one another, or to see one of them brutally beating up his wife, then strutting and marching about, arms and legs splaying in displaced exhibition, eyes bulging in defiance. Defiance of what? Morality, is it? Outraged, bewildered humanity, looking for something better than itself?

The contradictions and the complexities – the extremes – in people who are ordinary and who are abject.

I didn't go back to anybody's times for the resolution to my problem with John Connor (and consequently with the whole play), rightly so. A play is a play and it must have its say. The creative process consists mostly of sustained, intensive, plodding work that runs itself to earth every now and again. Then follows the full stop, the writer can't go on. Perhaps, perhaps, perhaps, this is interpreted as an act of humility on the part of the conscious mind and, in acknowledgement or as a reward, a higher authority enters. The play, or call it, inspiration. A moment of inspiration, magical to the writer can be meaningless to everyone else. In the case under consideration a moment happened one day in the form of two words combining, 'sacred' and 'strength'. No one as far as I know who has read or seen, acted in or directed *Famine* has commented on 'sacred strength' and there is no reason why anyone should. It is a matter between the writer and the play; and the thrill, or at least part of it, is in the surprise of the obvious. It is not necessarily infallible, but 'sacred strength' made thrilling sense to me, artistic and otherwise. John Connor stumbles on to his sacred strength: he dresses it in cant because he does not understand it: it is an instinct to survival, above morality as we know it, a resource greater than his own mere existence or his family's existence, so elemental that it is sacred.

These rare moments do not resolve everything, of course, but when they happen the writer continues the plodding pursuit with greater respect for the characters and the play.

As well as refusing Malachy romance with Maeve, the play deliberately refused to conclude Malachy's story. It took me some time to come to terms with this too. 'Some say Malachy is dead too: I don't know. Some say he's in America, a gang to him.' is the last reference to Malachy in the play. The line is loaded, albeit in subtext. Malachy is alive but the action of the play cannot accommodate all of his story because he is the violent *consequence* of famine. (As the play's different levels began to find the overall balance, I saw Malachy as a foretaste of the atrocities that were to follow in the Land Wars; I saw him, also, as a precursor in a direct line that led to Michael Collins, the great, decisive, guerilla leader who came seventy-or-so years later.) And, of course, Malachy is the personification of a revenge-theme taken up by other characters. Or, he has gone to America where, like other Irish emigrants, he becomes a gangster and fathers gangsters, like Shotgun Kelly or Legs Diamond – Capone-like. Whichever, he is a violent part of the future.

I don't particularly like 'messages' and I did not set out to say that the result of a shameful present is a violent future; it can hardly be said to be novel. I agree with it, of course; the play keeps coming up with it. (Even – though undesignedly – anticipating the outbreak of hostilities in Northern Ireland.) The Parish Priest, a sophisticated and educated man, finds it difficult to sustain his belief in idealism in view of the inhumanity he sees about him. Maeve's tears at the very end of the play represent hope, her line prior to his, however, is, 'There's nothing of goodness or kindness in this world for anyone but we'll be equal to it yet.' She is a sixteen-year-old girl. And, though senile, the affable Dan turns the loving Redeemer on his head: 'As Jesus was noble and denied he has long since been repaying the closed doors to him in Bethlehem!'

Finally, on *Famine*. I don't think that a play can do 'justice' to the actuality of famine: attempting to acknowledge that belief, and in writing-instinct, I concluded the action in spring 1847. The historical worst was yet to come, Black '47.

The Patriot Game is documentary drama. Its first aim is to tell the story of the Easter Rising in 1916, Dublin. Its theme is nationalism. The mystical conception behind the Rising was that the soul of Ireland could be redeemed in a blood sacrifice. It has been called a poets' rising. The insurgents – what amounted to a handful – seized central Dublin buildings, the Irish Republic was proclaimed and after a week of fighting came the surrender. The seven signatories of the Proclamation were executed as well as nine other leaders. The attitude of the populace, previously hostile to and derisive of the Rising, now turned to veneration.

It is natural and healthy to re-examine history but the hypotheses of what-might-have-happened-otherwise-had-the-Rising-not-happened by present-day revisionists remain − hypotheses. It happened. The swiftness with which the Irish government celebrated the 75th anniversary of the Rising, last year, 1991, is difficult to understand. It was the birth of the Irish nation. I believe in the individuality of races and cultures *and* I believe in internationalism; they are not contradictory. I believe that nationalism is an elemental and dangerous emotion, intrinsic to us all: but I believe that it is more dangerous not to acknowledge it or to pretend otherwise.

Thirteen young actors under a brilliant young director were brought together by the Abbey Theatre to perform the play. In a revival the company was reduced to nine. Nine actors appears to be the ideal: the cleaner matters become, the more compelling the ritualistic formality and declamatory nature of the piece.

The Famine and the Easter Rising are chapters in Irish history, the 1970s, in which *The Blue Macushla* is set, is a page. The 1970s was a period of comparative economic prosperity, the flow of emigration had stopped, Ireland joined the EEC. The level of sensational crime was high. This was due to a spill of violence from Northern Ireland and to ambivalent politics.

I returned to live in the Republic in May, 1970 after an absence of nine years abroad. An early experience following my return happened at a social gathering in the lounge of an hotel. Two men came in and started throwing their weight about for no good reason. I was told that they were Special Branch men of the Garda (Police). I wouldn't believe it at first: 'Special', to me, meant sophistication, greater finesse, intelligence. My *naïveté* was laughed at. Some time later I was driving in the heart of Dublin and a battered-looking car came alongside me: a fierce-looking man in civvies in the passenger seat was shouting at me, animal rage on his face, gesturing at me to stop, for no good reason. I stopped eventually, choosing the very middle of the street rather than pulling into the side: the more public, the more protection, I considered. For no good reason? I thought that the violent-looking man and the driver of the battered car must be the IRA and my politics had caught up on me. (I had expressed my revulsion of the IRA many times, mainly in pub-analysis.) It transpired that they, too, were the Garda's Special Branch. Whoever, whatever they wanted, fortunately for me, I was not it. The experience left me shaken, as it did my passenger. (I reported the above incidents to a minister I was acquainted with. He told me he wouldn't hear a bad word about a member of the Garda Force. It has since been established that the Garda were out of control in the 1970s 'at times'.)

I received a telephone call one night from a man who said he was a friend of a friend of mine; he said he wanted to discuss a matter, one that couldn't be talked about over the phone. I asked him over. A young man arrived, quietly self-congratulatory in the discovery of a cause. He was in touch with the IRA and had proposed my name to them as the writer of the TV documentary they were planning, to be released on St Patrick's Day, next year, in America. It is possible that he was living a cloak-and-dagger fantasy, but not probable. Whatever, he was sitting in my home, a gently-spoken bank clerk, like a man holding the cards, asking me to write a script for the Provos. I had heard about the sinister visitations. I didn't know how to deliver my direct 'no'; instead, I went into a rigmarole about the distinctions between the prose writer and the playwright, the creative writer and the commentator and that a documentary required skills that I did not possess, the skills of a journalist. He had my measure, I felt, smiled, but went into the night.

The foregoing are a few of the few personal experiences I had while going about my business; they are significant only in that they represent a type of genetic material for a play that, as yet, was nowhere in my mind. The bigger scene, which I absorbed rather than followed or studied, was as follows.

The troubles that had started with a civil rights protest march in Northern Ireland (1969) had escalated. Protestants and Catholics were at war again, the Protestants were called Unionists, the Catholics were now being called Republicans, Protestant Unionists and Catholic Republicans, to protect themselves from each other, formed para-military organisations, the UDA and the IRA respectively, these (as did the legitimate political parties) split and splintered into clones, their protective purposes now, sometimes, going into protectionism and other rackets; the British Army, including the SAS, came in to protect everyone; the CIA was believed (by the Unionists) to be in there also . . . Nothing was transparent. These events in Northern Ireland did not have to go far to spill into the Republic.

In the month of my return to Ireland (May, 1970) the 'arms trial' was happening. Two ministers of the Fianna Fail government were dismissed from the cabinet; they were then arrested on a charge of conspiracy to import arms for the IRA; they denied the charge and, after conflicting evidence under oath, they were found not guilty. The general belief in the country was that the alleged charge had taken place. (Fianna Fail in sub-title calls itself 'The Republican Party', meaning, as per the Constitution, an All-Ireland Republic; the party was born out of the Old IRA; elements within Fianna Fail retain 'an each-way bet on force'.)

Nothing was transparent in the Republic. The IRA were the baddies but who were the goodies? The populace was confused. Who was who and who was doing what in the country? There followed a celebration of deviousness. Criminal elements and opportunists took advantage of the situation. Though not on the scale of what was happening in Northern Ireland, but sensational in the Republic, there was a series of shootings, bombings, kidnappings, jail-escapes, bank robberies. The IRA went into Dublin slums and expressed sympathy at the conditions there; their visits were appreciated, no one else seemed to care. The bizarre detail too – though not an unprecedented phenomenon: the arrival of the occasional English figure on the scene, with English pedigree, to espouse the cause of Irish freedom; said to be political too, later: the disappearance of the famous race-horse, never to be recovered. There was much drunken talk about guns. The police force was out of control 'at times'.

In late 1976 I decided to take time off from writing to do other things. I wrote and read nothing during the next couple of years. One of my main sources of recreation was watching old movies on TV, preferring the gangster *genre*. There were 'foreign' films too (Fritz Lang's German-made *M*, for instance) but it was mainly James Cagney, Pat O'Brien, Edward G Robinson, Humphrey Bogart. I enjoyed the recurring situations, the recurring plots. Two poor kids from the gutter; they grow up and one becomes a gangster, one becomes a priest. The recurring characters: as well as the gangster and the priest-type, there was the overweight, urbane, phlegmatic one, the little guy with the hat who acted like a big guy, the big guy with the little brain, the *femme fatale* who, for all her hard-bitterness, would prove to be truer than the other woman who was *really* up to no good, who was a society or foreign dame. And the rapid-talking dialogue.

Two years of time off and doing other things were more than enough for me and, in the absence of another idea and to wean myself back to writing, I thought I'd like to put a live gangster movie on the stage. I launched myself into a draft without any idea of where I was going. I wanted to have fun. And, well, playwrighting is discovery in the process of doing. I don't remember what I discovered in the draft – perhaps that I had shot the bolt on the idea of putting a live movie on the stage. I knew that gangsterism in movies did not spring gratuitously out of the ground, that it had come out of American culture; I don't remember when it was I realised that I had discovered in it an apt metaphor for a play about Ireland in the 1970s.

Famine

To the memory of Jack and Winifred Murphy

Famine was first produced at the Peacock Theatre, Dublin, on 21 March 1968, with the following cast:

JOHN CONNOR	Niall Tóibín
MOTHER, his wife	Geraldine Plunkett
MAEVE	Máire Ó Néill
DONAILL	Francis O'Gorman
DAN O'DEA	Micheál Ó Briain
HIS WIFE	Máire Ní Gráinne
LIAM DOUGAN	Patrick Laffan
MARK DINEEN	Niall Buggy
BRIAN RIORDAN	Patrick Dawson
FATHER HORAN	Joe Dowling
MALACHY O'LEARY	Seamus Newham
MICKELEEN O'LEARY	Eamon Morrissey
FIRST POLICEMAN	Seán Mac Philip
SECOND POLICEMAN	Seamus Brennan
CLANCY, a merchant	Patrick O'Callaghan
CAPTAIN SHINE, a landlord	John Kavanagh
MR SIMMINGTON, an agent	Patrick Layde
FATHER DALY, Parish Priest	Peadar Lamb
JUSTICE OF THE PEACE	Harry Brogan
PARSON	Desmond Ellis
THE ENGINEER	John Richardson

Famine figures: Eoin White, Robert Browne, Gerald Woods, Dervla Mulloy, Biddy McGrath, Leslie Lawlor, David Byrne, Terry Farrelly, Mary Carlisle, Máiréad Rafferty, Jack Kelly.

Direction Tomás Mac Anna
Design Brian Collins
Lighting Leslie Scott

Characters

JOHN CONNOR, the village leader, aged about 45
MOTHER, his wife, about 40
MAEVE, his daughter, aged 16
DONAILL, his son, aged 10
DAN O'DEA, a villager, about 65
DAN'S WIFE, about 70
LIAM DOUGAN, a villager, mid twenties
MARK DINEEN, a villager, about 45
BRIAN RIORDAN, a villager, about 60
MALACHY O'LEARY, a villager, about 25
MICKELEEN O'LEARY, a villager, about 30
FATHER HORAN, a curate, about 35
FIRST POLICEMAN, about 50
SECOND POLICEMAN, about 30
CLANCY, a merchant, about 50
CAPTAIN SHINE, a landlord, about 50
MR SIMMINGTON, an agent for an absentee landlord, about 40
FATHER DALY, Parish Priest, about 65
JUSTICE OF THE PEACE, about 65
OTHER VILLAGERS

Time and place:
Autumn 1846 to Spring 1847 in rural Ireland.

Scene One

A Sunday afternoon, Autumn, 1846, in the village of Glanconor.

BRIAN is sitting on a ditch by the roadside outside John Connor's house. MARK is coming from John Connor's house to join BRIAN. Behind the ditch is the potato crop.

DAN and his WIFE enter on the road and go to John Connor's house. They pause in the doorway.

DAN.
  The Lord have mercy on the soul of the dead!

PEOPLE IN THE HOUSE.
  The Lord have mercy on us all!

  In the house, John Connor's daughter is being waked. DAN shakes hands with the chief mourners: JOHN, MOTHER (JOHN's WIFE), MAEVE and DONAILL; then he kneels by the corpse and prays. DAN's WIFE sits with MOTHER.

  As the following develops into a keen, JOHN leaves the house and stands outside the door. He is followed by DONAILL.

DAN'S WIFE.
  Cold and silent is now her bed.

OTHERS.
  Yes.

DAN'S WIFE.
  Damp is the blessed dew of night,
  But the sun will bring warmth and heat in the
  morning and dry up the dew.

OTHERS.
  Yes.

MOTHER.
  But her heart will feel no heat from the sun.

OTHERS.
  No!

DAN'S WIFE.
  Nor no more the track of her feet in the dew.

OTHERS.
  No!

DAN'S WIFE.
  Nor the sound of her step in the village of Connor,
  Where she was ever foremost among young women.

OTHERS.
  No!

DAN'S WIFE.
  Cold and silent is now her bed.

OTHERS.
  Yes.

  LIAM *enters. He shakes hands with* JOHN. *He stands in the
  doorway.*

LIAM.
  The Lord have mercy on the soul of the dead!

PEOPLE IN THE HOUSE.
  The Lord have mercy on us all!

  LIAM *shakes hands with the chief mourners, kneels by the
  corpse and prays.*

MOTHER.
  My sunshine, she was!

OTHERS.
  Yes.

MOTHER.
  I loved her better nor the sun itself!

OTHERS.
  Yes.

MOTHER.
  And when I see the sun go down
  I think of my girl and my black night of sorrow.
  But a dark storm came on
  And my sunshine was lost to me forever;
  My girl cannot return.

OTHERS.
  No!

MOTHER.
  Cold and silent is now her bed.

OTHERS.
  Yes.

DAN *leaves the house and stands with* JOHN *outside the door,
respectfully silent for a few moments.* JOHN *is staring vacantly
at the crop of potatoes.*

DAN. . . . A quare softness in it, Johnny? . . . A bad Summer? . . .
It was, a mac. Dry and drought and then the rain . . . But we
saved the oats?

JOHN. (*to himself*) How am I to overcome it?

DAN. Hah? . . . Oh now, she's in a better place: May she rest in
peace . . . What do you think of the piaties? (*Potatoes.*)

JOHN. (*to himself*) Oh, what does it matter!

He turns abruptly and goes into the house followed by
DONAILL.

DAN *joins* MARK *and* BRIAN *who are sitting on the ditch.*

DAN. How the men!

MARK } Hah-hah, Danny!
BRIAN } Dan!

DAN. Poor Johnny is upset. And he should be getting used to it now.

BRIAN. Oh, yis.

A silence.

MARK. (*nervous staccato voice*). But – but – but, ye see, last year the first crop failed but the main crop was good, and this year the first crop failed, but the main crop will be – will be – will be . . .

DAN. Hah?

BRIAN. Oh, you could be right.

LIAM comes out of the house and joins them. A silence.

MARK. But – but – but, we didn't see none of that quare fog we had last year?

LIAM. What?

BRIAN. No.

MARK. Isn't that what I'm saying? And that crop in there now – (*He points to the crop but then quickly changes his mind.*) That's what you'd call the ghostly fog. Last year. The clouds of it rolling –

LIAM ⎱ That wasn't why –
MARK ⎰ Not wanting to rise, but clinging to the stalks, and slow. And sure what piatie could grow right with it . . . We had nothing like that this year?

LIAM. We had the rain, we had the –

BRIAN ⎱ No faith now, we had narys the fog.
DAN ⎰ That's correct, Marcus.

MARK. Certainly! And – and – and I seen my own crop last year, and the stalks as black as – as – as – as . . .

DAN. And 'twas the fog caused that.

BRIAN. Oh, yis.

LIAM. Ach!

MARK. Yis! And what's on them in there now today but a few speckeleens the flies'd cause?

BRIAN. Oh, you could be right.

DAN. But tell me this, and tell me no more . . . (*Joking; lowering his voice, mysteriously.*) what caused the fog?

MARK. Cause 'twas a terrible year last year.

LIAM. (*winks at BRIAN, then*). What, tell us, Danny?

DAN. (*finger to his lips*). Oh, the less said about that party the better.

They laugh.

MARK. (*forcing a laugh*). The – the – the less said about the sidheog (*Or 'the fairies'.*) the better.

DAN. Ye won't heed me: Well, here's someone that ye'll heed (let ye ask his opinion).

BRIAN. (*looks off at someone approaching; then*). Oh, we'll be right enough.

FR HORAN enters.

FR HORAN. Bail o Dhia oraibh! (*God bless you!*)

MEN. Go mba shé dhuit. (*The same blessing on you.*)

FR HORAN. Our prayers for fine weather are answered, I'm thinking.

MARK. They are, they are, Father.

LIAM. If it isn't too late.

FR HORAN. Wha'? (*Looks at crop, but only for a moment.*) Trust in God.

DAN. There was nothing on them this morning getting up, d'ye know.

FR HORAN. Wha'?

MARK. Speckles.

LIAM. Do you think –

FR HORAN. Sure I'm not a farmer, Dougan.

MARK. Last – last – last year was the bad year.

FR HORAN. God is good.

DAN. And he has a good mother.

BRIAN. He has.

FR HORAN. He has, he has indeed.

LIAM. But would you say it'd be alright if we dug a few of them to see if –

FR HORAN. I saw you late into mass again this morning, Brian.

BRIAN. Oh –

FR HORAN. (*mimicking him*). Oh! Oh!

BRIAN. Aaa, I'm a slow sleeper, Father.

They laugh.

FR HORAN. (*leaving them*). Be good, men!

FR HORAN *goes into the house. A silence.*

MARK. Well, I – I – I heard of a priest one time that was a blister from the pulpit: They say he was one Sunday charging his flock about the drinking and the poteen. ''Tis the drinking,' says he, 'as makes ye go home and beat your wives and your childre, and neglect your crops and your duties, and shoot at the landlord,' says he, 'and miss'. And miss. (*They laugh*).

BRIAN. Oh now, that's only a yarn.

MARK. And miss!

DAN. He wasn't a home-produced priest anyway if he mentioned the shooting. Moral force, boys. They learn a different class of Latin now entirely.

LIAM. Moral force.

DAN. (*importantly*). The polocy. (*Policy.*)

LIAM. Daniel O'Connell's crowd in Dublin.

DAN. And the clergy all over.

BRIAN. Oh, we'll be alright.

DAN. And I heard 'tis the Queen herself, and not the Pope, is writing the books for all now.

LIAM. (*winks at* BRIAN). Correct. And doesn't she send a pound to O'Connell every week of the year!

DAN. To 'The Liberator' is it?

BRIAN. And a kiss every time she meets him.

DAN. Hah? (BRIAN *chuckles*.) Ara, hanam mo ndiabhail! May the divil sweep ye! (*They laugh*.)

BRIAN. (*chuckling*). Victoria!

LIAM. (*chuckling*). Victoria!

DAN. (*chuckling*). Vic-tore-eeaaaa!

MARK. Give over, will ye. Is it any wonder –

DAN. (*laughing*). Oh, you can always, Marcus, put a bag on your back, like many another done, and take to the roads if they fail.

BRIAN. Aw, whist, Danny.

Silence.

LIAM. But if we knew – Hah? If there was something we could – Hah? If there was someone to –

DAN. Someone to –

LIAM. Tell us what to . . .

DAN. Yis.

Instinctively, they look towards the house. JOHN comes out of house and stands outside the door, head bowed. DONAILL follows him, stands beside him, tugs at JOHN's coat.

BRIAN. And that's the second one he's lost.

DAN. But he'll think of something brave for us yet.

BRIAN. Oh, sure he will.

MARK. If – if – if it's needed.

DAN. If it's needed, boys. The Connors would do the brave thing always.

JOHN is conscious of the men watching him. DONAILL tugs at JOHN's coat again. JOHN turns on the boy, his fist raised as if to squash the boy into the ground.

JOHN. *(angrily)*. You're under my feet!

He pauses, his fist raised, seeing the boy's surprise and hurt. Gently.

Don't be under my feet, a mac.

He goes to the gable end of the house, trying to suppress his grief and perplexity.

FR HORAN comes out of house. He looks sympathetically after JOHN. He takes DONAILL's hand and leads him off, taking him for a walk.

FR HORAN. Is there but one true church?

DONAILL. Although there may be many sects, there is but one true church.

FR HORAN. Good man. And how do you call the true church?

DONAILL. The Roman Catholic Church.

FR HORAN. And why are we obliged to be of that true church?

DONAILL. Because none can be saved out of it.

FR HORAN. Good man. And who are those who do not believe what God has taught?

DONAILL. Heretics and infidels.

FR HORAN. Good. And . . .

FR HORAN and DONAILL have gone. Through the following, JOHN goes into the house.

BRIAN. Oh, he's bright enough with it.

DAN. Well, I remember in '17 – and the comical-est thing – I seen the youngsters and the hair falling out of their heads and then starting growing on their faces.

BRIAN. And in '36 –

LIAM. I seen the likes. I seen –

DAN   } You did not!
LIAM   } I did! – I seen –
BRIAN } The worse I seen –
DAN   } You did not! And in '22 –
LIAM   } I seen – I seen –
DAN   } You didn't! And in '22 – in '22 –
BRIAN } The worse I seen –
LIAM   } Well, I seen '36, didn't I? And '40, and '41!
BRIAN } The worse I seen was a child –
DAN   } In '22 – In '22 – In '22! I counted eleven dead by the roadside and my own father one of them. Near the water, Clogher bridge, and the rats. I'm afeared of them since.

BRIAN. A child, an infant –

DAN. And some I seen, green from eating the grass, and yellow and black from fever and the divil-knows-what.

BRIAN. A child under a bush, eating its mother's breast. And she dead and near naked.

MARK. But only speckles.

LIAM. And last year, '45.

DAN. Sure, you weren't here at all last year.

LIAM. Well, didn't my mother go last year?

MARK. She was old –

LIAM. Starved!

MARK. Old –

LIAM. Starved! To keep what few piaties we had for seed for that crop in there. Isn't it the same way John Connor starved that daughter of his that went last night. Wasn't that his plan? The meeting he called: to keep what little piaties we had for seed.

BRIAN. Oh, you're alright, Liam.

LIAM. And now a wake – Like we done! Flaithuil (*Generous.*) with food, drink and tobaccy. And cannot afford it in life or death! And what kind of plan is that?

BRIAN. We'll be alright.

DAN. Well, Daniel O'Connell –

BRIAN. We'll be alright.

DAN. Sure, he's a great man, the finest, 'The Liberator', sure, isn't he?

MARK. But only speckeleens.

DAN. Only speckles, Mark.

BRIAN. We'll be alright.

Evening is coming on and it is growing dark. MALACHY enters, glancing behind him a few times. He joins the men at the ditch.

DAN. Good man, Malachy!

BRIAN. Malachy, a mac!

Silence.

MARK. Hah? . . . But, sure – sure – sure, there's no sense at all in what ye're saying. How do ye know what's under them yet? They're not black. And there's no change in them in the last few hours. Ye see, last year the first crop failed but the main crop was good, but this year the first crop failed but the main crop – that crop in there – will be – (*To LIAM who starts to move.*) Stand your ground, Dougan, and don't go bringing any class of bad luck by rooting on a Sunday!

LIAM. (*annoyed*). Ach, I wasn't going near them! (*He sees MICKELEEN approaching.*) Here's your brother coming, Malachy.

MALACHY. (*to himself*). Chris-jays, if he keeps following me!

MALACHY *leaves as the hunchbacked figure of* MICKELEEN *arrives.*

MICKELEEN. (*shouting after* MALACHY). Pay your respects! Pay your respects! I'm not following you at all! Run! Run then! Off to England again! (*He glares at the group beside the ditch.*) What are the big men watching? (*Then he laughs at them.*) Why don't ye root a few and see? Can ye not see the foretelling spotted leaf? The sourness is still in the clay. Smell it! Smell it! Ye don't want to see, but in a day or three, the smell will blind ye into seeing!

He laughs, goes to the house and stands in the doorway.

The Lord have mercy on the soul of the dead!

PEOPLE IN
THE HOUSE. (*after a slight pause*). The Lord have mercy on us all!

MICKELEEN. (*standing over corpse*). She was lovely.

PEOPLE IN
THE HOUSE. She was.

MICKELEEN. She was civil.

PEOPLE IN
THE HOUSE. She was.

MICKELEEN. Even to the cripple . . . not like some. She was regal. And why wouldn't she? A descendent of the Connors, kings and chieftains here in days of yore. A true Connor, she was, of this village, Glanconor, called after the Connors. She's an angel now. She was an angel on earth. And we won't forget her. Or forget it for *them*. And blessed will be the day or the night when instruments will scald the rotten hearts of them responsible. And blessed will be the earth, cause 'twill refuse them graves, but spew up their packages for the fox and the dog, the rat and the bird.

MOTHER. (*looks to* JOHN *to reply*). . . . We know nothing of that kind of talk here.

MICKELEEN. You're a king, Seán Connor, and I'm sorry for your trouble, as ye were sorry for mine, when my mother and my father – that put this (*Hump.*) on me with his stick – rotted on the hillside. And my brother of the great stature was off roving, having his spate of pleasuring in England. And ye here, kings and all, afeared of the bodack landlord and his bodack agent to give the cripple and his mother and father shelter.

MOTHER. I'm asking you, Michael O'Leary, not to go bringing disgrace on the dead child's bed. (*She looks to* JOHN *again to reply.*) Welcome be the holy will of God.

JOHN. Let him talk. 'Tis his right to talk. He means no harm.

MICKELEEN. Phy (*Why.*) would I mean harm, Seán. I'm sorry for your troubles and for all your troubles to come. (*He sits abruptly*).

MOTHER. (*looking at* JOHN). We're thankful.

JOHN. We're thankful to ye all.

MICKELEEN. (*taunting*). Hah, Seán?

JOHN. Drink. Drink up. Pass round the pipes, Sinéad. Bring out more food, Maeve. Call the fiddler. 'Tis a poor class of a wake ye're giving *my* daughter.

MICKELEEN. But how will you overcome it, Seán? Or are you another pleb refusing to smell the sourness again?

JOHN. (*he goes to the corpse*). We can't send them off mean . . . She *was* regal . . . And – we – won't – send – them off mean, in spite of – in spite of – whatever! Welcome be the holy will of God. No matter what He sends 'tis our duty to submit. And blessed be His name, even for this, and for anything else that's to come. He'll grace us to withstand it.

MICKELEEN *laughs as* JOHN *goes outside.*

Preparations begin for the festive part of the wake. Talk grows louder, people laugh, smoke, eat and drink. Off, behind house, the FIDDLER *is playing a tune and the dancing has begun.*

Outside it is dark. The men at the ditch are reluctant to leave their vigil. JOHN *watches them.*

DAN. The sport is starting up. Will we be going over?

Silence.

MARK. But – but – but, and that government official that came by in June. The writing down he did, the Lord save us!

LIAM. A hundred of the same government officials came by and went, writing down, and things is only getting worse, and what do you reckon that means?

MARK. What – what – what do you reckon, Dougan?

LIAM. Ach!

JOHN. (*calls*). Are ye not coming over?

MARK. Ach! Ach, phat? (*What?*) Ach, phat, Dougan? Ye weren't the only ones had death in your house through the year – Ach, phat! – And – and – and your rent wasn't ruz in the middle of it.

LIAM. Well, maybe we weren't trying to do 'swanky' on it, white-washing the outside of our house.

MARK. And isn't that my business?

JOHN ⎱ Are ye coming over?
LIAM ⎰ 'Tis, 'tis, 'tis, that's your business, ach phat!

At this stage the mourners are coming out of the house, listening to the row.

MARK. Some people like the dirty word always!

LIAM. And they like splitting paupers' skulls wide open too!

JOHN ⎱ Is this what ye come here for?
MARK ⎰ Some people – some people like the dirty word. And the dirty deed. And it's men like some here, doubtin' – doubtin' – doubtin', no heed or faith to Him that's above, or what He can do, will make Him change His mind. And I seen men like some here heel cartloads of the finest of lumpers into hollows in the fields one time, and

there's some of us was ever careful and never wasted, and we're suffering for their likes.

LIAM. Stand away from me, Danny, I'll not touch the pauper.

BRIAN ⎫ You're alright, Marcus.
MARK ⎭ Pauper yourself, Dougan! Pauper yourself! With the dirty mouth! And where's the man with – the – dirty – word's proof? Are they black are they? Are they black? Are they? Are they? Are they black? Are they black?

JOHN. Is this yere respect for a dead Connor?

JOHN pushes them aside roughly and jumps over the ditch into the field. He roots some plants, scattering them about him, digging in the earth with his hands. Then he holds out his hands to them, showing them the blighted potatoes.

(*Quietly.*) Ach phat now?

Pause. They stare, dumbfounded, at his hands for a few moments, then at the field. MARK takes the bad potatoes from JOHN.

LIAM. What are we going to do?

DAN. . . . Hah?

MARK. We should have et (*Eaten.*) the seed.

LIAM. Maybe we should have sowed them deeper.

BRIAN. Maybe if we leave them for a while . . .

DAN. . . . Hah?

MARK. The fog if we expose them.

LIAM. John?

DAN. The sunshine might dry them – or – But it might damage them too if . . .

MARK. We should have et the seed.

DAN. Johnny?

JOHN. Dig them, first light, and maybe save some of them. Then we'll see.

MICKELEEN has pushed his way through the mourners. He starts to laugh.

MICKELEEN. Did ye think '46 wouldn't folly (*Follow.*) '45? That bad doesn't folly bad? That all is to be bad! That ye'll all folly my style of thinking yet!

MARK. Aa, get – get – get up off your knees, you gadhahaun!

And at the same time he throws the rotten potatoes at MICKELEEN.

Suddenly MARK's remark and action seem funny; excepting JOHN, the crowd, laughing and shouting, start to chase MICKELEEN off. The chase turns into a dance. The wake is in full-swing. The whole is a scene of revelry.

It grows lighter and the noise gradually subsides as morning comes on. The lid is put on the coffin, and as it is being carried off, followed by mourners, MOTHER keens.

MOTHER.
Life blood of my heart –
For the sake of my girl I cared only for this world.
She was brave, she was generous,
she was loved by rich and poor.
She was comely, she was clear-skinned.
And when she laughed – Did ye hear?
And her hair – Did ye see? –
Golden like the corn.
But why should I tell what everyone knows?
Why go back to what never can be more?
She who was everything to me is dead.
She is gone forever.
She will return no more.
No!
Cold and silent is her repose.

MOTHER exits following the others.

Scene Two

THE MORAL FORCE

Off, the noise of a convoy of corn-carts on a road. The noise continues throughout the scene.

The scene is the same as before. It is a few weeks later.

MARK, BRIAN *and* MICKELEEN *are standing or sitting on the ditch, watching the convoy, counting the carts.*

Contrasting with them, JOHN *and* MAEVE *are working in the field behind the ditch:* JOHN *is redigging;* MAEVE *is foraging with her hands.*

BRIAN. That's fifteen.

MARK. (*calling to* JOHN). The fifteenth one passing!

JOHN and MAEVE do not look up. MICKELEEN *laughs.*

MICKELEEN. Hah, Seán?

BRIAN. The sixteenth coming.

MARK. Sixteenth, coming!

MICKELEEN. (*calling*). Hah, Maeveen? Would you like a maum (*A handful.*) of oats out of one of them carts?

MAEVE. Would *you* get it for me?

MICKELEEN. (*laughs*). Oh, that's for the ports. To the ports of soft English bellies. Not that I'm saying yours isn't . . . soft.

JOHN. (*calls*). Look about you, girl. Them nettles yonder.

MICKELEEN. Hah, Seán? 'Twas another mistake to dig them too soon?

MARK. The seventeenth!

BRIAN. The eighteenth coming.

MICKELEEN. (*calling*). Don't stoop too low, Maeveen! (*She mutters something, not looking up.*) . . . Hah? . . . Where was your hand this morning when you woke up, Maeveen?

MAEVE. (*childish outburst*). Mickeleen Cam! (*Twisted.*) Mickeleen Cam! Mickeleen Cam!

JOHN. (*approaching*). Bí 'do thost, girl! (*Hold your tongue, girl.*) Is that a críochán (*Potato.*) over there?

MAEVE. A stone, a stone! You got everything good that was in it the last time you dug it.

JOHN. I got a few middling ones: Take them in.

MAEVE *takes the potatoes and gives them to* MOTHER *who is in the house.*

BRIAN. The nineteenth.

MARK. But why are they exporting it so early this year?

MICKELEEN. Hah, Seán?

JOHN. (*quietly*). Because I think they're afeared we'll eat it.

MARK. Begobs no fear of us doing . . . (*He breaks off, laughing nervously.*)

DAN *and* LIAM *arrive, an excitement about them: they are followed by* DAN's WIFE *who arrives a few seconds later.*

DAN. There's a cart –

LIAM. Pulling this way –

DAN. To join the convoy ablow (*Below.*) –

LIAM. And Malachy and others trailing behind it!

BRIAN. And the soldiers, no doubt, 'round it?

LIAM. No! –

DAN. Only a couple of the police, just, and the driver. Hah?

LIAM. There's enough of us in it.

DAN. Hah? Johnny?

MICKELEEN. Get the stones, get the stones!

MARK. Yis!

MICKELEEN. We'll leather the vastard peelers. (*Police.*)

JOHN. One cart won't do much for us.

MARK. We have a rights to live!

JOHN. Not of other people's property.

LIAM. (*incredulous*). . . . What?

DAN. What's upsetting you, Johnny?

JOHN. Where would the world be if any could come and take what he felt like?

LIAM. . . . What!

MICKELEEN. Stone the rotten bodacks!

LIAM. But what are we going to do?

JOHN. What's right!

The statement seems to surprise himself as much as it does the others.

. . . What's right. And maybe, that way, we'll make no mistakes.

LIAM. But –

JOHN. We done the likes before and where did it get us?

MARK. But the bad year it's going to be.

MICKELEEN. (*laughs*). 'Twill be the worst ever!

JOHN. They're always right: We'll be right too.

LIAM. But how are we to live?

JOHN. Go home: Redig: We dug them fields too fast and, I'm sure, missed a lot that's edible. And collect up whatever roots and nettles ye can.

MICKELEEN. Roots and weeds are for the pigs! –

JOHN. And not be using up whatever cabbage and turnips ye have left –

MICKELEEN. Get sticks, stones –

JOHN. I got a few críocháns in there today –

MICKELEEN. Look! It's coming –

JOHN. I'm calling a meeting tonight and a fair say for everyone! Then we'll see.

MICKELEEN. Look! It's coming! We'll stone them now while we're able.

JOHN. It's easy for you! All you want is to cause trouble. You have nothing to lose.

MICKELEEN. (*holding his crotch*). I've still my budgeen as good as another!

JOHN. Stand in off the road. I ask you gently.

MARK. (*taking a kick at MICKELEEN*). Stand in, you – you – you – you –

JOHN. (*restraining MARK*). 'Asy. 'Asy. (*To himself, as if to convince himself.*) It's not the way . . . 'Asy now.

The cart is heard approaching.

FIRST POLICEMAN enters, clearing stones off the road. Followed a few seconds later by SECOND POLICEMAN. As scene progresses a crowd gathers, including MALACHY, MOTHER and MAEVE.

FIRST POLICEMAN. (*wary*). Good day to ye!

MICKELEEN picks up a stone and throws it aside, as if helping the POLICEMAN.

(*To MICKELEEN.*) Stand in, a mac, there's a wagon passing in a minute.

MICKELEEN. We won't eat it.

FIRST POLICEMAN. Hah?

JOHN. Stand in, Michael.

SECOND POLICEMAN. What is it?

FIRST POLICEMAN. Clear the way like a good boy.

MICKELEEN. We won't eat it!

SECOND POLICEMAN. Move! Out of the way! Move in! (*He pushes MICKELEEN back.*)

JOHN. 'Asy, and he will.

MICKELEEN. (*sees* MALACHY *is close by*). Ara what? Ara what? Do ye think you're big gallant soldiers or what? (*The* POLICEMAN *hesitates.*) . . . They're afeared of us!

MARK. They're afeared we'll eat it! Yahoo!

SECOND POLICEMAN. Close up now, or I'll soon fasten your tongue.

MALACHY. (*stepping in*). Never attempt that, peeler.

LIAM. We're hungry! –

DAN. Hit him, Malachy! –

MARK. We're hungry – we're hungry – we're hungry! –

LIAM. Why should we starve? – And look at it!

The cart has stopped, off.

JOHN. 'Asy.

FIRST POLICEMAN. We've orders for no trouble now.

SECOND POLICEMAN. But we'll take trouble.

JOHN. 'Asy, let ye.

LIAM. Do ye want to starve us?

FIRST POLICEMAN. Back! Sure the real hunger didn't start at all yet.

MARK. We grew that oats.

SECOND POLICEMAN. And sold it – back! Back or I'll – If ye wanted to eat it ye should have done, and not sold it.

JOHN. (*losing control for a moment*). And what'd pay the rent for us then?

FIRST POLICEMAN. That's it, ye can't have it two sides!

MICKELEEN. Take it, and leather them! What are ye waiting for?

JOHN. Stop, will ye!

FIRST POLICEMAN. Think of yere homes let some of ye –

MICKELEEN. The cart! Break it! Smash it!

SECOND POLICEMAN *goes for* MICKELEEN, MALACHY *moves to intercept him.* JOHN *throws* MALACHY *back, pushes* SECOND POLICEMAN *aside, and grabs* MICKELEEN.

JOHN. (*to* POLICEMAN). Take yere cart the other way. There's no one here that'll hinder ye!

The Police are leaving, we hear the corn cart moving off, and peace is being restored as FR HORAN *arrives. He is too hot and bothered to see that the trouble is over.*

FR HORAN. What's going on here? Out of the way! Ye were going to show yourselves as wild savages, were ye?

JOHN. It's all over now, Father.

FR HORAN. What's the stick for, Dineen? Put it down at once! I command you!

JOHN. It's all over now.

FR HORAN. Stand back, Connor! Is it that ye wanted to go breaking the laws of God and man? Didn't I see ye and I coming down from the hill above.

LIAM. We're hungry.

FR HORAN. Stand where you are, Dougan!

MICKELEEN. The bodacks of vastards don't want us to live!

FR HORAN. Oh-ho, O'Leary, didn't I know you'd be in it!

LIAM. They're sweeping the country bare –

MICKELEEN. And are ye going heeding another that bids ye starve?

FR HORAN. Come down off the ditch, O'Leary.

MARK. We're going to starve?

MICKELEEN. Yis, that's what they want to do to us!

FR HORAN. Come down off the ditch –

MICKELEEN } They want to starve us! And look at it! Christ, the
 } wagon-loads of it!
FR HORAN } A curse on the first man to move! Are my eyes

deceiving me? Do ye realise the great God is above in heaven watching ye? And His blessed Mother this minute shedding down tears of sorrow. Merciful Jesus forgive us!

JOHN. It's all over now.

MICKELEEN. Christ, ye're letting it go!

FR HORAN. And if it be Thy Holy will, straighten that wretch on the ditch. Give us back our forbearance, our patience – Our saintliness, O'Leary! The fine character of this village –

MICKELEEN. There'll be no village –

FR HORAN. Stop!

MICKELEEN. Why should I stop? –

FR HORAN. Stop! –

MARK. Stop, O'Leary! –

FR HORAN. Do you believe in God at all, O'Leary? The one true God, or in His church, or His ministers, or in His goodness? And especially His goodness to you and tolerance: that He doesn't strike you down dead this minute! No wonder the hump is on you!

JOHN. It's all over now.

FR HORAN. I saw the devil here today. Weren't ye warned that it's in hard times he strikes most? Can ye forget the great God so easy? He knows about our grievances and He's taking account of them and He won't forget them! And won't we win in the long run?

JOHN ⎫ 'Asy, your reverence.
FR HORAN ⎬ Aren't we on the right path? The pride we had that
we could say we had no physical force men in this
parish. And we got our religious freedom that way,
in '29, O'Connell's way, without a blow struck –
Stay where you are, O'Leary! But that a proved

heretic can stand up here and start the devil's work:
Anarchy, fight, the pike, the gun! – Where would it
end? – Strike! – Maul! – Maim! – Wreck! – And
destroy! – Tear limb from limb! – Butchery! –
Murder! – Blood and destruction! – Let it flow on
this holy ground – Yis, Murder! – And ye were
ready to murder – Butchery and gore! What
advantage is worth a single drop of blood?

MICKELEEN. Jesus shed his blood!

FR HORAN. To think that he did, and for you!

MALACHY. (*sensing new danger; quietly to* MICKELEEN). Stop!

FR HORAN. Come down off the ditch, O'Leary!

MICKELEEN. The men of '98 shed their blood!

FR HORAN. Haven't we had enough trouble with you?

MICKELEEN. Were they murderers?

MARK. They were! They were! They were!

MALACHY. (*to* MICKELEEN). Stop, pleb.

MICKELEEN. And the priests – the real priests – who led and
fought and died – were they murderers?

FR HORAN. Oh, the twist is in your mind along with your body.

MICKELEEN. Answer that one!

FR HORAN. I thought the drop in you was black, but did I
think –

MICKELEEN. And when the tithe war was fought again' the
Protestants –

MALACHY ⎫ Stop pleb.
MARK   ⎬ Get him down!

MICKELEEN. There was little talk from ye about spilling blood!

FR HORAN. O'Leary, don't talk you about Protestants! Didn't you take the soup from them last year? Didn't you?

JOHN. 'Asy, 'asy –

MICKELEEN. I did! I did! But I didn't say the words for them.

FR HORAN. And damned your eternal soul! –

MALACHY. Others here took it! –

MICKELEEN. Because I pretended I couldn't talk English –

FR HORAN. You took the bowl of infidel soup –

MICKELEEN. And when they gave me their book to kiss –

FR HORAN. And entered into league straightaway with the devil –

MICKELEEN. I held it like this –

FR HORAN. And I say here and now –

MICKELEEN. But 'twas my *thumb* I kissed! My thumb!

FR HORAN. (*roars*). And – I – say – here – and – now, that the religion that has to depend on starvation to swell its puny misguided flock is double damned!

The crowd is angry, pressing forward towards MICKELEEN.

MAEVE ⎱	Souper! Souper!
MALACHY ⎰	Others here took it.
DAN ⎱	Did I take it? Did I take it?
JOHN ⎰	Stand back will ye!
MARK ⎱	Welt him! Welt him!
MOTHER ⎰	Knock him!
JOHN ⎱	Stand back!
MAEVE ⎰	Kick him!
JOHN	(*pushing* MAEVE *out of the crowd and shaking her*).
	What's coming over you?

FR HORAN. Keep back there!

MICKELEEN. (*above the hub-bub*). And I'd take it the same way again to stay alive!

FR HORAN. Keep back, I say! Keep – You would! You would!

Suddenly, he lashes MICKELEEN on the legs with his stick, MICKELEEN falls to the ground. The crowd close in, arms and legs working.

MARK ⎫ Welt him!
MOTHER ⎭ Kick him! Kick him!
MAEVE ⎫ Flake him! Flake him!
MARK ⎭ Kill him! Kill him!
MALACHY ⎱ Leigh amach é! Leigh amach é! (*Let him out! Let
         ⎰ him out!*)

FR HORAN has the stick raised again to hit MICKELEEN. JOHN wrenches it from him. MALACHY and JOHN fighting off the crowd. FR HORAN being tossed about in the middle of it.

FR HORAN. I n-aimm Dé! (*In God's name!*) . . . What's come over ye? . . . Stop!

JOHN. Let out the O'Learys! . . . Clear back! . . . Give over! . . . Have sense! (*Swinging the stick.*) Will ye stop now, will ye!

Eventually they stop, mainly through JOHN's swinging the stick about him in a circle to clear them back. MICKELEEN is unconscious on the ground.

FR HORAN. (*near tears*). Get him home will you, Malachy, for the love of God.

MALACHY. (*savagely, inarticulate*). 'Hat – phat – home – 'hat – phare?!

JOHN. Take him into the house. (*To LIAM.*) Help him.

MALACHY and LIAM drag MICKELEEN into JOHN's house.

Now, go home the rest of ye.

DAN. You'll think of something for us, Johnny?

JOHN. Go home! Have sense! Go on now! (*They start to move off.*)

FR HORAN. (*on the point of tears*). Off . . . ye vagabones . . . or I'll have ye up before . . . the parish priest. (*He turns away to hide his tears.*) . . . And if there's any more of this kind of . . .

JOHN. . . . . Go on now!

> JOHN, MAEVE *and* FR HORAN *remain.* JOHN *returns the stick to* FR HORAN.

Ara, they didn't mean it. They don't mean to be this way. It's only the hunger.

FR HORAN. Hold your tongue, Connor. Be off with you.

JOHN. (*to* MAEVE). Get inside!

> *He pushes her in front of him into the house.*

> FR HORAN *leans against the ditch, crying. The last sounds of the convoy of corn-carts fade in the distance.*

Scene Three

THE RESOLUTION

The scene is the same as before. Night.

JOHN *stands outside his house looking out into the night.*

MOTHER *comes out of house for a basket of turf. (In the house, are* MAEVE, DONAILL, DAN, BRIAN, LIAM, MALACHY *and* MICKELEEN.)

Silence.

JOHN. I don't think any of the others will come. I thought Marcus might, or . . .

MOTHER. Are they going to be there stuck in the hearth all night?

JOHN. We'll talk for a while and see what to do.

MOTHER. I want to feed the childre. Or do you see them anymore: the eyes getting bigger in their heads?

JOHN. Hah? . . . Surely we can share the weeds?

MOTHER. There's a can of the cow's blood in it too. And I doubt the same poor creature of a beast will stand up to much more bleeding.

JOHN. (*to himself*). I don't know what to tell them. (*He is about to go in.*)

MOTHER. Johnny.

JOHN. And the devil is ready to rule the world if we allow him.

MOTHER. What's meetings to do with us?

JOHN. And that will be worse for us as always.

MOTHER. Neglecting your own. What class of change is coming over you?

JOHN. Hah?

MOTHER. You're going astray on us.

JOHN. Hah?

MOTHER. We've lost enough of them.

JOHN. 'Hat? I'll look after them!

MOTHER. Will you? . . . There's no one inside there has anything to do with you but your own. Yis! That seafóideen (*Senile.*) O'Dea is wily. And, believe you me, them Dougans is foxy too, with more stores laid in at home than we'll ever hear of. Them all sparing their turf, while we put on the roaring fires for them.

JOHN. Ara, whist –

MOTHER. Yis! And them auld O'Learys, having them there, squinting with venom across the floor at each other. That's the country we have. They'll all live on their bitterness and devilry, and where will you be?

JOHN. I'll be – I'll be – And I've found my way to live too!

MOTHER. And where will *we* be then?

JOHN. What are you saying woman? . . . You're mistaking me. I'll do nothing wrong anymore. It's only by right that we can hope at all now.

MOTHER. What's right? What's right in a country when the land goes sour? Where is a woman with childre when nature lets her down?

JOHN. Oh, whist woman, you don't know what you're saying.

MOTHER. (*bitterly*). No.

JOHN. Is there a mark or a blemish on any of ours inside there?

MOTHER. We've lost two of them!

JOHN. Is any of them like the childre your father reared or my father?

MOTHER. We've lost —

JOHN. These times is to be different. Believe that! You must! There's lots can be done.

MOTHER. These times is for *anything* that puts a bit in your own mouth.

JOHN. 'Hat? . . . What are you saying?

MOTHER. Hoarding their fine stacks of turf.

JOHN. 'Hat?

MOTHER. In their yards: their turf: flour can be got for turf in the town.

JOHN. (*he gets the insinuation*). . . . What would you have me do?

MOTHER. Nothing!

JOHN. Then hould your whist! You're the one that's going astray, I think.

MOTHER. (*this time a plead to him*). I'm only asking then: don't get lost on us, in meetings or what's right, and forget us.

JOHN. But you're mistaking me. I'll do nothing wrong. (*She turns away from him.*) — I'm doing what I can. And if a time comes when something better is to be done, for you or childre, I'll do it. Be sure of that. And them inside has always come to this house. It's expected of me.

MOTHER *starts to fill her basket with turf.* JOHN *goes into the house.*

In the house, the elation of the corn-cart incident is still with them. DAN *is cavorting about, mimicking* FR HORAN. MAEVE, DONAILL, LIAM *and* BRIAN *enjoy his performance.* MALACHY, *dour and morose, mutters occasionally to himself, glancing at* MICKELEEN, *who lies on a bed of straw at his feet.* MICKELEEN *is fully conscious. There is a pot on the fire.*

DAN ⎱ 'The Mother of God shedding down tears of sorrow!
     ⎰ ... Murder! The pike! The gun!'

BRIAN ⎱ *(chuckling)*. Yis ... Sure yis ... Yis.
DAN   ⎰ 'I n-aimm Dé!'

LIAM ⎱ 'What's come over ye!'
DAN   ⎰ 'I command ye!'

LIAM ⎱ But the peelers were frightened.
BRIAN ⎰ Oh, they were, sure.

DAN   ⎱ 'Do ye realise the great God is watching ye?'
JOHN ⎰ Ye were lucky he didn't excommunicate the lot of ye.

DAN   ⎱ 'Stand back, Connor!'
LIAM ⎰ 'Stand back, Connor, when you're told!'

They laugh.

MOTHER *enters with turf.*

They become silent.

BRIAN. Musha, the creature was only trying to do his job.

MALACHY. *(to himself)*. Ary yis-yis-yis-yis-yis-yis.

Silence.

JOHN. Well, I don't think anyone else is coming.

DAN. You thought of something for us, Johnny?

JOHN. Well ... The thing now is ... I'm sure there's lots we can do, if we all think.

Silence.

Well, I was saying about redigging and collecting up –

LIAM. Sure the most of us has done that.

JOHN. Well, for them that hasn't. Everyone to be doing something more than waiting until . . . until . . .

DAN. Until what, Johnny?

He does not know.

LIAM. A plan, isn't it, we need?

JOHN. No. Yis. And some class of relief committee is meeting in the town to see about their plan.

DAN. (*defiantly*). But they can't stop us making a plan.

BRIAN. Oh, they can not.

JOHN. No, what I'm saying is –

LIAM. Something useful to be doing, John.

JOHN. Yes.

Silence.

DAN. Repeal!

LIAM. Ary, that's only alright for persons in the town to be interested in.

Silence.

BRIAN. We'll get nothing off the merchants.

DAN. (*chuckles*). We will not, Brian. Off Clancy or the others. We know that.

BRIAN. (*chuckles*). We do.

DAN. We do, a mac.

Silence.

(*To himself.*) Repeal and No Surrender, he says.

(*Suddenly, like a first realisation.*) Food! Food, isn't it we need?

BRIAN. Oh, not the greens.

LIAM. If we got chance of a sheep?

DAN. Yis!

LIAM. To *eat*, Malachy.

MALACHY. Eat or spike, what's it to me?

BRIAN. (*holding his stomach, beginning to laugh with a pain*). But . . . But let them . . . not get the taste of mutton on you –

DAN. (*laughing*). Or the smell of it on your breath itself, Brian –

BRIAN. Or – or . . . Or they'd soon have – (*Chuckling, he doubles up in pain.*)

DAN. Or they'd soon have you dancing a hornpipe in the air!

BRIAN *exits quickly.*

(*Laughing.*) God help you, Brian, a mac, with the 'looseness'.

Silence.

JOHN. Are ye thinking?

DAN. Oh, we are, Johnny, we are.

MICKELEEN. (*muttering*). What's it to Malachy Mór, the rover.

MALACHY. (*to himself*). Chris-jays!

JOHN. Do you want a speak, Michael?

MICKELEEN. I do, I do. There's a look of a sheep to Dougan there: a ram, I'd say, the way he's eyeing Maeveen.

LIAM. Ary, give over.

DAN. (*laughs*). Cripes, Mickeleen, if you had a body on you at all! 'Jesus shed his blood', says he.

JOHN. Ar, Danny!

DAN. (*laughing*). But there's no use running your head again' a wall, perticily a church wall!

JOHN. Stop, Danny.

DAN. Sure, all I'm saying is the priests are worse off nor ourselves and we'll get nothing there.

JOHN. I was wondering, maybe the Agent.

LIAM. I was thinking of him for a job.

DAN. . . . A job with Simmington, is it?

LIAM. (*angrily*). Well, if there's nothing else.

DAN. To go evicting people for him is it?

LIAM. (*angrily*). Well what do *ye* say?

DAN. Tumbling houses on your neighbours for him, is it?

LIAM. (*angrily*). Well, what do *ye* say? What do *ye* say we can do?

JOHN. No, what I was saying, what I was thinking, us all go down to him and explain. To allow us time for the rent money.

DAN. And hasn't he the rent demands out already? And persons flying from them. And upwards on a thousand 'round the Lodge gates, night and day, and sorry the satisfaction any of them is getting, but a crack of the coachman's whip, for fear they'd touch the carriage, and maybe pass on a fever.

JOHN. Oh, I don't class every man as bad at all as ye do. Simmington is a civil man enough.

DAN. Well, aren't you the changed boy, Johnny.

JOHN. 'Hat?

DAN. The head of the bull, boys, the hind-quarters of the mule, and the smile of an Englishman!

JOHN. (*angrily*). Sure, there's only one answer to everything in the back of yere minds, but ye won't convince me.

LIAM. What?

DAN. Hah?

JOHN. If we got time for the rent – If we could use the rent money. And some of us had extra expenses this year, and maybe haven't enough to pay it – Oh, carry on!

LIAM. Hah?

JOHN. (*angrily*). Well, we'll withstand it!

DAN. Sure, we'll have to.

LIAM. But how?

JOHN. Yis!

LIAM. What?

JOHN. Aye!

LIAM. Hah?

JOHN. Wait on.

LIAM. For what? Hah? You said a plan.

JOHN. Yis, I said – Yis – I – That's what I – *we'll withstand it!* (*Turns angrily on* MOTHER *who is stirring the pot.*) What are you foosthering at it there for? You're knocking the good out of it with your poking. Coinnigh amach uaidh! (*Stand back from it! To himself.*) There's more ways to live besides food, and it's not yere way.

BRIAN *enters.*

MICKELEEN. (*to himself*). Vastardeens and spailpeens.

MALACHY. (*restraining himself*). Chris-jays! (*To* JOHN.) If we had guns is it?

JOHN. For what?

MALACHY. Chris-jays, for what!

JOHN. Yis for what?

BRIAN. Oh, that's all done away with now.

JOHN. Is it that we're not dying fast enough for them? Always back to the same thing, always the same answer.

MALACHY. Lord, the Connors is getting very saintly of late.

JOHN. 'Hat? Wouldn't you live for a year on the price of a gun? Wouldn't it pay your rent?

MALACHY. Pikes then, sticks, and get the Cosackbawn men above with us.

JOHN. And where will it get us now?

BRIAN. . . . Oh, the Cosackbawns is cute.

DAN. They're well able to go up there, Brian.

BRIAN. They'll be alright.

MALACHY. Chris-jays, ye're talking!

JOHN. Yis, we're talking!

MALACHY. Well, tell me then who's fault is it? (*They do not appear to understand. He waves his arms about his head.*) Who's fault? All the — Why? — All over — The corn — Poor people, strangers — All over the country — Why, all over, who's fault?

BRIAN. Oh, sure —

MALACHY. Naaw! Ye're talking. (*Pointing at* MICKELEEN.) And the polotician there: and he's blaming me. And I know what ye're saying about me too.

MICKELEEN. 'Tis the sheeps' fault!

MALACHY. What? . . . 'Tis! 'Tis the sheeps' fault, 'tis!

He swings and kicks out at MICKELEEN. MICKELEEN *retreats;* MALACHY *pushes him out of the house.* MICKELEEN *stays outside the house, taking shelter somewhere from the cold until the end of the scene.*

MALACHY. Keep on trying me now and I'll give you what I gave you last week! (*He returns to the others.*) And if I did spike them sheep — and stakes through their sides and into the ground — And I'll spike a dozen more — But it's better nor yere moaning.

JOHN. You're getting the right to talk now, Malachy, and only that. And I'm giving you the right: remember that too.

MALACHY. Tell me then who's fault?

JOHN. The blight.

MALACHY. Naaw!

JOHN. The blight — the blight!

MALACHY. Naaw! Nor do you believe that. Nice homecoming from England I had: me mother and father dead, the house tumbled and the holding gone. And when there's nothing, ye're blaming me. There's no blame or shame on me. I went off to England to gather enough to get on top of the rent. He (LIAM.) went with me, and stayed away as long, and there's no one blaming him. I dragged piaties out of that holding — out of the rocks – good years and bad. And the two bad years ye're talking about! Ary yis!

JOHN. Fight what?

MALACHY. That's it! That's what I'm asking.

LIAM. The soldiers is it?

MALACHY. The – soldiers – is – it, yis – is – it, ate them if you like!

JOHN. I'm not listening to ye at all. Carry on.

JOHN *motions them to continue, that he is not interested.*

BRIAN. Oh now, the soldiers don't do much on us indeed.

MALACHY. They're there!

DAN. Hah?

LIAM. Us? The thousands of them?

MALACHY. Not soldiers then – Soldiers! – Anyone! I – know – we – can't – them – all! Some of them. One now, and maybe two after a while as we get better. But make such a job of that one he'd count for ten.

DAN. (*excited*). Yis! We could, we could!

LIAM. (*excited*). John? John? – Hah?

JOHN. I'm not listening to ye at all.

DAN. (*looks at* JOHN *and* BRIAN. *He starts to chuckle*). . . . We'd fight one time, but we were better fed. Suidhe síos (*Sit down.*) Malachy, a chuid. You're stout. And all the O'Learys were ever in it were stout.

BRIAN. They were.

DAN. Well, they were . . . (*Feeling sorry for* JOHN.) And all the Connors.

BRIAN. Well, they were.

Silence.

MOTHER. (*apologetically; giving hint to leave*). It's late, Danny.

DAN. Hah? (*Then sympathetically*.) You're alright, Sinéad; we understand, a gradh. (*The others rise with him*.) We can be talking tomorrow. We'll have the conversation whatever, boys.

JOHN. (*suddenly, angrily*). And do ye think they'll get the better of me? I'm telling ye now, so I am! (*Misinterpreting their standing up*.) 'Hat? Sit! Ye'll heed me!

BRIAN. We will as always, John.

JOHN. See if ye'll live by yere bitterness or yere fight this time against them.

LIAM. But what do you say we should do?

JOHN. I say – I say – Something useful to be doing until . . .

LIAM. Until what?

JOHN. Until *help* comes! Help, yis, help, that's it. Help will come, it will come, it will have to come if we give them no excuse not to send it.

LIAM. But they swept the country bare today: do you think they'll refill it?

JOHN. What else is there?! – No, what I'm saying is, last year wasn't as bad as this year is to be and they sent meal to parts.

LIAM. But I think they do begrudge doing the likes and do be in no hurry.

BRIAN. Oh yis, the polocy.

JOHN. But won't they have to send it to all over this year? The ways we are. They'll have to, because there's nothing else.

LIAM. But when?

JOHN. Soon. It'll depend on – Important things. The Government, the Deal, the Policy, Business – The Policy.

BRIAN. Oh yis.

LIAM. Politicians, far away.

JOHN. Yis, far away now, but – It wasn't given to us to understand. A bitter man or a hungry man, or a dying man doesn't understand. But they're there, and for our good, and it's better we understand that. They have rules that they must follow, and we have one: to live and be as much at peace as we can with them, as with God. (*He pauses. Then, defiantly.*) Well that's what I believe. I believe that. Help will come, because it's right. And what's right must be believed in if we're to hope. And there's nothing to be gained by listening to the contrary if we're to live at all in times like these.

Silence.

MOTHER. It's late.

DAN. We'll be off.

MOTHER. May God go with ye now.

JOHN. What? . . . (*He realises why they are standing.*) Sit – sit – sit. We'll all have a share. No one ever went hungry from the house of a Connor. Sit, and don't offend us. (*To MOTHER.*) We're only sorry to be able to offer so little.

MOTHER. 'Tisn't the sweetest smelling –

JOHN. 'Hat?

MOTHER. . . . . But there's nourishing in it. Sit. (*They sit.*) 'Tisn't too much cooked, but 'twill last longer in the stomach that way. (*She turns on MAEVE and DONAILL who have come up around the fire.*) Clear back out of my sight and don't be looking in the mouths of people!

MALACHY *moves towards the door.*

JOHN. Malachy, I understand what you're saying, but it's not the time.

MALACHY. We'll all look out for ourselves then?

JOHN. No.

MALACHY. We all know our own know then?

JOHN. No. You can stay the night by the hearth if you will.

MALACHY. The blight took only half the food.

MALACHY *exits.*

MICKELEEN. (*who has been crouched at the gable-end of house, rises; following* MALACHY). Vastards, the big men. But they'll soon be a reduction. And I'll live in spite. I'll live in spite of all.

MICKELEEN *exits.*

DAN. Let them off. They'll be following each other 'round all night, roaming the hills, and not speaking till they start drawing kicks on each other.

LIAM. . . . But there must be *some one thing* at least we can do? Until what you say, John.

MOTHER *allows a suitable pause for the men to come up with a suggestion; then.*

MOTHER. There's a pile of auld boards outside the back. Couldn't ye, before someone else starts it, band together and make coffins and maybe sell them to the countryside.

DAN. (*pleased*). Yis. They'll be in demand. They will.

JOHN. Take up the pot.

DAN. You have a head on you, Sinéad, you have, God bless it! The meeting is closed, boys.

Scene Four

THE LOVE SCENE

A few weeks later. Night. A wood.

Occasional moonlight through the rolling clouds. A shaft of light falls on a bush. Under the bush, the corpses of a woman and her two children. A little away from them, the body of a man lying on the ground. It grows darker. The man groans. LIAM enters furtively. He roots under a bush on the opposite side of the stage. He produces a bag from the hole he has dug. He takes a handful of nuts and an apple from the bag. He buries the bag again. A second groan. LIAM gasps. He is about to run when he hears footsteps approaching from another direction. He hides.

MAEVE *enters. Her harshness, in the early part of the scene, would be more suited to a bitter old hag.*

LIAM, *hiding, makes an owl-hooting sound, a curlew whistle . . .*

MAEVE *stops for a moment, looks around defiantly, is about to move again.*

LIAM. There you are, Maeveen!

MAEVE. (*harsh*). Mickeleen Cam!

LIAM. Hillo-Hillo-Hillo?

MAEVE. The huncy pleb!

LIAM. Hillo-Hillo-Hillo!

MAEVE. 'Tis not! . . . Malachy?

LIAM. 'Tis a gintleman – You scoundrel – How dare you – Good evening!

MAEVE. Shleeker!

LIAM. Hillo!

MAEVE. Vastard!

She is about to move off. Another groan from the darkness.

LIAM. (*urgently*). Hillo-Hillo-Hillo! Will you marry me, Maeveen?

Silence.

We have nothing to lose.

She hides somewhere. LIAM comes out of hiding to follow her.

Maeve? . . . Maeve? (*She confronts him.*) . . . Hillo!

MAEVE. Dougan! Sly, rotten, foxy breed!

LIAM. (*unsure*). Ar, sure, go then, you childeen . . . Sure, you're only a slip . . . (*Approaching her.*) Although, I might be making a grave mistake . . . You're purty right enough: I can see that . . . but slender.

MAEVE. (*snarls*). You'd fatten me!

LIAM. I – I – It's a wonder you're not afeared out here alone and all sorts of creatures coming and going through the countryside. A minute ago I thought I heard a –

MAEVE. What's the shleeker's business out here?

LIAM. I was hoping maybe to get a glimpse of you.

MAEVE. The luck is on me, as always. The vastard shleeker is a prize!

LIAM. Well, what's yours?

MAEVE. Oh, I was down in Quilty's house to see if they'll march to the town with my father: But they're all off to America: And I stayed with them, preparing the sea-store for the voyage.

LIAM. And was there no sport in it?

MAEVE. Crying and whinging when they should be laughing.

LIAM. (*slipping his arm about her*). And do you tell me you couldn't find e'er a man to folly you home?

MAEVE. (*shakes off his arm*). What's on yeh!

LIAM. I fear you're not affectionate.

MAEVE. Chris-jays, there's a lot to give me cause.

Silence.

He puts the apple in her hand. Feeling dejected he sits. He starts to crack the nuts. He is no longer paying her attentions.

She looks at the apple; she wants to be grateful; she can't.

LIAM. Your sister liked me.

MAEVE. It didn't stop you wandering.

LIAM. . . . You look like her.

MAEVE. And leaving her.

LIAM. . . . I know.

MAEVE. And she's well rotten now.

LIAM. . . . She was gentle . . . Like Malachy Mór, I meant to stay away only the one season. But the appetite I had, and the wailing that was here.

He hands her some nuts. She looks at the apple in one hand, the nuts in the other. She takes a bite of the apple.

MAEVE. (*a nervous, involuntary giggle*). It's sour.

She eats more of the apple. Progressively, she becomes a sixteen-year-old girl again.

. . . Was there no hunger at all in England?

LIAM. There was. But I seen no man die of starvation there.

MAEVE. . . . If I went away I wouldn't come back.

LIAM. Aa, you would. Though I don't know why.

MAEVE. I wouldn't . . . The waiting here. Waiting for what? . . . Look at the moon trying to get out, Liam . . . And the bailley and his gang came for the cow last Monday cause we hadn't it for the rent. And they were just taking the cow out of the yard when the rates man came with his demand. And, the wind up, the bailley and the rates man were nearly coming to blows over whose right it was to the cow. And my father trying to make peace between them. (*Laughing.*) The cow just munching grass.

LIAM. (*beginning to laugh with her*). And who got the cow in the end?

MAEVE. The bailley, cause he came first . . . The cow just munching away for herself . . . Infidel and dirty and all as Mickeleen is, he's clever too. But now, my father saying we'll march to the town, legal, and explain to them, so they'll hurry up sending us meal. Will you march?

LIAM. . . . I got a job from the Agent today. (*He looks at her, afraid of what her reaction will be.*)

MAEVE. You'll get bread every day.

LIAM. He's recruiting a gang: I don't know what for.

MAEVE. (*continues eating*). Oh Lord, I envy Peggy Quilty off in the morning, and we're to be here waiting, and rooting over the same old fields.

LIAM. What else could I do? He gave me the job because he said he never had anything against my father.

MAEVE. My father saying something good will happen soon.

LIAM. And I overheard them saying the word 'demolition'.

MAEVE. And saying we'd be different people if someone came along and put the bit in our mouths.

LIAM. There's no one thing else I can do.

MAEVE. And my mother saying what's coming over my father, and saying he's soft. And I think the same. And I do be watching him thinking. And I do be wondering what does he be thinking about. And my mother saying the only things sowed anymore will be in the graveyard. And there's something coming over her. And I do hear her going out in the middle of the night with the turf basket and coming home and lying down again at dawn, cold and wet from the dew. And never seeing her shiver. But she got flour for a basket of turf the other day and the belly on Donaill swole after. (*She laughs.*) And I thought of Nora Reilly that swole and died after drinking the sup of milk . . . And I want my father to let *me* go, but he won't.

LIAM. Where?

MAEVE. But I think I might go myself.

LIAM. Where would you go to?

MAEVE. America.

LIAM. Where would you get the ticket money?

MAEVE. Oh, I'd snake on to one of them numerous ships and hide.

LIAM. (*laughs*). They'd ketch you and drown you.

MAEVE. Let them then, and I'd pray for their forgiveness while they were about it.

LIAM. Well, you're an awful girl.

MAEVE. I might be.

LIAM. Y'are.

MAEVE. And you're a fox.

LIAM. Did you ever kiss a fox?

MAEVE. No. And I don't want –

He pounces on her. He kisses her.

LIAM. You're purty right enough. . . . Did you ever kiss anyone that was in England?

MAEVE. Once only. (*He kisses her.*) Twice. (*He kisses her again.*) Three times.

They laugh. He starts to sing. She joins in singing with him.

LIAM.
As I roved over on a Summer's morning,
A-speculating most curiously,
To my surprise, whom did I espy,
But a charming fair one approaching me;
I stopped a while in deep meditation,
Contemplating what I should do,
Till at last recruiting all my sensations,
I thus accosted the fair Colleen Rua.

Are you Aurora or the Goddess Flora,
Artemidora or Venus bright –

Through the above the moon has come out again, revealing the corpses of the family under a bush. A groan from the prone figure of the man. LIAM and MAEVE move apart.

MAEVE. (*whispers*). Chris-jays!

MAEVE *runs off.*

LIAM *sees the corpses of the family and stands there as if transfixed by them.*

Scene Five

THE RELIEF COMMITTEE

*A few nights later. A room in the Town Hall. The Relief
Committee is seated around a table: CLANCY, a merchant;
CAPTAIN SHINE, a landlord; Mr Simmington, AGENT for an
absentee landlord; PP (Parish Priest) Father Daly; FR HORAN;
and JP (Justice of the Peace) who is acting Chairman.*

*In the street outside, crowds are calling for 'Food! Food! Food' and
'Work! Work! Work'.*

JP. I'm sorry to say we still have had no reply to the presentment
we made to His Excellency, the Lord Lieutenant, to begin public
works to relieve this appalling distress which God has chosen to
inflict on us. Whether we presented for too much work, or
whether the process of examining our application is such a slow
one, I don't know. I have written to them daily stressing the
urgency of our needs. I have asked them could we start on part
of the work now. I have myself drawn up the plans for building
a new road and submitted a copy to them and asked could we
start on that . . . (*He gestures despairingly.*) . . . We are not
being treated fairly. I'm sorry. I'm at a loss.

PP. Food supplies?

JP. No. They still say no. Trade must be protected. They're treating
this as if it were some minor upset. I did receive that pile of
government pamphlets and I have examined them, but they are
totally inconsequential since we cannot eat them. I don't blame
them out there, I don't blame them at all. Have you any
proposals, gentlemen?

AGENT. Well, the Captain and I –

CAPTAIN. Perhaps our Catholic friend, the merchant, Mr Clancy,
could suggest something?

CLANCY. (*mutters*). I don't know.

PP. Well, I don't know what you're doing on this committee.

CAPTAIN. Looking after your own interests, Mr Clancy? Seeing
that the free-trade guarantee the Government has given you is
not violated, hmm?

PP. Isn't it a great pity all the landowners wouldn't meet and see
what they could do?

AGENT. But that's exactly what the Government wants us to do.

PP. Yes?

AGENT. But, I think, your reverence, when you hear our
proposal –

CAPTAIN. No, wait, Simmington.

PP. If ye meet ye'd admit the responsibility is it?

CAPTAIN. You think the responsibility is ours?

FR HORAN. Ye own the whole country.

CAPTAIN. I'm quite aware of the limits of your thought: 'the
wealthy tyrant landlord'.

AGENT. (*attempting a joke*). I believe we're held responsible for
the bad weather.

PP. No, Mr Simmington, we all know that the Government causes
that.

JP. Gentlemen –

CAPTAIN. Well, I suggest you start pointing your finger at them
for a change, or at yourselves.

PP. If that's your proposal, Captain, we'll bear it in mind.

JP. You have some – any – proposal, Captain? Mr Simmington?

CAPTAIN. Father Daly? . . . We wanted first to see what
suggestions the representatives of the great Papist majority could
come up with for the country . . . Well, I have talked with
Simmington here and he has contacted his absent employer, and

we have arranged to borrow £10,000 between us and make it available to the tenantry on our respective estates.

JP. Oh, my dear Captain –

CAPTAIN. We have arranged to *borrow* this money.

PP. (*not taking bait*). I'm sure you deserve every credit, Captain, and when we hear how you propose to spend it –

CAPTAIN. But that the 'wealthy tyrant' has to borrow! Aren't you surprised? Our Papist friends are so informed about the wealthy tyrant's side of things in their speeches and sermons and letters to the press.

JP. Ah – well – ah – (*He looks at* PP *to reply.*)

PP. You seem to want to talk, Captain, and since you're going to borrow the money, and if you think it's the right time –

CAPTAIN. Do you know anything about the law of entail, Daly? Or encumbrances? Or do you only know about 'the industrious but oft-abused tenantry' causing that din up and down the town out there?

AGENT. (*wanting to restrain him*). Captain –

CAPTAIN. I can say with all sincerity that I have done as much honest toil in my life as any man. All I expected was fair play – from the Government and from my tenants. But the Government's imagination goes no further than rates. Aw, but the oft-abused tenantry are more resourceful. They have their feast-days and pattern days and celebrating-misery-days. The weeds must be allowed to thrive and flower and blow across on to the crops of the industrious. There *is* a particular minority *sect* in this community that responds to encouragement, but they, like myself, must suffer the nettles, sorrel, docks –

FR HORAN. The present food of your tenantry.

CAPTAIN. Is that why they grow them? . . . How many lambs blinded by the thistles every year? And did you ever try to get an honest day's work out of one of them? And their times of sowing: a month after the proper time. Not for want of encouragement. But why not publish these facts? The superstitions and witchery, fences and walls to be knocked. How many sheep spiked wantonly every year? Would you expect it of the black man? Ignorance, deceit, rent evasion, begging. This county alone would furnish all England with beggars. Filth, the breeding of disease. But, are they so naturally this way – so naturally destructive? Hmm? And the scrawls on the grubby little bits of paper, threatening the life of the landlord or his wife.

FR HORAN. Well, I can tell you –

PP. (*restraining him*). Father Horan.

CAPTAIN. What can *you* tell any man? I, too, could be off in 'the gaming houses of Europe'.

PP. Your would-be assassins are in more imminent danger, Captain.

JP ⎫ Gentlemen, if we could –
CAPTAIN ⎰ But are they so *naturally* this way, Daly?

PP. You're not the worst of them, Captain.

CAPTAIN. I admire – I admire – your composure, Daly. Coming in here this evening I passed some of their pig-sty dwellings and the chimneys are gone. I insisted all houses have chimneys. But the chimneys are gone, the chimneys are knocked down and the holes blocked up. What for? Is it that the fairies don't like heights? Or was the banshee getting caught up in them in her frequent entrances and exits, or was it the Pope?

FR HORAN. The rents were ruz because of the chimneys!

PP. Father Horan!

CAPTAIN. Travesties of the beautiful countryside.

FR HORAN. And the houses were cold because of them.

PP. Father Horan! I agree with a lot you say, Captain.

CAPTAIN. Of course. You can't deny it here.

PP. It will be a slow process.

CAPTAIN. Yes, there's a slow process in operation. And we've grown soft.

JP. Please, could we, perhaps, get back to –

FR HORAN. It's just that you don't understand the Irish yet.

CAPTAIN. What?! But I am Irish, stupid priest! And don't speak until you are spoken to. You are not a member of this committee. Or I wasn't consulted about your co-option if you are. My family goes back several hundred years.

FR HORAN. To some time of conquest, no doubt, *your honour.*

CAPTAIN. Yes? But I didn't steal your land, boy.

FR HORAN. It was stolen, it was stolen! And time won't make the theft right.

CAPTAIN. It seems I've committed a felony. I'm the receiver of stolen goods. Must I give it back?

FR HORAN. I didn't say – Yes! Yis! Yis!

CAPTAIN. To primitive man?

FR HORAN. To the people! To the people!

PP ⎱ Father Horan!
JP ⎰ Gentlemen!

CAPTAIN. This is, indeed, a strange country: There are Irish and Irish who aren't Irish.

FR HORAN. Yis! – Great Irish! – Who will yet legislate for themselves!

CAPTAIN ⎫ Is there a –
PP ⎬ Father Horan!
FR HORAN ⎫ The Union will be repealed!
JP ⎭ Gentlemen, please, I must ask you –

CAPTAIN. Is there a pure Irish race somewhere, or are you referring to the monkeys roaming the hills out there? Monkeys who could now be men, but for the popery that keeps them apart!

FR HORAN. We can wait! We won't forget the past! Your breed will go! You'll see!

CAPTAIN. There it is! That's what I wanted to hear!

PP. Father Horan, I forbid you to say another word!

CAPTAIN. There it is! They can wait! There's their slow process! Do they want to be helped, are they so naturally evil, or is there some cunning power directing all this, some malicious conspiracy, directed by the Roman anti-Christs that would have the well-meaning robbed and reduced to squalor and filth on a level with their own.

PP. (*to* FR HORAN). You have a lot of sick calls to make. I don't think you should waste your time here. Tell them outside to pray.

FR HORAN *leaves*.

Well, Captain, you bought the right, and now, if you've got your pound of flesh, maybe we can –

CAPTAIN. No, sir! I thought it was timely to let you know that we are aware of what's going on.

PP. Fair enough. Just, it struck me more like the babbling of a drowning man.

CAPTAIN. No, sir! No, sir! And half the countries of the world have been conquered as long ago as Ireland has, and conqueror and conquered have managed to work together and prosper without any fine-cut distinctions of nationality or unending vicious conspiracy.

PP. There's no conspiracy: I'm not going arguing nonsense with you. But I'll say one thing, the fine-cut distinctions you talk about might be due to the fact that men like you still behave like conquerors – No-no-no, Captain – Listen, I'll be off too if I'm only hampering the real business of the meeting. I'll call later to the Chairman and –

JP. For heaven's sake, gentlemen, please! Could we be seated again.

FR HORAN. (*off; calling to crowd*). Kneel! Kneel! . . . Now, pray! Pray! (*Hushed murmuring of prayers.*)

JP. . . . To remind you, gentlemen, that yesterday, a whole family was found dead in a wood about seven miles from here. No one knows who they are or where they came from. At this moment there are seven or eight funerals waiting outside the cemetery . . . Could we hear your proposal or plan, Captain?

AGENT. Perhaps, Captain, if *I* outlined what we have in mind . . . (*He smiles at meeting, the most amiable of men.*) It's a simple little plan, gentlemen. Well, as the Captain said, the country must be saved no matter what the cost. Now, the way we see the situation is this. Are we to receive relief in the form of food supplies from our free-trade, or free-for-all, government? No. Can we expect permission to begin public works. Yes. *Sometime* in the future. But even with the sanctioning of Public Work, will the building of a road or a wall absorb half the labour force around here or fill one quarter of the bellies? Well now, what else have we? Yes, we hear of the charitable organisations and we know of the costly, dangerous and unselfish nature of their administration, but what can they hope to achieve against such odds of numbers? Indeed, many people maintain – and dare I disagree? – that well-meaning though these organisations might be, the fact remains that alms-giving is contrary to the spirit of industry we should like to see fostered in this country. But that is just a by-the-way.

CLANCY. Hear – hear!

JP. What is your proposal, Mr Simmington?

AGENT. The Captain and I are pointing out that all doors seem to be closed on us, and that –

PP. What is your plan, Mr Simmington?

AGENT. All this, your reverence, to avoid wasting time on possible argument later on.

PP. (*suspicious*). What?

AGENT. Can any thinking man, your reverence, seriously believe that we can hope for constructive help in the immediate future from our Government?

PP. Yes, yes, but, what do you propose to do?

AGENT. It was only the other day I was saying to Captain Shine that I should like to say we are dealing with *faction* politics, not party politics. That at the moment one faction in the Commons is saying there is no distress here: that that belief has come from the famed Irish imagination. While another faction says we've got *famine* here, but of such magnitude that it is impossible for them to deal with it. And yet another: that if we have a problem, it's ours, we created it, and solve it we must alone; that they are sick and tired of dependent Ireland; that we have arrived at the stage, they say – humourously – where an Irish gentleman cannot marry off his daughter without first seeking the advice and aid of Government. But I must mention one last group. I speak objectively, and with all due respect to any individual's political leanings. The Irish MPs of O'Connell's party. The statements of this group amount to the belief that if the people starve patiently the result will be a speedier repeal of the Union between Great Britain and Ireland.

PP. Very good, Mr Simmington, now how do you propose to spend this money?

AGENT. I'm coming to it, your reverence.

PP. How will you import speedily enough such large quantities of food to –

CAPTAIN. What?

AGENT. Well, your reverence, we think it may not be a question of importing food.

PP. What?

AGENT. You see, what we first of all tried to make our Government see is the recurring hopelessness here when all the while prosperity is there for the taking in other parts of the world.

PP. What? – For who? – What are you saying?

CAPTAIN. He's saying, Daly –

AGENT. I'm saying, your reverence, the world is opening out. New continents with untold natural wealth are waiting to be reclaimed by the brave pioneer hand –

PP. Food! Soup! Meal! –

AGENT. Huge tracts of land waiting to be tilled, to produce food, unlimited food for everyone. A new world that promises –

PP. Clear them is it?

AGENT. No.

PP. What then?

AGENT. Aid them to emigrate.

PP. This is what ye worked out?!

CAPTAIN. We are prepared to spend –

PP. Yes, Captain, ye are prepared to spend. If I had known the measure of your scheme ye would not have made your fine humbug speeches. Ye had no right. Indulging yourselves in your high-fallutin' ráimeis that showed up your hypocrisy and ignorance as much as your arrogance.

CAPTAIN. I'm afraid I don't understand your attitude.

PP. I'm sure you don't!

AGENT. Your reverence –

PP. I didn't think you would. You're not Irish! – You're not Irish!

CAPTAIN. What can you offer them?

PP. What can I offer them? You – you talk about new continents, land to be reclaimed, and not a farthing to clear a stick or a stone off all the land that lies about ye here in a state of nature. Not a farthing piece to drain a drop of water off all the acres and acres of bog.

AGENT. We're offering a great number of people an alternative to death.

PP. And we've been watching the tricks of the *adventurer* too, Mr Simmington, this while back, agent, or part-owner, or whatever you are now of your absent employer's estate.

JP. I see merit in the scheme.

PP. Well, there's a smell off the merit. (*Turns on* CAPTAIN.) Yes, Shine – Yes, Shine, they're poor people, ignorant, demoralized and dirty, moulded and shaped that way by England and by England's tools, the landlords, over the past five or six hundred years. Colonization and poverty! And all we can see after all those centuries of British rule and justice is a Union flag flying proud over an empty government meal depot up the road there and a mob of howling peasants around it.

JP. We understand, Father Daly, but we must think of the moment now. It's a solution.

PP. Clear them! Get rid of them! And that's the extent of relief that can be offered in this modern year of 1846?

JP. Large numbers are emigrating voluntarily, so to speak.

AGENT. Oh, there's no question of compulsion.

JP. No – no, of course not.

PP. (*to* CLANCY). Have you anything at all to say, Clancy? Didn't you make fortune enough last year? Is there any spirit in you at all other than greed that would make you close down your whiskey houses and throw open your big stores now, instead of waiting for starvation prices to soar higher?

AGENT. Your reverence –

PP. What are ye addressing this at me for?

AGENT. What else can be offered them?

CAPTAIN. What can *you* offer them?

PP. (*viciously*). A captain, a captain! And sure little schoolboys with any background get that rank straightaway on entering the army! (*He turns away, wincing at his own malice.*)

AGENT. Father Daly –

PP. Well, I have faith in humanity! – I have faith in – What are ye addressing this at me for?

AGENT. Well, frankly, the unfortunate relationship that has grown up between landlord and tenant.

PP. In spite of yere gentle encouragement . . . Aaa, I see, now! And ye need the help of the clergy in clearing a reluctant peasantry off the land they were born in and love?

AGENT. . . . Well, if you insist on putting it that way.

PP. (*a last try*). Would nothing induce ye to spend the money here?

AGENT. It's not a matter of spending the money here. Common sense. It's getting worse every year: This tillage system is hopeless: The country is a workhouse.

PP. But this great sum. Couldn't it be used for –

CAPTAIN. Rates cost us more yearly.

PP. . . . Rates cost ye more?

AGENT. (*forcing a laugh, trying to cover the blunder*). Yes, who would have thought?

PP. It's cheaper to clear them! . . . *Who* are we saving?

AGENT. It may not appear obvious now, but it's the only hope for the country.

PP *turns away from them.*

Short silence.

JP. Well . . . I feel . . . I think . . . Have you decided on a?

CAPTAIN. Canada.

JP. And when do you think?

AGENT. It will take a month to complete arrangements.

JP. Do you intend the offer for a particular class?

AGENT. No. It's to be a general offer, though, generally – I mean naturally – the most needy will get preference.

JP. And I expect a number of those who might accept have leases or made improvements: do you propose to?

CAPTAIN. What?

JP. Would you compensate them?

CAPTAIN. Good God, man, you might as well propose compensating the rabbits for digging holes in the ground! I've never seen half of them before.

JP. How many do you propose to – to – to emigrate?

AGENT ⎱ Two thousand.
CAPTAIN ⎰ Three thousand.

JP. . . . I see.

Short silence.

AGENT. (*forces a laugh*). But, though neither am I of the Catholic Church, it was only the other day that I thought that emigration – and such as we propose – could be considered a means towards spreading that faith throughout the world. Though, I think better of mentioning it now. But still.

PP. Not bad, Mr Simmington, but I'm not as naive as you think . . . I did think a minute ago of something in its favour. (*He looks at* CLANCY.) Your scheme would relieve those poor people out there of all sight and dealings with the accursed gombeen man whose fate, I feel certain, is more assured than the fate of Judas. (*He turns away again, wincing at his own words.*) . . . But I think now of the long sea voyage, in the ships that are coming to be known as coffinships. And at the end of the journey, opportunity, maybe. But I see them, a herd of innocents, starved and diseased, thrown up on a foreign shore, the sacrificial offerings of a modern world. This prosperous Christian world. I wonder is there another part of the world today stricken like ourselves? And I wonder is there a body of leaders, principled men, believing in an ideal for the world and letting a great chance go by. Because this is an opportunity, and the leaders should be rushing forward to grasp it with all the love and help they've got to further the hope of the ideal. Otherwise, better stop talks of ideals entirely and say that life is based on a lie; otherwise, what can be expected of evolving man. (*The others are showing signs of impatience.*) If it was needed for a war against the Afghans! But, maybe I've been a simple old fool all my life. Maybe economies can only survive and cater for the catastrophe of war. Ye're impatient, gentlemen.

AGENT. Time.

PP. Yes, time is against us too. And I have no answers. But the future will answer us all.

JP. Well, I suggest, that perhaps the best thing to do would be to interview them individually. That is when you've gone further with your preparations.

AGENT. But it would be – nice – if we could tell them something tonight.

JP. Well, perhaps, if they were told generally about the scheme now.

AGENT. Certainly.

JP. It would give them time to be thinking about it.

AGENT. Excellent. Would Fr Daly like to address them? (PP *shakes his head.*)

CAPTAIN. But, surely to God, man, you can't tell them to refuse?

PP. If we could at least keep God's name out of it. Consider only that I'm not your enemy. The decision will have to be theirs.

Scene Six

THE QUARRY

A few weeks later. A rise overlooking a quarry. Night.

A rabbit cooking over a small fire. MALACHY *has collected a pile of stones. He weighs one of them in his hand. He carries them off, and returns with an armful of twigs which he places in readiness beside the fire. His movements are deliberate; an air of cool and ruthless detachment about him. He hears a noise off. He hides.*

MICKELEEN *enters and waits.* MALACHY *reappears; he realizes that the errand he has sent* MICKELEEN *on has not been successful.* MICKELEEN *laughs. Though his speeches are bitter and taunting, he is wary of* MALACHY.

MICKELEEN. They won't come up . . . I say the scarecrows won't come up to visit you. They have lots to be doing. Still talking about the emigration: Connor wondering is it right to take it. Hah, Seán? . . . And I told them you'd have a sheep for them to eat. (*He laughs.*) But they doubted even Malachy Mór'd manage to steal one and all the bodacks of guards Simmington has. And, for why, they asked, did you pick a place on the rise beside the quarry for a meeting and chance catching a fever from one of the workhouse paupers buried ablow. On that account, I said, 'twould be safest from the peelers. But the fire cooking it, they said, would of a certainty be sure to be seen by the peelers patrolling the glen and they'd have to drop in on us. (*Laughs.*) But to thank you kindly . . . Christ, a noble plan to trick your army up here.

MALACHY. (*quietly*). Eat, Michael.

MICKELEEN *takes a piece of the rabbit. He starts to kick some ashes on the fire to damp it down,* MALACHY *growls, then starts to kindle it.*

MICKELEEN. Ara what? . . . And they were talking about Liam Dougan too as is now a top bodack of a vastard for Simmington. And they're sorry for Brian Riordan because some thief has all his turf near stolen, all to the few cíaráns. Hah, I said, maybe the dispossessed Learys took it? The small bandy cripple and his brother of the great stature that's handy at the deserting. The Learys is bad, I said; they'd take a snail from a blind hen, I said . . . (*Notices fire is brightening up.*) Not that I fear any parish tyrant of a rotten peeler – We're doing no harm – but if they come up here now and remember me – cause I'm easy remembered – from the day of the corncarts.

MALACHY. (*putting sticks on the fire; to himself*). Ar yis, yis, yis, yis, yis.

MICKELEEN. (*looking into quarry*). The wind blowing down
there – Curse of Christ! Curse of Christ! – going astray in its
direction blowing, throwing all classes of rotten fevered paupers'
diseases up on top of us. (*Glances at the brightening fire again.*)
And the peelers too is looking for some gallant rebel that stoned
to death the soldier's horse that used be straying at night.

MALACHY (*quietly; looking into quarry*). Lime, Michael, the
quick-lime: it burns them, diseases and all: the paupers, and the
odd stray one they pick up dead in the fields.

MICKELEEN. Connor, I said, Seán, I said, don't you reckon
they'd have blessed the smaller quarry in Clonshee if they
expected your sort of help to come. (*Suddenly soft.*) Connor.
The meal will come. Johnny Connor. (*Suddenly harsh again.*)
Seán! – Vastard! – Pleb! – Lúdramán! – He'd make a one
seafóideach with his class of talk!

MALACHY. Over there, wasn't it, Tomás and Mary Leary rotted
on the hillside, yourself in attendance, Michael, this time last
year?

MICKELEEN. (*looking into quarry again*). I often heard tell of one
being buried alive. How many would you say to fill it?

MALACHY *moves off, looking down into the glen.*

MICKELEEN. (*nervously, to himself*). Ara what? . . . You'll not
clear your conscience this night! You'll not –

MALACHY *enters.*

MALACHY. But 'twas a good plan, Michael. I thought to myself,
since Connor is scattered, myself to be leader. Five men, cripples
or no, would have done easy. (*Pointing to where he would have
positioned them.*) One there, one behind the boulder, one in the
hollow yonder against the furze, myself there on the ledge in the
quarry, and yourself running, making enough noise for us all.
The peelers hearing you would stop there. They don't expect
revenge. And we'd have two guns, the start of an army to see
whose fault.

A noise off. MALACHY *motions* MICKELEEN *to be quiet, and
he moves off cautiously to investigate the noise.*

MICKELEEN. . . . Ara what? Ara what? . . . Fine plan, fine plan – Christ! The big stature. And deserting us again tomorrow. Like the other vastards and spalpeens. Go, let ye, one way or the other. My name is on no list for going. Show yere bodies to the world. Hop a stone off a man's head and ye're free. And the cripple is left to all these ghosts and the hills.

MALACHY *enters.*

MALACHY. Whist! They're coming. When I give you the word –

MICKELEEN. Ara what?

MALACHY. Stand still till I give you the word. Then make noise running as if – (*He grabs at* MICKELEEN.)

MICKELEEN. (*dodges him*). Ara what? Christ! Ara what?

MICKELEEN *escapes and runs off.*

MALACHY *stands motionless for a moment. The police can be heard apparoaching.* MALACHY *starts to mutter to himself, his determination beginning to falter.*

MALACHY. Chris-jays . . . Chris-jays . . . Chris-jays.

He starts to run, in several directions, growing confused. He kicks ashes on the fire and races off.

FIRST *and* SECOND POLICEMAN *enter. They wait, until the fading noises of* MICKELEEN *and* MALACHY *are gone. They search about the place for a few moments. Then they relax.*

FIRST POLICEMAN. They're well gone.

SECOND POLICEMAN. Two of them, I'd say.

FIRST POLICEMAN. Let them keep going.

SECOND POLICEMAN. A rabbit.

FIRST POLICEMAN. (*warms his hands at fire*). Lord, it's bitter cold, Ciarán.

SECOND POLICEMAN. There's no fight in them.

FIRST POLICEMAN. What did we do to deserve to be out in a place like this?

SECOND POLICEMAN. Be thankful to God you have a job at all.

FIRST POLICEMAN. Well, it's not that they're giving us much trouble. But it's bitter cold, Ciarán.

SECOND POLICEMAN. There's no spark in them. Times I'm ashamed of them. I wouldn't starve so quiet, I'm telling you. And the fearful army of spectres they'd make.

FIRST POLICEMAN. Gobs, I'm not going to complain about that.

SECOND POLICEMAN. That's what I'd like.

He goes to the quarry and looks down into it.

FIRST POLICEMAN. (*takes a bottle from his pocket*). Do you think it's a famine? They're saying it is. (*He takes a drink; then, philosophically.*) Oh, what can stop a famine!

SECOND POLICEMAN. What's down there?

FIRST POLICEMAN. What can stop a famine! It's a quarry. I wish it was Spring. (*He is taking another drink.*)

SECOND POLICEMAN. No, a neat pile of stones on the ledge there, like as if –

At this moment MALACHY rushes out of the darkness, arms outstretched. He pushes SECOND POLICEMAN into the quarry, jumps on FIRST POLICEMAN and kills him with a stone. He takes FIRST POLICEMAN's gun and races off.

Scene Seven

THE INTERVIEW

A week later. The rent office.

AGENT sits inside the window of the rent office, a list of names before him. On a table outside the window is a similar list for the marks or signatures of those being interviewed. AGENT has a long pointer for indicating where the signatures should be made. (These precautions are taken in fear of fever contagion.)

LIAM is outside the rent office, acting as the AGENT's usher.

A crowd of people (on or offstage) are waiting to be interviewed.

A MAN, *standing outside rent office, puts his mark on the paper that is on the table and is waved off.*

AGENT. Incomprehensible, some of them. (*Adding numbers on his list.*) Six hundred and eight and six is six hundred and fourteen . . . Now, next area. Glanconor village. John Connor. He's some sort of village elder, isn't he? (LIAM *nods.*) We'll get his acceptance first. Call him.

LIAM. John Connor! . . . John Connor!

JOHN, *now looking more dead than alive, enters and stands at the table.*

AGENT. Connor. You've decided? (*He glances up at* JOHN's *abject expression and decides for himself in the affirmative.*) How many of you? – Look the other way when you speak. (JOHN *obediently turns his head away from the* AGENT.) Good man. Make sure you do not breathe in this direction. How many of you? Wife, children, grandparents.

JOHN. Four.

AGENT. Look the other way, man! . . . Four.

JOHN. But –

AGENT. Put your mark there.

JOHN. Ah –

AGENT. What?

JOHN. (*apologetically*). I can write, your honour.

AGENT. Look the other way – Look the other way! You can write. Good man. Sign there. (*Adding numbers on his papers.*) Six hundred and fourteen and four –

JOHN. I don't know.

AGENT. What?

JOHN. If I was sure.

AGENT. If you were sure.

JOHN. I'd go if I was sure.

AGENT. Oh now, my good man, I haven't to go through all this again, have I?

JOHN. (*appears to be in a daze*). No.

AGENT. Of course I can't compel you to go.

JOHN. Yes, your honour.

AGENT. What?

JOHN. No, your honour.

AGENT. I can't compel you to go.

JOHN. No, your honour.

AGENT. I can't compel you.

JOHN. No, your honour.

AGENT. Have your clergy spoken against it?

JOHN. No, your honour.

AGENT. There you are then.

JOHN. No, your honour.

AGENT. Stop! Are you listening to me at all?

JOHN. Maybe to wait a while longer.

AGENT. You're some kind of village leader aren't you? Are you possibly the man who led the Glanconor people to join that mob in town a few weeks ago?

JOHN. To explain, your —

AGENT. To explain. Well, maybe we'll forget that.

JOHN. I'm confused.

AGENT. Indeed you are. Aren't you hungry — Do you like starvation — Do you want to die in the fields — Quicker still in the workhouse — Do you want to die of fever?

JOHN. No, your honour.

AGENT. Hmm?

JOHN. I had it once, your —

AGENT. What?

JOHN. The workhouse were built for paupers, your honour.

AGENT. Yes –

JOHN. We're farmers.

AGENT. Farmers. And you should know by now that the land you hold is no good except, possibly, for grazing. All the good land waiting for you in Canada. You look a sensible man.

JOHN. Naaw.

AGENT. What?

JOHN. (*neurotically*). Only what's right, I must do only what's right.

AGENT. You want to do the right thing, of course you do –

JOHN. Yis, your honour, only what's right –

AGENT. Turn your head the other way!

JOHN. And for the Glanconors. And if you can explain, and that it's right, and explain the reason, we'll go.

AGENT. The reason? (*He laughs at* JOHN.)

JOHN. (*first trace of defiance*). I could have gone years ago, my father could have gone, my grandfather –

AGENT. The reason. Aren't you starving?

JOHN. Naaw!

AGENT. Aren't you starving? –

JOHN. Naaw!

AGENT. Isn't your wife starving? Your children?

JOHN. . . . . I'll look after them.

AGENT. Will you? . . . I think you're just being stubborn, Connor. And selfish.

JOHN. But we've been here so long. Waiting.

AGENT. And now help has come. Isn't this the answer to your prayers?

JOHN. If you can explain to me the reason why it is.

AGENT. (*losing control*). Aw, listen here – (*He controls himself, forces a laugh.*) I think I know what's wrong. You're afraid to go, afraid of the water like some of the others.

JOHN. We sowed the crop, it failed again: that's all.

AGENT. A big man like you. There, Connor, put your mark there.

JOHN. (*defiantly*). I can write!

AGENT. Now listen here – listen here – listen here – listen! Who else will help you if I don't? You're not one of those expecting government aid are you? What? Well, you can forget that.

JOHN ⎱ That can't be. We're peaceful, we're doing no wrong –
AGENT ⎰ That can be! That is!

JOHN. We sowed the crop, it failed again: that's all.

AGENT. There will be no government aid, no aid, so who else will assist you if I don't?

JOHN. There's a God above still we hope.

AGENT. Will He pay the rent for you, will He pay the rates?

JOHN. I've paid my rent! The oats! – And the cow you took! – The cow! – And how long will the voyage take? – And to what part of Canada? – And how many acres will we get? – And does anyone know we're coming? – And how hot or how cold is it there? And will there be any compensation for –

AGENT. Get back from the window, I'm not spending any more time on you. I expected your gratitude because I am the only one who has pity on you. You will receive help from no other quarter – Don't shake your head! By signing that paper you will be doing the right thing: I can assure you it's God's will. Is that sufficient explanation for you?

JOHN. He gave me a will too.

AGENT. Alright, Connor, listen carefully. Every man of you on my estate – *my* estate! – is a half-year's rent in arrears –

JOHN. Begging your pardon, but isn't that the way it always was?

AGENT. By law – by law, on that account, there isn't a man among you I can't have out on the roadside in the morning. I'm not going to have some staying and some going. I'm not going to be ruined by half measures after my years here. Do you understand that? . . . Now, sign there.

JOHN *looks at him.*

Turn your head the other way.

JOHN. (*does not obey*). We'll withstand it!

AGENT. Turn your head!

JOHN. We'll live!

AGENT. Look the other way!

JOHN. I won't go.

AGENT. Why? (*Shouts.*) Why? – Why? – Why?

JOHN *keeps looking at him.* AGENT *hits him with the pointer.*

Get back, Connor! Get away, get away!

JOHN *walks away, much more alive than dead.*

Next! Next! O'Dea, Daniel O'Dea!

LIAM. Daniel O'Dea, Daniel O'Dea! . . . Daniel O'Dea!

AGENT. Dineen, Marcus Dineen!

LIAM. Marcus Dineen! Marcus Dineen!

AGENT. Malachy O'Leary!

LIAM. Malachy O'Leary!

AGENT. Riordan! Brian Riordan!

LIAM. Brian Riordan! . . . Brian Riordan!

AGENT. Connor, Connor, get Connor back here!

But JOHN *has gone.*

If crowd is on stage, DAN, DAN'S WIFE, BRIAN and MICKELEEN follow JOHN.

MARK remains, waiting to accept the offer.

Scene Eight

ALBERT O'TOOLE

JOHN's house and the road outside. DAN and MICKELEEN are outside the door, looking off. They move in and out of the house.

A little away from them, also looking off, are MOTHER, MAEVE and DAN's WIFE.

The house is almost bare of furniture and effects. A few coffins are stacked in a corner, one of them painted red. JOHN is working doggedly on another – a coffin with a trap-bottom. DONAILL is beside him. BRIAN sits by the fire; he remains silent throughout.

MICKELEEN. (*calling*). Hah, Seán?

DAN. (*looking off*). There's no sign of them moving yet . . . There's the widdy and her brood. (*Calls.*) Johnny! And, aw, will you look at himself! Marcusheen! . . . He's looking up this way. Pull back or he'll see you. (*They stand in the doorway.*) Johnny! . . . The crowd of them!

MICKELEEN. What's the matter, Seán?

DAN. I never thought to see a Glanconor go without as much as a shake hands. Comical. (*Joins JOHN.*) Yis, we must struggle on whatever. We're upset. (*Proud.*) But we refused their offer, John. We did. We did.

JOHN. I don't understand it.

DAN. Hah? . . . (*Referring to coffin with trap-bottom.*) Oh, never fear, Johnny, this melodian will be our saviour yet. (*Pointing at red coffin.*) Wouldn't you think that would attract anyone? But, when the customer hasn't it for the real article, this contraption. And when we were only paid for three, was it? Two? Four? Hah? Oh, maith go leor, who could refuse a dead man –

(*Laughs.*) or woman. The dead must be protected, if only for a time. I'd prefer the wolf any day to the rat.

JOHN. (*to himself*). Am I doing right or wrong?

DAN. (*looks at* JOHN's *work; laughs*). Isn't it simple as life and death itself!

JOHN. (*angrily*). Heed me!

MICKELEEN. (*calls*). Don't let it best you, Seán.

JOHN. Them is the sides nailed: Now which do I nail fast, the top or the bottom?

DAN. The bottom.

JOHN. But didn't ye say a trap bottom? – Sure, you won't heed me! Whichever you nail fast, the open end will always have to be up to receive the corpse: but then if the open end is to be the trap bottom, you have to turn the coffin over: but then you'll be carrying them on their faces, carrying them on their faces.

DAN. Nail down the top and you'll understand. You're not working so tasty as you were. (*Goes to fire.*) There's none of us is, Brian, no, a mac. (*Surveys the bare house.*) And there's nothing left to sell – (*He laughs.*) Save, if we pawn one of the women. Are they still there, Mickeleen?

MICKELEEN. Yis, na vastards!

DAN. Carney buried the wife in a bag last night. Now! And never came anear us. A person'd soon go rottening through a bag. The maggots is the boyos to the dead. But isn't the rat worse to living dead? Hah? A strange little animal. Buried Nell Carney in a bag. But, isn't it the same with this style – Lord, a chuid, style: trapdoors in coffins, a Thighearna! (*Lord!*) 'Tisn't the most natural, we know, but the journey to the graveyard, tuigeann sibh, (*Ye understand.*) to be respectable in the eyes of the world.

JOHN. Hold it for me.

DAN. (*helps* JOHN). We'd want a couple every day to struggle it out until . . . until . . . Hah? And they're in it too, if only they'd come to us.

JOHN. Why do you keep talking?

DAN. I'm holding it . . . I'll be in that red vessel myself yet, if you don't go before me, Johnny. (*Laughs.*) Or maybe Mickeleen'd fly before any of us!

JOHN. Why do you keep talking?

DAN. I'm holding it!

MICKELEEN. Here he's up! Marcus!

MICKELEEN *draws back into the house.* MOTHER, MAEVE *and* DAN's WIFE *pull back also.* DAN *and* MICKELEEN *peep out the door.*

Look at him! He thinks he's secure now! The Dineen breed, and all his breed before him! His grandfather one time that stole the spade that was the only livelihood to Peadar Bane. His sister that used to give belly to the soldiers at the fairs in Turlough.

DAN. The peacock! Look at the strut of him!

MICKELEEN. The dirty breed!

DAN. The Dineens how-are-yeh!

MARK *enters timidly, slowly, his eyes on the road all the while. He waits.*

JOHN. 'Hat? – Go out to him – Didn't we just refuse? Go out to him.

MICKELEEN. Let the spalpeen go now.

JOHN. Go out, can't you, Danny, bid the man adieu.

DAN. . . . Aaaa . . .

JOHN. What's coming over ye at all?

JOHN *comes out to* MARK, *followed by* DONAILL, MICKELEEN *and* DAN. BRIAN, *trance-like, follows.* MOTHER, MAEVE *and* DAN's WIFE *approach.*

Go mbeannuighthe Dia dhuit, a Mhark! I knew you'd come up to see us before going.

MICKELEEN. What's delaying yere departure?

MARK. A crowd above in Cosackbawn is inclined to renege and the bailley is gone up to tumble their houses and bring them down.

MICKELEEN. And your own will be levelled before duskess. (*Dusk.*)

MARK. What's to signify in that now?

Not having an answer he looks to JOHN *to supply one.*

MICKELEEN. Oh, we bid the deserters farewell.

JOHN. (*to* MARK, *gently*). You're not going alone whatever.

MARK. But the ones that were nearest ever to me?

MICKELEEN. And Albert O'Toole will be after you.

MARK. Who?

MICKELEEN. From Pullanoar.

MARK. I don't know the man.

MICKELEEN. Don't you? Well, whether you do or no, he refused Simmington *and* the Captain. And Danny O'Dea there refused. And they threatened John Connor here with whips about arrears, but he wouldn't be – transported.

JOHN. Stop now! – Oh but I wouldn't go for them alright.

MARK. But why are ye staying?

MICKELEEN *and* DAN *look to* JOHN *to reply.*

JOHN. (*losing control*). That's why! – That's why! – That's why!

MICKELEEN. And you'll be no sooner gone when the roadworks will be starting up.

JOHN. And help – the meal – it's coming, it's coming.

MARK. But all that's dying.

JOHN. Yis, but the roadworks, and – but did you hear about Albert O'Toole threatening them?

MARK. Sure, I don't know the man.

MICKELEEN. Did you hear about Albert O'Toole threatening them? –

JOHN. Did you? –

MARK. Sure, we never knew anyone from Pullanoar –

JOHN. But did you hear – did you hear –

MARK. But Tom Fada is going and the widdy and hundreds –

JOHN. But did you hear – (*Urging* DAN *to speak.*) Danny.

MICKELEEN. The only journey I'll be making, says Albert O'Toole –

JOHN } He did, he did.
DAN } Will be direct to hell, chasing your vile souls there.

JOHN. He did, he did!

DAN } By the five crosses, says he –
MARK } But, sure, we never knew anyone from –

DAN. By all that's before ye, behind ye, above ye, ablow ye, and all about ye –

MARK } Sure I don't know the man.
MICKELEEN } I'll live to see ye transformed to dung.

DAN. And they arrested him.

JOHN. Do you know that? –

MICKELEEN. Do you, Dineen? –

DAN. Do you know that? –

MICKELEEN. And do you know that when Father Daly –

DAN. The parish priest himself –

MICKELEEN. Heard that the peelers had him, and his wife barely cold in her deathbed, up went his reverence and got his release for the duration of the funeral –

JOHN. Do you know that? –

DAN. And that was maith go leor until whatever cullermuggerin' the ophans had 'round the grave as the mother was going under, but they were laughing whatever, and 'Hacka!', says Albert, hitting the eldest putack a smather and stretching him on the clay, and then off with him racing, 'cross the fields, na police air a thóir (*Chasing him.*) nor did they ketch him – No! – till he was halfway through the Lodge windy, and a lump of a stone to him to get at Simmington.

JOHN. He'll be remembered.

DAN. He'll be remembered –

MICKELEEN. There's some brave men yet –

DAN. Sure, he's a hero.

MICKELEEN. A great man –

DAN. A hero –

MICKELEEN. Not a bodack of a vastardeen of a deserter!

JOHN. Stop! (*Realising he has lost control of himself.*)

MARK. But – but – but, Australia they'll send him to.

MICKELEEN. Will it? –

DAN. Will it now? –

MICKELEEN. It's all the same: Canada or Australia.

JOHN. Stop.

MARK. . . . Sure I'm not happy to be leaving ye. I'd renege myself but I can't watch any more of them die on me. (*He produces his ticket.*) And they do say it's prosperous. And no dealings there with landlord or bailley. A famous country next to America that the English has little or no to do with.

MICKELEEN. The same English is stuck everywhere.

The sight of the ticket has a quietening effect on them.
MOTHER *examines it.*

MARK. They'd take more yet. They'd take ye now. There's time.

JOHN. (*conscious of* MOTHER's *eyes on him; examining the ticket*). It looks legal enough.

MARK. Johnny? They'll wait an hour for ye. They'll have ye out anyway because they're going making a grazing range out of the whole village. They let me up so as to tell ye.

JOHN. (*hands ticket back to* MARK). You'll be alright, Marcus, we wish you well.

JOHN *shakes hands with* MARK *and returns to house, followed by* DONAILL; *he resumes working on the coffin.*

MARK *starts to cry.*

MARK. We'll be shifting anytime now . . . Oh Lord, and I'm afeared of the water. And I had a dream. Goodbye to ye, I'll do nothing wrong, I'll do nothing wrong. And I dreamt Canada was at the bottom of the ocean. And some say the captain and sailors is ojus drinkers. They won't let herself up. To be leaving ye all. And my own childre ablow, and what will Glanconor mean to them after six months out of it, or the fields, or the hazel beyond . . .

He exits through the speech.

MOTHER, MAEVE *and* DAN's WIFE *move off to watch* MARK's *departure.* BRIAN *continues motionless, standing outside, like something forgotten.*

DAN. He was nice. Poor Marcus . . . (*As he goes into house.*) I'd go myself but I'm too old . . . And I was counting for herself last night, all that's gone, dead, left, or disappeared and I don't know how many I counted.

JOHN. (*finishes the coffin*). I don't understand it.

DAN. You put them in the usual way, like this, and then turn the coffin over and . . . (*He sees the problem.*)

JOHN. Carrying them on their faces.

MICKELEEN. (*coming into house*). Hah, Seán?

DAN. Maybe if you'd put the handles on the other –

MICKELEEN. What's the matter, Seán?

JOHN. (*turns suddenly and catches MICKELEEN by the throat*).
I'm standing over you now, Michael, the likely way 'twill always
be: I've never afflicted you because God himself chose you for
misfortune: But don't keep on, for I'd not want to use on you
the sacred strength I'll always have kept aside! (*Releases
MICKELEEN and turns back, glaring at the coffin.*)

DAN. Just for carrying them to the graveside, sure.

JOHN. (*grabs DONAILL and lifts him up*). Open it! Now which
way his face?

MICKELEEN. Down.

JOHN. 'Hat?

MICKELEEN. Down! Down! And turn it over.

They put DONAILL into the coffin face down.

JOHN. Close it. Put the clasp on.

MICKELEEN. Turn it over . . . Now he's right ways up.

JOHN. Lift it . . . Walk . . . Stop . . . Loosen the catch.

*The catch is loosened and DONAILL tumbles out on to the
floor. He stays there whimpering. DAN, MICKELEEN and
JOHN laugh.*

DAN. I knew it wouldn't best you, Johnny.

MICKELEEN. 'Tis fit for man, woman or child, Seán.

DAN. And a fourpence is not unreasonable for such a serious
journey.

JOHN. (*lifting DONAILL to his feet*). Aw, musha, a mac, it's only
a bit of sport we're having. Run down to your mother, there's
mo bhuachaill. (*My boy.*)

He leads DONAILL outside, DONAILL runs off.

JOHN *stands beside BRIAN who has remained outside since
MARK's departure, JOHN is looking off into the distance,
vacantly. MICKELEEN comes to JOHN's side, looks off also,
but is puzzled.*

MICKELEEN. . . . . But what thing is it ye're waiting for? John?

JOHN. Not for you, *Mickeleen.*

Scene Nine

THE ASSASSINATION

A few weeks later.

LIAM, *the foreman on the roadworks, is walking along a stretch of new road that is being built. LIAM is giving instructions to the workers, men and women.*

Standing by, not hired, a group of people including JOHN, BRIAN, DAN and DAN's WIFE. This group in a block, motionless, silent, staring.

LIAM. (*to a worker*). Level that patch, step nimble, don't be leaving it all to the roller . . . (*To another.*) Break them smaller or you'll get no day's task marked up for you. (*To another.*) Root out them bushes . . .

JP *who is engineer of the works enters. He is followed by MICKELEEN. There is something strange in MICKELEEN's attitude. In fact he is considering warning JP that MALACHY is coming to shoot JP.*

Sir, this stretch will be ready for the roller next –

JP. (*turns to MICKELEEN*). My good man, what are you following me for?

LIAM. Clear off, O'Leary!

MICKELEEN *exits.*

JP. (*turns to LIAM*). Yes?

LIAM. This stretch will be ready for the roller on Thursday.

JP *sighs over the sorry plight of the workers and the futility of the works. LIAM misinterprets JP's attitude.*

It's not my fault if they're not doing the work. And some of them are complaining that the stones are field stones, not quarry stones. They're not able to work, sir.

JP *sighs again looking at the group standing by.*

LIAM. I've told them, but they won't go away for me.

MICKELEEN *has entered again, this time from another direction, and is watching* JP.

JP. (*sees* MICKELEEN). What does that man want? What is he following me for? (*Calls to* MICKELEEN.) What do you want, man? There's nothing here for you. I can't employ you if you haven't got a work permit. (*Continues to* JOHN's *group*.) I cannot employ you. Listen, I believe the government will reconsider its policy, I am very hopeful and maybe – soon – food will be distributed. (*No reacton from group*.) . . . Listen, the Quakers have set up a soup kitchen in Shaftstown: they require you to say or do nothing: it's a long way, I know, but you will get soup there. (*No reaction*.) . . . Have you permits? Then be off, be off with you! If this interference continues I shall have to call the soldiers. I'll have to call the soldiers, I will, and all work will be suspended. (*To* JOHN.) I haven't the power to employ you, man.

JOHN. Did I ask?

JP *and* LIAM *move away*. MICKELEEN *nervously looking after them and looking off*.

MICKELEEN. Hah, Seán? Why should I protect anyone? And I don't know what thing it is you're waiting for. Hah, Seán?

DAN. Talk for us, Michael.

MICKELEEN. Mickeleen Cam, Micheleen Cam! Twisted and humpy, mind and body, a codger the cripple, talk for the big men? Ask King Johnny. You're brand of right is only keeping yourself standing straight, Seán? Your defiance will splinter if you move, Seán, will it?

JP *and* LIAM *are returning*.

LIAM. O'Leary!

MICKELEEN. Why should I protect anyone? It's plain as day there's no one giving. Hah, Seán? The work is it ye want? Then take it! Take it! Let it be a practice for ye at taking!

JP ⎫ Please, please, my good man –
LIAM ⎭ O'Leary! Mickeleen -

MICKELEEN. (*to* JP). Run, run, vastard, run for your life!

LIAM *looks off, sees* MALACHY *approaching, then races away.*
MICKELEEN *shouts 'Run' again to* JP *and goes forward, arms
outstretched to stop* MALACHY *who is entering.* MALACHY *is
carrying a gun, he has his face blackened and he wears a
woman's dress over his clothes. He sweeps* MICKELEEN *aside,
levels his gun and shoots* JP. JP *falls to his hands and knees.*
MICKELEEN *watches* MALACHY *running away. He knows he
will not see* MALACHY *again.*

JP *crawls on hands and knees to* MICKELEEN'*s feet.*

JP. Help me . . . Help me.

MICKELEEN, *laughing and crying, starts to kick* JP.

MICKELEEN. But why should we starve like dying plants! Hah,
Seán? Humpy slaves can be tyrants too! Hah, Seán? (*Crying,
continues kicking* JP.) Hah, Seán? Hah, Seán? . . .

Excepting JOHN, *the group close in on* JP *kicking him, falling
on top of him and on top of each other, taking his boots and the
contents of his pockets.* MICKELEEN *comes free of them and is
crying, looking off in the direction* MALACHY *has taken.*

Scene Ten

THE KING AND THE QUEEN

That night.

MOTHER, MAEVE *and* DONAILL, *and their belongings, on the
roadside beside the ruin of their house.*

Off, approaching, JOHN, *drunk, muttering to himself and
shouting defiantly.*

JOHN. (*off*). Hale and hearty still! . . . Still standing straight! . . .
They won't get the better of me! . . . (*Entering.*) I'm Connor of
Glanconor! (*The sight of the ruined house stops him only for a
moment.*) . . . It won't best us, a chuid!

MOTHER *does not lift her head.*

MAEVE (*harshly*). Where were you?

JOHN. 'Hat, girl?

MAEVE. I was searching, I couldn't find you – A gang of them, they came.

JOHN. 'Asy!

MAEVE. Every house, and Danny's – Father Horan trying to stop them.

JOHN. They won't best *me*!

MAEVE. They said the rent, the rent, arrears, the rent. The bailley – We couldn't stop them – I couldn't find you – We're to move.

JOHN. And the whiskey hut Clancy set up is tumbled too!

MAEVE. Didn't you know this would happen?

JOHN. What are you saying?

MAEVE. But you done nothing!

JOHN. 'Hat? (*Surprised and offended by her remark.*) . . . Root out them doors! Root out them doors and we'll make a shelter. Go on. (*She does not obey. He addresses* MOTHER.) Is Donaill asleep? . . . 'Tis a relief to him. Wurra, mo chailín, hut-tut, not another word now. Look! I brought ye something. (*He produces a bottle of whiskey.*) Whish – whish – whish anois now, not **another word from you, Sheeny, but drink down a blogam and you'll see the good of it. And we'll give a taste to the putackeen** when he wakes. Go on, Sheeny. (MOTHER *and* MAEVE *drink a little.*) They killed the engineer, then tumbled the whiskey hut. But I done nothing wrong. Nor won't. I got that bottle off Danny. They won't get the better of me! (*To* MAEVE.) Not too much now, mo pheata, or 'twill hurt you. (*He sets about building a shelter.*) I'll throw up these doors and won't we be secure against anything that's sent. And in a day or two I'll find better place where they can't shift us so easy. Sure, the Springtime is on us and look at all the holdings that'll be going. We'll be better off than ever. Cause we'll last it. (*He is finding it difficult to lift the door to make a roof for the shelter he has built; he chuckles to himself.*) Oh, bo-bo-bo-bo-bo! Maeve, come here and help me. (*She doesn't. He lifts the door, completing the shelter.*) . . . If we had a dog now, like the rambling man, we'd have place to keep our feet warm. But sure any dog left in it

would only eat the toes of a one. Hah? What am I saying? In
with ye there now. Sure, there's lots can be done. (MAEVE
retches. He moves towards her.) Oh bo, mo pheata!

MAEVE. (*harsh*). Leave me alone!

MOTHER. (*harsh*). Leave her be!

MAEVE *exits.* MOTHER *carries* DONAILL *into the shelter.*
JOHN *carries in their possessions.*

JOHN. And the meal is to be given out.

MOTHER *pauses in what she is doing until he adds.*

Yis, Sinéad: The Policy: they're going changing their minds.

They lie down in the shelter.
Silence.

MOTHER. Don't go asleep.

JOHN. Hah?

MOTHER. . . . Did you say your prayers?

JOHN. . . . Ary, phy – why – why wouldn't I. I said them coming
home. I – Don't – Whisht.

Silence.

MOTHER. Don't go asleep.

JOHN. Wurra, Sheeny –

MOTHER. All of Glanconor. Father Horan trying to stop them.
And the same man is gone strange from all that's dying without
the oil . . . Johnny?

JOHN. Wurra, Sheeny, we'll be on top of the wheel yet. We'll be
right with the Springtime. Draw in closer. We'll be – Hah?
Weren't the Connors kings here once. Hah? And still. And still.
And always married queens. Didn't we? There was enough of a
hoult in you one time. And there will again, big and round, like
any queen. You'll see. Uroo, mo vourneen –

MOTHER. No, no, stop, stop.

JOHN. And the giggling of you, the Lord save us, nights. Draw in closer. Pull in Sinéad. Sheeny, mo chuid. The childeen is asleep. Hah? And sure, she's off walking out there. And, sure, you don't want to freeze.

MOTHER. (*sits up, pulls away from him*). We should have went! They're there now, eating their nough, Marcus and the rest. The only wonder is we're still alive . . . They say it isn't too hard to get to England . . . Do you hear? England isn't so far away.

JOHN. Far or near.

MOTHER. But what's to become of us? No roof, no plan. How can we escape, and the fever on top of it now? There's hundreds making safe voyages . . . Johnny? And I don't know what I do be thinking, walking over the dead scattered about. I can't pray. And I want to tell you about Brian's turf.

JOHN. Whist. Sleep.

MOTHER. His turf. I stole it –

JOHN. Don't.

MOTHER. I as good as killed him. I stole his turf for flour.

JOHN. I'm not listening to you.

MOTHER. God knows I'm not fit to die yet!

JOHN. Whisht – 'Asy – You don't understand.

MOTHER. But what's the use in –

JOHN. I don't know!

MOTHER. We'll all die here.

JOHN. Then let us!

MOTHER. Shhh! You're only being stubborn.

JOHN. Stop.

MOTHER. The childre –

JOHN. Don't.

MOTHER. The –

JOHN. I'll look after them! I'll – Don't keep on.

MOTHER. Just, it's a quare thing if you'll allow –

JOHN. Jesus – Stop – Christ – Woman! Isn't there enough trying to best me besides you! It won't get me. I don't understand it myself, but I have to live. Someone has to live. So don't keep on. Or that other strap rambling out there. Saying I'm doing nothing. Cause – I – will – live! I'm doing what I'm doing. How else can I? That holding is mine. That holding – *All* that land was Connors' once! And I'll not go. Not for landlord, devil, or the Almighty himself! I was born here, and I'll die here, and I'll rot here! . . . Cause there's food to be . . . The road-making is to . . . Cause there's . . . Cause I'm right.

Scene Eleven

THE QUEEN DIES

A few evenings later. JOHN, *seated motionless, in the ruin of his house.* MAEVE *is somewhere about, looking off occasionally for the return of* MOTHER. DONAILL, *asleep, in the shelter. In a second make-shift shelter on the opposite side of the stage is* DAN, *sitting up in a bed of straw, laughing and rambling away to himself. His* WIFE, *Cáit, is dead beside him.*

A fire favours DAN'*s side of the stage. At the end of the scene,* JOHN'*s side of the stage is in darkness,* DAN'*s is dimly lit by the fire.*

DAN. What year was I born in? 1782 they tell me, boys. There's changes since, Brian? There is, a mac. And Henry Grattan and Henry The Other and prosperity for every damned one. Hah? Yis – Whatever that is. (*Laughs.*) Oh, I'm alright, and herself is worse. Máirtín Hynes in Annagh Cross will forge me a pike in the morning. For the rebellion, Máirtín. There's a rising . . . Whisht! Who's in it? . . . Can't I hear ye breathing? . . . Oh, be off – be off – be off. I've things to be doing. We have things to be doing, Cáit . . . Is she dead? With your tight black face. Lord have mercy or divil mend her: (*Laughs.*) one of the two will be on the lookout for you. If I'm old enough for a spade, Máirtín, I'm old enough for a pike, Máirtín. Though I never killed. But we had the sport, 1798 yis, out all hours under the bushes. But she was sprightly. She could sing . . . She could sing . . . Why do

I keep talking, Johnny? And how many said that to me? And why do I? (*Laughs.*) Because! . . . Oh, what way was she ever, but cold. Cold, boys. Her feet worse nor the dog's nose through years prodding me into the grave. Rise up, you bony óinseach, and kindle the fire! . . . I'm afraid of the sleep in case of the rats, Daniel, said Mother. Isn't it comical? And the comical small piaties in '17 and, oh, a Thighearna, an t-ocras mór, an droch shaoil! Your father was better man with spade nor two cross Connors, four Dougans, or seven Dineens. (*Laughs.*) And isn't he dead now, Mother? Yis. Lallys' side of Clogher Bridge, near the water, 1822, and little on him for the maggot after the rat had pleased himself. But the C'ronor said he was drunk on poteen. I suppose he was. But I liked him, in spite of all.

MAEVE. She's coming.

DAN. Whisht! . . . But do you remember the wind, the big wind blowing? 1839. What didn't it blow? (*Laughs.*) That's how you lost your hair, Simon? What was I saying? Oh, but do you remember the wedding – Oh, long before the wind – the Union, Brian, in 1800? The marriage to start off a brand new century and prosperity for every damned one. And Rosaleen without a dowry. But isn't a good woman better nor the finest dowry? And with a good man, a dry bed, and pulling together . . . A strange little animal, the rat.

MOTHER *enters, a piece of bread in her hand. She puts the bread in front of* JOHN. *She crawls into the shelter to look at* DONAILL.

The fine suit they put on me one morning, with Murty Dineen, and we laughing to be taken voting, like the forty shilling farmers. We laughed. Well, we did. And took them off us again at noon and were each given a sixpence by a man by the name of Bully MacKiernan. Bhí go maith, is ní raibh go h-olc, till once at the fair of Turlough, Turley Connor – Yis, father to Johnny – split the Bully with a granite stone, and that put paid to the voting.

MAEVE *has been watching* MOTHER. *Cautiously, she moves to where the bread had been left and takes it.* JOHN *does not appear to notice, though she is directly in his line of vision.* MAEVE *starts to wolf down the bread.*

Oh, the Connors were nobles and not to be bested; the Connors would do the brave thing always . . . Cáit? And weren't you alright a minute ago?

MOTHER *comes out of shelter; she sees* MAEVE *eating the bread. She rushes at* MAEVE. *They struggle. The remaining piece of bread falls.* MAEVE *breaks away from* MOTHER *and runs into the shelter.* MOTHER *tries to salvage some of the crumbs but seeing the futility of it, she abandons it.*

JOHN *rises when* MOTHER *and* MAEVE *are struggling. He does not want to see or hear what is going on before him.*

DAN *continues to speak, softly keening for his wife, during* MOTHER's *speeches.*

MOTHER, JOHN *and* DAN *form a kind of trio with* MOTHER *speaking lead.*

Cold and silent is now your bed, damp is the blessed dew of night but the sun will bring warmth and heat in the morning and dry up the dew. But your heart will feel no heat from the sun. No. Nor no more the track of your feet in the dew. No. Nor no more the sound of your step in Glanconor where you were ever foremost among women. No. Cold and silent is now your bed.

My sunshine you were. I loved you better nor the sun itself. And when I see the sun go down I think of my girl and the black night of sorrow. For a storm came on. And my girl cannot return.

Life blood of my heart, she was brave, she was generous. She was comely, she was clear-skinned. And when she laughed – Did ye hear? And her hair – Did ye see? – Golden like the corn. But why should I tell what everyone knows? She is gone forever, she will return no more. Cold and silent is her repose.

MOTHER. The bread, the bread, the bread for your father! If he goes what's to happen to us? Connor! Move! Ketch her and scald her! Oh, Lord in heaven, you strap! The crumbs I went through hell to get! Take up the stick! – Take up the stick! The fourteen miles again today: this time off charitable people: their books I was prepared to kiss, though they never asked me. Connor, will you move now, or are you still engaged, defying all, standing in the rubble of what you lost? What bravery! But he's doing what's right he says. Right? Our noble men can afford what's right. Will I keep stealing from the dying?

JOHN } *(turning away from her; an undertone)*. Don't keep on.
MOTHER } You'll listen! Come forward to view your handsome childre. The cruit on one, the twist to her every part, her eyes without notion of a tear. And the belly black and swole on your heir. Did ever the vicious Connors of yore foster their likes? The leaders and chieftains!

A little movement from JOHN, *leaning forward, to move off.*

You forgot us! – You forgot us! . . . He wouldn't go, no. For why? Yis, we know – we've understood! – but how, Lord, did he think us to live here? No rights or wrongs or ráiméis talks, but bread, bread, bread. From where, but myself – Not him, not You – but always the slave, the slave of the slave, day after day, to keep us alive for another famine.

A little movement from JOHN, *stooping, to pick up a stick. He hesitates.*

Take it up, yis, take up the stick!

JOHN } *(a strong undertone)*. Don't keep on.
MOTHER } Jesus Christ above, what's wrong at all, and all the clever persons in the world? Biteens of bread are needed only. Life blood of my heart: hunger, childre, pain and disease! – What are we going through it for? Take us then! Take her – Take him! It's nothing new to You to take them, and roast them in hell if that's what You want them for. For there must be other ideas in Your mind. Well, they're there for You now, for You, Policy or the Blight.

JOHN *takes up the stick.* MOTHER *fears he will not use it. She pauses, holding her breath.*

DAN's *voice rising for a moment, 'And when she laughed – Did ye hear? And her hair – Did ye see? – golden like the corn . . . ' Etc., to end of keen. '. . . cold and silent is her repose'.*

MOTHER. (*quieter more intense*). Johnny. Are they to have my life so easy? Would that be right? . . . Johnny, I've understood your defiance, the hope you picked out of nowhere. I've understood all along but it's not of my kind, nor can it ever be. Now they have me prone, and I can only attack your strength. But you will protect yourself. They gave me nothing but dependence: I've shed that lie. And in this moment of freedom you will look after my right and your children's right, *as you promised*, lest they choose the time and have the victory. (*She goes into the shelter and lies down.*)

MOTHER, MAEVE *and* DONAILL *are now in the shelter which is almost completely in darkness.*

JOHN *moves to the shelter. We hear the stick rising and falling. After a moment* MAEVE *rushes out of the shelter and off. The sound of the stick, rising and falling, continues for a few moments.*

DAN *resumes his rambling talk.*

DAN. Whisht now a minute and riddle me this. Bhí fear is fear is fear . . . Sure I seen O'Connell once! Yis, yis, yis, The Liberator – didn't we, Brian? We did. And we waved, and he waved. And he smiled. On top of his horse. The lovely curly head on him. He did, did, waved with his hat. Aaaa, but the day we got our freedom! Emancy-mancy – what's that, Nancy? – Freedom, boys! Twenty-nine was the year and it didn't take us long putting up the new church. The bonfires lit, and cheering with his reverence. Father Daly, yis. And I gave Delia Hogan the beck behind his back. I had the drop in and the urge on me. (*Laughs.*) Oh! – Oh! – Oh! – Oh! that's alright, said Delia, winking, but the grass is wet . . .

JOHN *comes out of darkness and walks off. He has killed his wife and his son.*

Whisht . . . A strange little animal. The auld is to be deserted, Daniel, said Mother. Yis, I said, and married herself that the Colonel had spoiled. Oh, we were both past 'Collopy's Corner' and I had doubts I'd knock any rights out of her. And didn't. And didn't. No one to tend me now? As Jesus was noble and denied, he has long since been repaying the closed doors to him in Bethlehem! He has. And all the doors that's closed and black throughout today will have to be repayed . . . Cáit! Cáiteen! Well, you're a divil like myself. (*He laughs.*) Well you are! A dancer, a topper! Well, isn't she? And she'll be first asked at wake or wedding to sing. Oh, I married the blackbird, boys, I did, I did. I married the blackbird, boys. I did. I did. . . .

Scene Twelve

THE SPRINGTIME

Before and as the lights come up:

JOHN. Sheeny, Maeve, Donaill! The meal, it's come! Marcus, Liam, Brian, Danny! It's come! Cáit, Malachy, Mickeleen! It's come! . . .

It is Spring, 1847. JOHN is on a rise (or at some remove from MAEVE and LIAM whom we see later); a strange isolated figure; perhaps he has lost his senses: who can say? He walks off. MAEVE is looking down at a corpse, MICKELEEN. LIAM enters, a piece of bread in his hand.

LIAM. The meal, it's come. (*He offers the piece of bread to her.*)

MAEVE. No. O'Leary is the only name I'd accept anything from.

LIAM. Some say Malachy is dead too: I don't know. Some say he's in America, a gang to him. Whichever, this country will never see him again.

MAEVE. It'll see his likes.

LIAM offers the bread to her again.

No. There's nothing of goodness or kindness in this world for anyone, but we'll be equal to it yet.

LIAM. Well, maybe it'll get better.

MAEVE. No.

LIAM. And when it does we'll be equal to that too.

He puts the bread into her hand. She starts to cry.

The Patriot Game

for Nell

The Patriot Game was first performed at the Peacock Theatre, Dublin, on 15 May 1991, with the following cast:

CONNOLLY	Paudge Behan
COUNTESS MARKIEWICZ, WIMBORNE	Hazel Dunphy
MALLIN, O'BRIEN	Bronagh Gallagher
PEARSE	Aidan Gillen
CLARKE, FRIEND, COWEN, JIM	David Gorry
MCDONAGH, JOHNSTONE, MICK	Pat Kinevane
PEARSE'S MOTHER, EVANGELIST, PLUNKETT	Paula McFetridge
BIRRELL, MACNEILL, MAXWELL	Michael McMonagle
BALLAD SINGER	Sarah Merrigan
MACDERMOTT, MOLLY, ASQUITH	Fionnuala Murphy
NARRATOR	Nell Murphy
HOBSON, NATHAN, REDMOND	Timothy Reynolds
CEANNT, BIDDY	Rachel Rogers

All other parts were played by the cast.

Directed by Alan Gilsenan
Set and Costume Design Kathy Strachan
Lighting Tony Wakefield

The play transferred to the Tramway Theatre, Glasgow on 4 September 1991 with Declan Conlon as MacNeill, Birrell, Maxwell; David Gorry as Connolly; George Heslin as Ceannt, Jim, Redmond; Frankie McCafferty as McDonagh, Mick; Alison McKenna as Asquith, McDermott and Wimborne; Rachel Rogers as Clark, Biddy.

Scene One

PEARSE, *a young actor, comes in with a gramophone, places it somewhere and winds it. A distorted version of 'God Save the King', the British National Athem. He begins to dance – at first to the music; his dance begins to grow wild, out of control, frustrated, hysterical.*

The NARRATOR, *a young actress, comes in and watches from a distance. She is wary of* PEARSE, *both frightened and fascinated by him and, to conceal this, she tries to affect a detached superiority. (Offstage, he could be a boyfriend or a brother who gets out of control.) The narration appears to her to belong to another age and in her modern-day image (leather-jacket and white dress) one suspects that she takes liberties with it – 'yeh?' She is determined to keep control of herself; she loses her resolve every now and again, as in her very first line; she doesn't like the emotion of nationalism, 'it doesn't exist'.*

'God Save the King' has unwound itself. PEARSE *is leaving.*

NARRATOR. Stupid! . . . (*Dismissively.*) He's playing Patrick Pearse. Lookit, you wouldn't know right where to start the story. (*Finds her spot.*) Here. The Disgraceful Story of 1916, by Tomás Macamadán (son of the Idiot). Hi! You could start on the day seven hundred years ago and more when England first put her foot in Ireland and has it there still. Which makes us England's oldest colony. Which makes she take us for granted. Which is a mistake. To be sure. Or you could begin with Home Rule. Jesus, Home Rule. Was anything ever more talked about, Jesus. And the time a few years ago when the Home Rule Bill looked like being passed at last and in Ulster, up there, the Proddy Boys were sayin', we want none of it, Home Rule means Rome Rule. An' they could be right. But, we'll organise they said, we'll arm, we'll fight England – we'll fight by Christ but not by the Virgin, England – in order to remain part of England. Isn't it a good one?

Well, they did – organised an' armed – and when the gurriers down here – by Christ *and* the Virgin – saw the Proddies gettin' away with it, they did the same, and the Irish Volunteers were formed. Jesus.

The Volunteers are forming under MACNEILL.

The potential was there – potential, yeh? – for a civil war or rising. There was no civil war so you may forget the Ulster crowd. There was a rising and it revolved round the Irish Volunteers organisation. Jesus.

That's Eoin MacNeill, professor of Early Irish History at the university and therefore valuable at the head of any organisation.

MACNEILL. (*addressing the Volunteers*). Volunteers! Nil aon tinteán mar do thinteáin féin! (*They applaud.*)

NARRATOR. (*terminating the applause*). But! 1914: England warring with Germany and the old saying appeared again: 'England's difficulty is Ireland's opportunity.' The smell of freedom was in the wind, but the way to make the most of the opportunity was not agreed upon.

MACNEILL. On behalf of the Volunteers – I'm the bossman! – the way to make the most of the opportunity is this: We'll get our Republic by building up and up and up and up the strength of the Volunteers, we'll recruit an' organise them – Not for defiance? –

NARRATOR. Defence! –

MACNEILL. So (*that*) when the great world war is over and the great world peace conference on, we'll present ourselves –

NARRATOR. In millions! –

MACNEILL. And say we're a belligerent nation – Yeh? – and will get our Republic that way. Sensible, reasonable, logical?!

VOLUNTEERS. Yeah!

PEARSE. But!

MACNEILL. Wha', won't we?!

VOLUNTEERS. Yeah!

PEARSE *and* MACDONAGH *now stealing away to form a conspiratorial bunch with* CEANNT, MACDERMOTT, PLUNKETT *and* MACDONAGH.

NARRATOR. But! There was an organisation within the Volunteers' organisation and they were only using MacNeill as a respectable front. This was a secret, oath-bound society called the IRB and they were only biding their time until they controlled the Volunteers.

PEARSE. (*conspiratorially*). Níl aon tinteán mar do thinteáin féin.

NARRATOR. Patrick Pearse, the poet sure, was on the executive council of the Volunteers, and his henchman, MacDermott, was a paid organiser who made speeches up and down the country, enlisting men morroya (*mar dhea: in pretence*) for the Volunteers, but, really, investing in them the principles of the IRB and fixing-up his own men in the senior positions.

CLARKE. (*joining IRB group*). We have asserted arms six times in the past three-hundred years.

NARRATOR. Aul' Tom Clarke, a tobacconist. He'd spent fifteen years already in an English jail. And there was Eamonn Ceannt from the Treasury Department of the Dublin Corporation. Joseph Plunkett, another poet an' a descandenta (*of*) Blessed Oliver – yeh? An' Thomas MacDonagh, another poet.

PEARSE. (*conspiratorially*). The way *we* say to go about things is this: the Establishment of an Irish Republic by force of arms.

IRB. (*hushed*). Yeah!

CLARKE. But when?

PEARSE. When we control them sure, the Volunteers. An' when we start the fight, *everyone* will join in!

PLUNKETT. Oh they will, they will!

PEARSE. Won't they?!

IRB. Yeah!

NARRATOR. And there was a third group, an army two hundred strong, formed by the Unions during the 1913 strike, to protect the workers from police brutality. Led by James Connolly.

CONNOLLY. (*entering*). World change is needed, world revolution!

NARRATOR. He was an internationalist.

CONNOLLY. (*cynically*). Níl an tinteán mar do thinteáin féin!

NARRATOR. But the nationalist side of his nature would get him. From the age of eleven he was many's the thing in his time: cobbler, tramp, navvy, soldier, writer — oh he knew well about hardship. So, the rich, or the poor indeed themselves, couldn'ta thought much of'm. (*Of him.*)

CONNOLLY. We of the labour movement, we of the Irish citizen Army say the time is ripe — Nay, the imperious necessities of the hour call loudly for, demand, the formulation of a committee of all the elements outside as well as inside the Volunteers, to consider means to take and hold Ireland and the food of Ireland for the people of Ireland.

NARRATOR. (*representing* CONNOLLY'*s* AIDE *and the Irish Citizen Army*). Hear-hear!

PEARSE *and* MACDERMOTT *have rejoined* MACNEILL. CONNOLLY *is now approaching them, offering his hand to the Volunteers.*

MACNEILL. (*refusing hand*). Really, Connolly.

CONNOLLY. You cannot legalise revolutionary action. Audacity alone can command success in a crisis like this.

MACNEILL. You're too aggressive for us and you haven't much support anyway. Really, Connolly, you used to be such a pacifist.

CONNOLLY. Constitutional action in normal times, revolutionary action in exceptional times: these are exceptional times.

MACNEILL. The duty of the Irish Volunteers will be defensive and protective!

MACDERMOTT. We will not contemplate aggression.

PEARSE. (*expected to say something*). We will not contemplate domination.

CONNOLLY. Thank you, *gentle*men I'm glad to know where we all stand.

CONNOLLY *walks off, winking at and nudging his* AIDE; *simultaneously,* PEARSE *is doing similarly to* MACDERMOTT; *and, importantly, innocently,* MACNEILL *dismisses the Volunteers.*

MACNEILL. Volunteers! Níl aon tinteán mar do thinteáin féin!

NARRATOR. (*now translates this Gaelic wisdom*). 'There's no fireside like your own fireside.' One fella foolin' the next and the next foolin' himself. And there were other groups – Groups?! Don't be talkin'! – all coming under the general heading Sinn Féin, We Ourselves, all aiming more or less at the same thing, self-determination, all baking their own little buns instead of, all together, making one fine big solid cake.

But, between Volunteers, IRB and the Irish Citizen Army, a revolution there would be – and there'd be no good in it.

Scene Two

PEARSE *comes in dreamily, singing to himself* 'Óró 'sé do bheatha bhaile'. (*The song simply means: Welcome home now that summer is near.*) *He has come in unnoticed by the* NARRATOR. *He has a quietening and unnerving effect on her at first; then she uses the narration in a cynical way, as if to taunt him. He continues, dreamily impervious.*

PEARSE.
Óró 'sé do bheatha bhaile
Óró 'sé do bheatha bhaile
Óró 'sé do bheatha bhaile
Anois ar theacht an t-Samhraidh.

NARRATOR. Anois ar theacht an – The son of an *Englishman* – The mother was Irish all right, but he's the son of an Englishman – Yeh?

PEARSE. Óró 'sé do bheatha . . . Since the wise men have not spoken, I speak who am only a fool,/A fool who in all his days hath done never a prudent thing:/O wise men, riddle me this: what if my dream come true?/And millions unborn shall dwell in the house I have shaped in my heart, the noble house of my thought . . . Óró 'sé do bheatha bhaile . . .

NARRATOR. He'd be dreamin' a lot, d'yeh know, an' lookin' at pictures he had of Cuchulainn an' the likes, heroes of ancient times, being warned by old Druids not to – whatever else in the world they did wrong, d'yeh know? – not to take up arms or they'd die young – d'yeh know?

PEARSE. I care not if my life have only the span of a day and a night if my deeds be spoken of by the men of Ireland.

NARRATOR. Oh yes, and he swore on bended knees at the age of twelve – or was it six? – or was it three? – with his little brother Willie that he'd give his life to free Ireland – (*To* PEARSE.) Yeh?

PEARSE. Óró 'sé do bheatha bhaile . . .

NARRATOR. Oh and some said he could easily be a saint – Oh but they said too he'd never make a fist of anything because – though, yes, a poet sure – he was a lawyer too that didn't practise because he was an idealist – a schoolmaster too, but wasn't the school he had founded up to its eyes in debt? – wasn't the girl he was to marry drownded? – and sometimes, to look at him, you wouldn't think he was of this world at all – (*To* PEARSE.) Yeh?

PEARSE. (*impervious*). Anois ar theact an t-Samhraidh.

NARRATOR. . . . (*contains herself.*) The IRB.

The IRB *has come in.*

CLARKE. Agenda.

MACDONAGH. Just one point: a date for our rebellion.

MACDERMOTT. There's more to it than just a date.

CLARKE. Have it out. (*Discuss it.*)

PEARSE. Yet to depend on ahm.

CEANNT. If the British try enforced conscription here.

CLARKE. What if they don't?

CEANNT. Well, supposing, if.

CLARKE. Why if? That isn't our policy, that's MacNeill's classa talk.

MACDERMOTT. Force of arms.

PLUNKETT. We aren't ready.

MACDONAGH. Preparations.

MACDERMOTT. Perfecting the organisation.

MACDONAGH. And we need money.

CEANNT. America.

PEARSE. Arms.

PLUNKETT. Germany.

CLARKE. Send who to Germany?

MACDERMOTT. Casement?

PLUNKETT. Casement.

CEANNT. And we must have control of the Volunteers.

MACDERMOTT. That's goin' well.

MACDONAGH. Twenty thousand men at least to start the fight.

CEANNT. And hope the rest of the country joins in.

PEARSE. They will.

MACDERMOTT. Blindly? I don't know.

PEARSE. But sure I know they will.

PLUNKETT. How d'yeh know?

PEARSE. I just know sure. The spirit of revolution is buried in them for seven hundred years.

CEANNT. That's a long time for it t'be buried.

PEARSE. Once the fighting starts you'll see.

CLARKE. N-a-a-w.

PLUNKETT. . . . . Yeh?

CLARKE. N-a-a-w, we'll have to go and wake them up.

MACDONAGH. Yeh?

CLARKE. But not to arouse suspicion, yeh know?

PLUNKETT. Yeh?

MACDERMOTT. How?

CLARKE. Speeches.

PLUNKETT. Speeches.

MACDERMOTT. Leave the date of our rebellion for the moment, so.

CLARKE. Get on with it.

They leave.

NARRATOR. So all they needed was men, money, arms, a date to start the fight and whip up national spirit with speeches.

Scene Three

The others (off) as they enter, are singing in chorus 'Óró 'sé do bheatha bhaile': this time it is like a militant dirge and growing in volume. And there is a drum and a flag – the flag held/arranged as if draping a coffin.

NARRATOR. They brought the body of an aul' Fenian back all the way over the sea from America. A fine day, a big day out, hardly a space for a relative mourner itself . . . A Ghaedheala.

PEARSE. A Ghaedheala, ná bíodh brón ar éinne atá ina sheasamh ag an uaig seo, act bíodh buidheachas againn inar gcroidhthibh do Dhia na ngrás do cruithigh anam uasal áluinn Dhiarmuda Uí Dhonnabháin Rosa agus thug ré fhada dhó ar an saol seo.

Ba chalma an fear thú, a Dhiarmuid!

It has seemed right before we turn away from this place in which we have laid the mortal remains of O'Donovan Rossa, that one among us should, in the name of all, speak the praise of that valiant man, and endeavour to formulate the thought and the hope that are in us as we stand around his grave.

We stand at Rossa's grave not in sadness but rather in exaltation of spirit that it has been given to us to come thus into so close a communion with that brave and splendid Gael. The clear true eyes of this man almost alone in his day visioned Ireland as we of today would surely have her: not free merely, but Gaelic as well; not Gaelic merely, but free as well.

This is a place of peace, sacred to the dead, where men should speak with all charity and will all restraint; but I hold it a Christian thing as O'Donovan Rossa held it, to hate evil, to hate untruth, to hate oppression, and hating them, to strive to overthrow them. Our foes are strong and wise and wary; but strong and wise and wary as they are, they cannot undo the miracles of God who ripens in the hearts of young men the seeds sown by the young men of a former generation. And the seeds sown by the young men of '65 and '67 are coming to their miraculous ripening today. Rulers and Defenders of Realms had need to be wary if they would guard against such processes. Life springs from death; and from the graves of patriot men and women spring living nations. The Defenders of this Realm have worked well in secret and in the open. They think that they have pacified Ireland, they think that they have purchased half of us and intimidated the other half. They think that they have foreseen everything, think that they have provided against everything, but the fools, the fools, the fools! They have left us our Fenian dead, and while Ireland holds these graves, Ireland unfree shall never be at peace.

A volley is fired, the thuds of clay on the coffin are Militant drumbeats. And the Rosary.

NARRATOR. Haily (*Hail*) Mary, full of grace, the Lord is with thee, blessed art thou among women, and blessed is the fruit of thy womb, Jesus.

CHORUS. Holy Mary, Mother of God, pray for us sinners now and at the hour of our death, Amen.

MOLLY. Sacred heart, but isn't he the lovely speaker?

MICK. (*farmer*). A noble talker, ma'am.

BIDDY. Holy Mary, Mother of God – but would yiz know what's up with them at all?

MICK. Amen – They have to be doing something, ma'am, sure.

MOLLY. Featherin' their own nests – thy womb, Jesus.

MICK. Holy Mary, Mother of – God rest the dead anyways: He was a good man they say and brave?

BIDDY. Death, amen – It's all the same to him now whatever he was.

MOLLY. Yiz're doin' well on the farms, mister?

MICK. Holy – hah?

JIM. Yiz're doing well down the country, wha'?

FARMER. Oh we are, thank God, we are – Now and at the hour of our – what with the high prices for the stock and the grain an' the exportin' wholesale since the war started: we'll be made-up if it lasts, an' secure if the Volunteers don't go upsettin' us.

JIM. Holy Mary, Mother of God – I was thinkin' myself, maybe, of joinin' up, maybe, an' maybe goin' out foreign for a while – of our death, Amen – but I might get shot.

MOLLY. Hail Mary, full of grace – An' why wouldn't yiz join up like the others. Yiz're still in time cause they're lookin' for more.

BIDDY. Holy Mary – An' off with yiz to Flanders or Belgium an' yiz might meet our Liam or Sean or Timmy out there an' the fine separation allowance your missus'd have every week without fail. True for yiz, mister, the country'll be remade if the war lasts out.

CHORUS. Name of the Father, Son and of the Holy Ghost, Amen.

They disperse/retire. CONNOLLY *is coming in.*

Scene Four

JIM, MICK, MOLLY *and* BIDDY *come in during the following to listen to and heckle* CONNOLLY.

NARRATOR. And Connolly was goin' his own road, bent on his own class of international revolution, but losin' his personal battle to nationalism.

CONNOLLY. Should the working class of Europe, rather than slaughter each other for the benefit of kings and financiers, proceed tomorrow to erect barricades all over Europe, to break up bridges and destroy the transport service that war might be abolished, we should be justified in following such a glorious example.

MICK. Yahoo!

CONNOLLY. Or perhaps Ireland may yet be the one to set the torch to a European conflagration that will not burn out until the vulture classes that rule and rob the world are finally dethroned. In America, in Russia, in Scotland, in Europe –

MICK. Them're middlin' foreign places, sir!

BIDDY. What's he sayin'?!

JIM. What do we know about Europe?!

MOLLY. What about Robert Emmett?!

MICK. An' Wolfe Tone an' Patrick Sarsfield?!

MOLLY. What about Parnell?!

CONNOLLY. They're dead. The Stuttgart resolution says –

BIDDY. Rabble raiser!

CONNOLLY. The Stuttgart –

JIM. What about the workin' man?!

CONNOLLY. The cause of the workers and the cause of Ireland are not antagonistic but complementary! The cause of the workers here and there and all over the world is the same!

BIDDY. Ireland unfree shall never be at peace!

MICK. What about Home Rule?!

CONNOLLY. The Irish Question at bottom is an economic one and –

MOLLY. What about Ireland?!

JIM. What about Ireland?!

BIDDY. Ireland!

MICK. Ireland!

MOLLY. What about Ireland?!

CONNOLLY. (*angrily*). Ireland as distinct from her people means nothing to me, and the man who is bubbling over with love and enthusiasm for 'Ireland' and can yet pass unmoved through her streets and witness all the wrong and the suffering, the shame and the degradation wrought upon the people of Ireland – yea, wrought by Irishmen upon Irish men and women – without burning to end it, is a fraud and a liar in his heart, no matter how he loves that combination of chemical elements he is pleased to call 'Ireland'.

A stupid pause, then a cheer goes up and they leave.

CONNOLLY. (*to himself*). So be it, then. Let us forget Europe and clean up this mess of nationalism first. Yeh, what about Ireland.

Scene Five

NARRATOR. And the others were pleased with the National spirit they had seen at O'Donovan Rossa's funeral. Casement was off in Germany looking for guns and men. And letters and messengers were back and over, to and from America and the funds were swellin' as a result. There was trainin' an' drillin' with what they had, and the odd poem, too, was bein' written at the same time. Epitaphs – yeh? They were nearly all poets sure.

MACDONAGH.
His songs were a little phrase
    Of eternal song,

Drowned in the harping of lays
  More loud and long.

His deed was a single word,
  Called out alone
In a night when no echo stirred
  to laughter or moan.

But his songs now souls shall thrill
  The loud harps dumb,
And his deed the echoes fill
  When the dawn is come.

PEARSE.
  I have turned my face
  To this road before me,
  To the work that I see,
  To the death I shall die.

PLUNKETT.
  Rougher than death the road I choose,
  Yet shall my feet not walk astray,
  Though dark, my way I shall not lose
  For this way is the darkest way.

Scene Six

NARRATOR. A mock attack on Dublin Castle.

  CONNOLLY *gives a signal and a group from the Citizen Army
  comes out of the shadows to carry out a mock attack. A*
  SENTRY – *played by* NARRATOR – *watches and is amused.*

SENTRY. Ar, is that you, young Quinn? Go home outa that or I'll
  tell your mother about you!

  They run off. CONNOLLY, *grim, remains for a moment.*

CONNOLLY.
  Youth of Ireland, stand prepared;
  Revolution's dread abyss

Burns beneath you
All but bared.

Scene Seven

NARRATOR. And in Dublin Castle the English weren't asleep
neither. Begod.

LORD LIEUTENANT. Egad! Did yeh see them out there, by
George? If I had any power here besides a damned title!

CHIEF-SECRETARY. No-no-no, Lord Lieutenant, it's only the
war and the excitement of war. No-no-no and bless my soul! On
behalf of Dublin Castle – I'm the bossman – personally, I would
feel dishonoured, if I did not say that this is a grand little
country.

UNDER-SECRETARY. Close enough to London, Chief-Secretary,
for the odd weekend there, far enough from Westminster for the
job to be cushy.

CHIEF-SECRETARY. Grand. And the Irish Literary Revival
Movement. I envy the rest of you. I'd prefer to spend a lot more
time in Dublin, but as a member of the cabinet – Yeh?

UNDER-SECRETARY. And Chief-Secretary, you're liked.

CHIEF-SECRETARY. I'm liked, Under-Secretary. The way I do get
the odd old concessional act passed for them now and again and
not too rarely at all, mind you.

UNDER-SECRETARY. Can I have a drink, Chief-Secretary?

CHIEF-SECRETARY. (appreciatively). 'I will arise and go now
and go to Innisfree.' (He likes the rhythm; he likes Yeats.)

LORD LIEUTENANT. I don't like it, egad, manoeuvring right
outside our gates.

COMMANDER-IN-CHIEF. I think I'd like to disarm them.

UNDER-SECRETARY. What arms?

CHIEF-SECRETARY. And thereby throw down a challenge to
them? Hmm? And wouldn't you then have to disarm the Ulster
crowd, up there, as well?! Yeh see?!

COMMANDER-IN-CHIEF. I'm a shagging soldier, Gus! (*What am I meant to do?*)

CHIEF-SECRETARY. Pshaw!

UNDER-SECRETARY. Pshaw!

LORD LIEUTENANT. Pack them off to the front where they belong! Work off their excess energy there!

CHIEF-SECRETARY. No-no-no, gentlemen. Interfere and you're sure of bloodshed, aren't you?

UNDER-SECRETARY. Correct.

CHIEF-SECRETARY. *And*! Westminister doesn't want America to get the wrong impression and start thinking that there's dissatisfaction here. Lose the Irish American vote and you may forget the Yanks ever joining the allies.

LORD LIEUTENANT. Bloody Yanks.

UNDER-SECRETARY. Hear-hear.

CHIEF-SECRETARY. They won't be neutral much longer. But no-no-no, I wouldn't worry about a tiny minority here – Pshaw! They're negligible, as Redmond said to me.

UNDER-SECRETARY. And he should know, Chief-Secretary.

COMMANDER-IN-CHIEF. Merely trying to avoid a few riots, Gus.

CHIEF-SECRETARY. Gotcha. (*Or winks, in understanding.*)

LORD-LIEUTENANT. March some troops up and down, what? Overawe the disaffected.

NATHAM. And that's a good idea, Lord Lieutenant.

CHIEF-SECRETARY. (*appreciatively*). Interesting people: they appreciate the maintenance of order but have an inveterate prejudice against the punishment of disorder.

UNDER-SECRETARY. Can I have a drink, Chief-Secretary?

CHIEF-SECRETARY. (*continues absently, appreciatively*). Hmmm? Nil *aon* tinteán mar do *thinte*áin *féin*. (*He loves the rhythm.*)

Scene Eight

NARRATOR. Another day out, another good day, another day in the world war, another contest for recruits. Speeches, songs, promises. Asquith, the man himself, was over, sure. And Redmond was there, the most popular man in the country. Pearse, Connolly and MacNeill. All looking for men for their wars, revolutions or whatever. The recruitin' battle was on.

ASQUITH *first, then* REDMOND, *then* PEARSE, CONNOLLY *and* MACNEILL *have taken their places.*

MACNEILL. A chairde!

PEARSE. A chairde Gaedheal!

CONNOLLY. Brothers!

ASQUITH. Friends!

REDMOND. Fellow countrymen! May I start by saying that there is today in Ireland a feeling of friendliness towards England and a desire to join hands in supporting the interests of England, such as was never found in the past. May I venture to say that?

PEARSE. A chairde, we want recruits because we have undertaken a service which we believe to be of vital importance to our country and because that service needs whatever there is of manly stuff in Ireland in order for its effective rendering. We want recruits because –

MACNEILL. In recruiting, training, arming and equipping the Volunteers as a military body, the men of Ireland are acquiring the power to obtain the freedom of the Irish nation.

ASQUITH. Speaking here in Dublin, I address myself for a moment to –

CONNOLLY. Comrades, should the day ever come when revolutionary leaders are prepared to sacrifice the lives of those under them as recklessly as the ruling class do in every war, there would not be a throne or a despotic government left in the world.

REDMOND. Ireland has a heartfelt sympathy with the objects of this war and she will bear her share of the burdens and sufferings with alacrity and with gallantry. Already, as you are no doubt aware, I declared in the House of Commons that Ireland was bound in honour to take this course.

ASQUITH. Friends –

PEARSE. We want recruits because we have a standard to rally them to. It is an old standard which has been borne by many generations of Irishmen, which has gone into many battles, which has looked down upon much glory and upon much sorrow.

ASQUITH. Friends –

CONNOLLY. Is there one British organisation that claims for Ireland, or would even allow Ireland, the same right to determine her national fate as all the British peace parties insist upon being secured for Belgium?

ASQUITH. Friends –

MACNEILL. The Volunteers are a defensive body but, make no mistake, though we are a defensive body, we would resist suppression, resist disarmament, resist – fight – enforced conscription.

ASQUITH. Friends! My friends! I am asking Ireland to contribute with promptitude and enthusiasm a large and worthy contingent of recruits to the second new army of half a million which is now growing up, as it were, out of the ground.

CONNOLLY. All those mountains of dead, all those corpses mangled beyond recognition, all those arms, legs, eyes, ears, fingers, toes, hands; all those shivering putrefying bodies, once warm, living and tender parts of men and youths.

MACNEILL. We declare that Ireland cannot with honour or safety take part in foreign quarrels otherwise than through the free action of a national Government of her own.

ASQUITH. And what we should like to see is an Irish Brigade – or better still, an Irish Army Corps. Don't be afraid that by joining the colours you will lose your identity and become absorbed in some invertebrate mass, or what is perhaps equally repugnant, be artificially redistributed into units which have no national cohesion or character.

PEARSE. We want recruits because we are sure of the rightness of our cause. We want recruits because we believe that events are about to place the destinies of Ireland definitely in our hands.

MACNEILL. What? What's going on?

ASQUITH. The call which I am making is backed by the sympathy of your fellow Irishmen in all parts of the Empire and of the world.

CONNOLLY. All, all are part of the price we pay for being an integral part of the British Empire.

REDMOND. Now is our chance, the test has come. And I say for myself that I would feel personally dishonoured if I did not say to my fellow countrymen that it is their duty to take their place in the fighting line in this contest.

PEARSE. We want recruits because we have work for them to do – We want recruits because soon we will be able to arm them – We want recruits –

CONNOLLY. Because Ireland is rotten with slums. Nations that know not the powers and possessions of Empire have happier, better-educated, better equipped men and women than Ireland has ever known, or can ever know as an integral part of the British Empire.

ASQUITH. I have only one more word to say –

REDMOND. Trust the Old Party –

PEARSE. Redmond has dined too long at English feasts –

MACNEILL. What's going on? –

ASQUITH. Though our need is great, your opportunity is also great –

REDMOND. Remember, Home Rule is on the way, you'll see –

CONNOLLY. That pitiful suspended abortion, hung up on a nail! Join the Irish Citizen Army! –

ASQUITH. There is no question of compulsion or bribery –

MACNEILL. Join the Irish Volunteers! –

REDMOND. Join the British Forces! – A fight for England is a blow for Irish freedom!

PEARSE. Nationalism is not a negotiable thing! –

CONNOLLY. Show the world that, though Redmond may sell Ireland, he cannot deliver the goods! –

ASQUITH. What we ask, what we want! –

PEARSE. We want recruits! –

ASQUITH. What we believe you are ready and eager to give is! –

PEARSE. Because we are absolutely determined to take action! –

ASQUITH. Is! –

CONNOLLY. Ireland has no foreign enemy but England! –

ASQUITH. The! –

CONNOLLY. Don't take the shilling! –

ASQUITH. The! –

PEARSE. We want – we want – we want! –

ASQUITH. The free will offering of a free people!

Pause. They listen. Who has won the contest? The NARRATOR has been waiting, has wound the gramophone: 'It's a long way to Tipperary', ASQUITH/REDMOND have won. They disperse/ leave, happy, frustrated, angry – as appropriate.

Scene Nine

In contrast with his dreaminess in Scene Two, PEARSE comes in, screaming his frustration and rage.

PEARSE.
Beware of the thing that is coming!
Beware of the risen people!
Who will take what you would not give!
Fools, did you think to conquer the people,
Or that law is stronger than life, or
Than man's desire to be free?

> We will try it out with you, ye that
> Have harried and held!
> Ye that have bullied and bribed!
> Tyrants, Hypocrites, Liars!

The others come in. It is tense, urgent.

CLARKE. Agenda.

PEARSE. Quick.

MACDONAGH. Just one point: a date for our rebellion.

PEARSE. When – when – when?

PLUNKETT. I say in seventeen.

PEARSE. No. No.

CEANNT. Autumn – in October?

CLARKE. No. No.

MACDONAGH. Summer – in July?

MACDERMOTT. No. No.

PEARSE. Quick – quick – quick.

CEANNT. What about Spring time?

PEARSE. . . . Easter resurrection.

PLUNKETT. Easter resurrection.

CLARKE. Yes, but hush.

MACDONAGH. Warily, go warily.

MACDERMOTT. Caution.

CLARKE. We'll be ready.

PEARSE. Our surprise.

CLARKE. But shhh.

CEANNT. Shhh.

MACDERMOTT. Shhh.

MACDONAGH. Shhhh.

PEARSE. Easter.

CLARKE. . . . Get on with it.

Scene Ten

CONNOLLY, *depressed, with an* AIDE. (NARRATOR).

CONNOLLY. The war is supposed to be our opportunity, and it has ruined everything. National dignity is gone. Self respect is gone. Deep in the heart of Ireland has sunk the degradation wrought upon its people.

AIDE. The Volunteers have plans.

CONNOLLY. The Volunteers, the Volunteers, the Volunteers! If *we* had a few thousand men.

AIDE. But they have plans. For a rebellion. They do!

CONNOLLY. (*cynically*). Do they?

AIDE. Yes! Our own intelligence –

CONNOLLY. *When* are they going to rise?

AIDE. We can find out . . . Well, what should we do?

CONNOLLY. Let's become poets and *eat* poetry. Words! . . . (*He gets an idea.*) Words? I wonder. I wonder now . . . If they really have a plan – If – perhaps we can speed it up. And if they have, ensure that their 'rising' has a more solid basis than middle-class aspirations. (*He smiles/laughs and in the manner of a Town-Crier with a handbell.*) Hear ye, hear ye!

NARRATOR. Connolly had a ruse – Yeh? He'd force himself on Pearse and the others whether they liked it or not. The rising wasn't going to be that private. But wait a while for that.

The recruiting wasn't going well for Pearse and the IRB. But they had *some* men and some money and some arms. The date was set. And they still had this great belief, faith, that as soon as the first shot was fired, the whole country would rise up and come out with knives and forks.

Only a few months to go to Easter Sunday, when the short lifespan of a night and a day would be over.

Scene Eleven

PEARSE *is talking to himself. His* MOTHER *comes in a little later.*

PEARSE. What is this thing called patriotism? I don't know.
  Nationalism? I don't know. Nationalism is not a negotiable
  thing. Good. Is it selfish? Ask him who adores what is God.
  Good. Can you eat it? Write it? Smell it – catch it – see it – stop
  it – find it – lose it – trust it? Can you trust it?

  I have not gathered gold;
  The fame that I won perished;
  In love I found but sorrow
  That withered my life.

MOTHER. Is this where you are, Pat?

PEARSE. 'Tis . . . (*To himself.*) The beauty of the world hath made
  me sad, this beauty that will pass . . . (*To* MOTHER.) Am I a
  great failure, Mother?

MOTHER. (*shakes her head. Then, quietly*). Don't do anything
  rash, Pat.

PEARSE. How beautiful is all that has been created by God. Look
  at the slanting sun and the play of its shadows on the hills . . .
  The day is coming. Soon that will be no more for me.

MOTHER. . . . And your brother?

PEARSE. He'll be shot too . . . (*To himself.*) Can you trust it? Yes.
  Can you trust it? Yes! Can you trust it – can you trust it?

  Of wealth or of glory
  I leave nothing behind (me)
  (I think it, O God, enough)
  But my name in the heart of a child.

  (*He starts to cry.*) . . . Can you trust it?

  He whispers the first few lines of the following; MOTHER
  repeats them. He leaves. MOTHER *continues.*

MOTHER.
  I do not grudge them: Lord I do not grudge
  My two strong sons that I see go out

To break their strength and die, they and a few
In bloody protest for a glorious thing.
They shall be spoken of among their people,
The generations shall remember them,
And call them blessed.

(*The poem was written by Pearse for his mother; the sentiments contained in it, therefore, are his – male – and not necessarily the sentiments of a mother. The actor playing* MOTHER *is free in interpretation to question the sentiments: e.g., 'The generations shall remember them and call them – blessed?'*)

The NARRATOR *appears but finds that she has nothing to say.*

Scene Twelve

CONNOLLY, *in the manner of a Town-Crier, comes in ringing a bell.*

CONNOLLY. Hear ye, hear ye! Revolution, revolution! Hear ye, English, hear ye, Irish! The time for Ireland's battle is *now*! The place for Ireland's battle is *here*! The Citizen Army is now ready to start alone! Even if it's only a street fight! The great appear great because we are on our knees! Let us rise! Do you believe freedom will be achieved without fighting for it?!

PEARSE *arrives and watches from the shadows, his face aghast at* CONNOLLY's *behaviour;* MACNEILL *arrives from another direction but only shrugs and leaves.*

CONNOLLY. England's weakest point is at the point nearest its heart! We are in that position! In this crisis of your country's fate, your first allegiance is to your country and not to any leader, executive or committee!

PEARSE. (*from the shadows; removed from* CONNOLLY). But – !

CONNOLLY. Words!

PEARSE. But – !

CONNOLLY. Words!

PEARSE. But – But! – But!

CONNOLLY. Words! Too many mouthers about war in times of peace! Too much canting about restraint in times of war! Too many would-be Wolfe Tones, too many hysterical perfervid patriots, too many comic-opera revolutionaries preaching revolution and practising compromise and doing neither thoroughly!

PEARSE *goes off angrily, purposefully, during the above.*

England's difficulty is Ireland's opportunity! We'll start without guns and get them later! Revolution, Revolution, Revolution! Hear ye English and beware! Revolution, Revolution, Revolution!

Figures – the IRB *– have come in to abduct* CONNOLLY.

Scene Thirteen

CONNOLLY *and his captors, the* IRB.

PEARSE. (*angrily*). And stupid manoeuvres outside Dublin Castle. Broadcasting threats to cause a little riot and have the authorities arrest us all before we can lift a finger. We cannot allow anything or anybody that threatens well-laid plans. You've been asked before to moderate your – recklessness – but who can talk to you? We can't tolerate it, we won't tolerate it. Nobody will be allowed to jeopardise an insurrection that is being carefully organised.

CONNOLLY. (*calmly*). What do you propose to do? Because with or without me, the Citizen Army will march on Dublin Castle within a week.

The others are startled by this.

PLUNKETT. (*to himself*). But, good God . . .

CONNOLLY. Check on it if you wish. (*He's bluffing.*)

PEARSE. (*aside to* PLUNKETT). D'you believe him?

PLUNKETT. He has us over a barrel.

MACDONAGH. . . . An alliance?

CONNOLLY. We could form an alliance if you can break through your refined distrust of the mob.

PEARSE. Are-you-prepared-to-listen?!

CONNOLLY. And to talk.

MACDONAGH. Talk then.

CONNOLLY. After you: you're all very good at talking.

PEARSE. (*trying to control himself*). Elaborate plans are already in operation for the liberating of Ireland and the proclaiming of a republic.

CONNOLLY. What *kind* of a republic?

PEARSE. Oh call it our 'independence' then. The country cannot be anything till it's free.

CONNOLLY. Political and social freedom are not –

PEARSE. Unrelated things, we know that!

CONNOLLY. Well since no one has ever heard your policy other than something based on a morbid idealising of the past.

PEARSE. (*shouting*). The establishment of an Irish *Republic* by force of arms – our brief and sufficient policy for now! If you are worried about later, I can assure you that the new army of Ireland will be the last to suppress the Labour Movement.

CONNOLLY. Oh? The rabble say thanks.

MACDONAGH. . . . . If you would stay your hand a while longer.

CONNOLLY. For what?

MACDONAGH. We brought you here to ask you to stay your hand.

CONNOLLY. To *ask*?

MACDONAGH. We're *telling* you then to stay your hand!

CONNOLLY. Who's rash? Your own speeches and propaganda haven't exactly been prayers.

MACDONAGH. There's a line.

CONNOLLY. Where is the cautious MacNeill, your leader?

PLUNKETT. You are not talking to McNeill now.

CONNOLLY. . . . (*is pleased with the implication*). I'm neither rash nor cowardly. I'm worried about this bide-your-time doctrine, this waiting-for-the-right-moment that has crippled a dozen risings in the past.

MACDONAGH. Premature risings are known to have failed too.

CONNOLLY. Are you waiting for the British to swoop?

PLUNKETT. Your recklessness is the greatest danger of making that happen.

MACDONAGH. Do you think we are the kind of men to let this chance slip by?

CONNOLLY *shrugs.*

PEARSE. We have chosen the right moment.

CONNOLLY. 1950? Or when the war ends? The right time was during the Boer war. The right time was 1913 when, if Labour and the Unions had any support from the likes of you, the British Government could have been crippled at will. The right time is now, with fighting spirit, which is more important than any theoretically perfect organisation.

PEARSE. Words are lightly spoken.

CONNOLLY. Yes, they are.

PLUNKETT. What could your few numbers do anyway?

CONNOLLY. We can die. If needs be.

PEARSE. We'll strike.

CONNOLLY. When?

PEARSE. Easter Sunday.

CONNOLLY. (*they await his reply*). . . . God grant, Pearse, that you are right.

NARRATOR. Connolly had forced himself on them and he was ready with his life – Yeh? (*Sings.*) 'Oh words are lightly spoken . . . '

SINGER.

'O words are lightly spoken,
Said Pearse to Connolly,
'Maybe a breath of politic words
Has withered our Rose Tree;
Or maybe but a wind that blows
Across the bitter sea.'

'It needs to be but watered,'
James Connolly replied,
'To make the green come out again
And spread on every side,
And shake the blossom from the bud
To be the garden's pride.'

'But where can we draw water,'
Said Pearse to Connolly,
'When all the wells are parched away?
O plain as plain can be

SINGER AND NARRATOR.

There's nothing but our own red blood
Can make a right Rose Tree.'

Scene Fourteen

NARRATOR. The preparations were speeding up and in earnest. Good enough. And Dublin Castle wasn't worried.

ATTACHE. (*played by* NARRATOR). From Military Intelligence, sir.

UNDER-SECRETARY. Yes?

ATTACHE. (*reads*). The general state of Ireland, apart from recruiting and apart from the activities of the pro-German minority, is thoroughly satisfactory and very free from ordinary crime.

UNDER-SECRETARY. (*signs document*). 'Very free from ordinary crime.' File it away.

NARRATOR. A smooth road, all was fine, good enough. Now the next thing on the list was to get the men in high fightin' fettle, so, cute enough of them, they forged a document that they said was stolen out of Dublin Castle.

Scene Fifteen

The IRB/MACNEILL/UNDER-SECRETARY.

CLARKE. (*dictating*). Disarm the Volunteers.

PLUNKETT. (*forging the document*). Disarm the Volunteers.

CLARKE. Take over all their meeting houses.

PLUNKETT. Take over . . .

CEANNT. Arrest the leaders –

MACDERMOTT. Us!

They laugh.

CLARKE. Make copies, spread it about, (*To* PEARSE.) take it to MacNeill.

PEARSE. (*to* MACNEILL). Did you see this, Eoin?

MACNEILL. What is it, Pat?

PEARSE. 'Tis bad, bad, bad.

NARRATOR. Dublin Castle:

ATTACHE. Did you see this, sir?

UNDER-SECRETARY. What is it, Henry?

ATTACHE. Read it, sir, 'tis bad.

UNDER-SECRETARY. Rubbish!

NARRATOR. Listen:

UNDER-SECRETARY. An utter and total fabrication!

NARRATOR. But who'd believe Dublin Castle! And MacNeill swallowed the ruse like a greedy dog'd butter. Listen:

MACNEILL. To all Volunteers: Be on the alert, stand at the ready, resist suppression for all ye're worth!

NARRATOR. Aw, they gave it great pub-liss-itee (*Publicity.*) and the fighting men of Ireland were rearing to go as a result. Bhí go maith (*Good enough.*) – Yeh? It was now Holy Week and there were only a few more days to go to Easter Sunday.

Scene Sixteen

PEARSE, PLUNKETT, MACDONAGH, MACDERMOTT, CEANNT *with an imaginary map of Ireland. The* NARRATOR *assumes the manner of a spy and eavesdrops on the following.*

PLUNKETT. (*indicating on the map*). Dublin: We take the main buildings, here, here, here, here, here. The GPO will be our headquarters. We form a defence line around the suburbs here (*A circle around Dublin.*) to stop English reinforcements getting in. We hold the main buildings until our troops arrive from the country. The German arms will be landed here (*Kerry coast.*) and distributed up along here (*The River Shannon, as far as Donegal.*) That line will then come eastwards, dealing with any opposition – barracks and so on – eventually, converging on Dublin and joining us.

NARRATOR. There's always an informer. (*And goes out.*)

PLUNKETT. In case pressure proves too great for us here, we retreat this way, northwards, and continue the fight in the hills.

An irate MACNEILL *comes in, accompanied by an* AIDE – *the* NARRATOR.

MACNEILL. What's going on – what's going on – what's going on? Are you mad, Pearse? I've just heard you've issued orders for an insurrection.

PEARSE. What?

MACNEILL. Don't mind what – Is it true?

PEARSE. Yes.

CEANNT *and* MACDONAGH *leave/retire as if with papers/ maps.*

MACNEILL. My God! – You would lead an unarmed country –

PLUNKETT. We're not unarmed –

MACNEILL. To useless and hopeless slaughter! Where is the logic, the reason, the common-sense, the sanity?

PEARSE. I've always admired your reason and your logic: Your arguments are unanswerable in reason and in logic: But I know I'm right.

MACNEILL. Who's the chief of the Volunteers? Who is chief-of-staff? The way my authority has been flouted! The deceit, the tricks, the lies of the thing!

PEARSE. You were deceived; it was necessary.

MACNEILL. How I've been used!

PEARSE. Yes, you have been used, but if you will listen to us now.

MACNEILL. And that bogus order about our suppression!

PLUNKETT. It was necessary.

MACNEILL. And I issued orders to the Volunteers for you! I alerted them for the slaughterhouse.

MACDERMOTT. Not for the slaughterhouse.

PLUNKETT. We stand a good chance.

PEARSE. Our plans will be carried out.

MACNEILL. Will they? We'll see. There will be *no* insurrection. There will be no waste of lives for which I, as *leader* of the Volunteers, am directly responsible. I'll not allow a half armed force to be led out –

PLUNKETT. If you'd care to listen –

MACNEILL. I'll do everything in my power – short of informing Dublin Castle – to stop an insurrection!

PEARSE. If you –

MACNEILL. I will *not* listen! What is our policy?

MACDERMOTT. Mr MacNeill, *we* control the Volunteers. Most of the officers take orders from us. You can do nothing. It's too late. We can count on at least 10,000 men, and when the fighting starts we believe that Redmond's supporters will join in. If they do, we shall then have over 100,000 men rising.

PLUNKETT. Any moment now we expect a landing of arms from Germany. Including artillery. And an expeditionary force of Germans. And that is only the start. Our plans are well laid. It's too late to turn back. It would be more dangerous to turn back now.

PEARSE. . . . We intended to acquaint you of our plans, but. (*'what could we do?'*) . . . We're after the same ideal.

PLUNKETT. So? (*'What are you going to do.'*)

MACDERMOTT. What do you intend to do?

MACNEILL. (*Bluster*). The only basis for successful revolution is widespread popular discontent. I see no such condition existing in Ireland.

PEARSE. We disagree.

PLUNKETT. So?

MACDERMOTT. What're you going to do?

MACNEILL. That-is-for-me-to-consider-and-decide-upon! (*And he leaves.*)

AIDE. (*to* PEARSE). No man has the right to fight or to ask anyone else to fight to carve a niche for himself in history.

CLARKE. (*coming in*). Ye should have arrested MacNeill. He could do us untold damage.

All going out.

MACDERMOTT. What d'you think?

PEARSE. Everything will turn out alright.

NARRATOR. No lie in it: Untold damage MacNeill did do.
Howandever. (*Enjoying the misfortune.*) Things were not goin'
well at all, an' the miadh (*Misfortune.*) started to fall heavier.
The eve of the risin' an' the first thing: Three Volunteers flew off
a cliff in their car on the way to meet the German arms – Yeh?
The next thing, a ship did come, the 'Aud', but 'Aud' and arms
finished up under the water, scuttled herself after being
apprehended by an English boat. And on top of that – (*Laughs.*)
Casement was arrested, barely off a German sub that landed him
in Kerry. The story got to MacNeill and that did it. His pen was
out.

Scene Seventeen

MACNEILL. Woodtown Park, Rathfarnham, Co. Dublin.
Volunteers completely deceived. All orders for special action are
hereby cancelled and on no account will action be taken.
(*Signed.*) Eoin MacNeill, Chief-of-Staff. (*He hands the order to
his* AIDE.) What d'yah think a tha'?

AIDE.
Bide your time, your worst transgression
Were to strike and strike in vain;
He whose hand would smite oppression
Must not need to strike again!

NARRATOR. And he wasn't content with that. He knew that the
officers getting his messages would be mostly Pearse's men: He
had to get through to the rank-and-file: So, he composed a
longer an' a better notice an' put it in the *Sunday Independent*
that everybody'd be readin'.

Simultaneous with MACNEILL, *Volunteers prepared for battle
are entering, reading aloud incredulously the notice in the
'Sunday Independent'.*

MACNEILL. Owing to the very critical position all orders given to
the Irish Volunteers for Easter Sunday are hereby rescinded, and
. . . (*etc.*)

FIRST VOLUNTEER. No parades, marches, or movements of the Irish Volunteers

SECOND VOLUNTEER. Will take place. Each individual Volunteer will obey this

THIRD VOLUNTEER. Order strictly, in every particular.

NARRATOR. That did the job — yeh?

FIRST VOLUNTEER. What's this? —

SECOND VOLUNTEER. What's that? —

THIRD VOLUNTEER. What on earth is going on?

NARRATOR. That put paid to the Rising plans.

FIRST VOLUNTEER. What's this? —

SECOND VOLUNTEER. What's that? —

NARRATOR. It did the job so well that Pearse sent off his own despatches —

PEARSE'S VOICE. I confirm MacNeill's despatches! —

NARRATOR. Not to have some units mobilising and other units not. (*Pleased.*) Yeh? Jesus, the confusion! A funny class of Easter Sunday. (*She goes to the gramophone.*) Christ is risen!

The Hallelujah Chorus.

The Volunteers' earlier incredulity has now become confusion and frustration: they are shouting and jeering, throwing down their packs, their arms, breaking their guns.

FIRST VOLUNTEER. Owing to the very critical position! —

SECOND VOLUNTEER. All orders given to the Irish Volunteers! —

THIRD VOLUNTEER ⎱ Are hereby rescinded!
FOURTH VOLUNTEER ⎰ Are hereby rescinded!

FIRST VOLUNTEER. O King that was born to set bondsmen free!

SECOND VOLUNTEER ⎫ O King that was born to set bondsmen
free!
THIRD VOLUNTEER ⎬ O King that was born to set bondsmen
free!

FOURTH VOLUNTEER. In the coming battle help the Gael!

FIRST VOLUNTEER. Up the Republic! —

SECOND VOLUNTEER. Up on your sister! —

THIRD VOLUNTEER. Me hand on your drawers! —

FOURTH VOLUNTEER. God save Ireland!

Scene Eighteen

PEARSE, CONNOLLY, CLARKE, MACDONAGH,
MACDERMOTT, PLUNKETT and CEANNT dejected.

   Pause.

CONNOLLY. So?

PLUNKETT. Oh.

CEANNT. MacNeill.

MACDONAGH. (*absently*). What?

CLARKE. (*sighs*).

MACDERMOTT. (*sighs*).

CEANNT. Confusion.

CONNOLLY. Send us a hole to swallow us up.

   Pause.

CONNOLLY. So?

PLUNKETT. Oh.

CEANNT. I could cry.

MACDONAGH. What?

CLARKE. Oh what does it matter.

MACDERMOTT. I didn't think MacNeill'd do it.

PEARSE. I forgot the papers. Yes, I forgot the papers.

Pause.

CONNOLLY. But you confirmed his orders?

PEARSE. Yeh.

CONNOLLY. Good.

CEANNT. I could cry, I could cry.

CLARKE. What does it matter.

PLUNKETT. Orders and countermanding orders.

CEANNT. Orders confirming countermanding orders.

PLUNKETT. Orders flying hither and thither, like . . . (*Cannot find the simile.*)

MACDONAGH. Dying leaves astray on the wind?

PLUNKETT. Something like that.

SENTRY. (*voice off*). Commandants! Some men out here want to know what to do with some gelignite.

PEARSE. (*vaguely*). Ahm . . . what?

MACDERMOTT. I'll deal with it. (*He leaves.*)

Pause.

NARRATOR. So what'll ye do, lads?

CONNOLLY. So, what do we do?

PLUNKETT. We, Sinn Féin.

CEANNT. And the spirit was there.

MACDONAGH. Oh, the spirit was there.

CONNOLLY. But what do we do?

CEANNT. The spirit was there.

MACDERMOTT. (*returning*). Well, whatever we do, we had better decide. In more ways than one we are sitting on more than a haul of gelignite.

Pause.

NARRATOR. So what'll ye do, lads?

CLARKE. Fight! . . . (*Explodes.*) Oh! Are ye surprised, *ye* Sinn Féin? Sinn Féin, IRA, IRB, Citizen Army, Volunteers, National Spirit! *Fenians! England* has no right to be here!

CONNOLLY. . . . The only failure is the failure to strike.

NARRATOR. With your few numbers? – For Jesus' sake!

CONNOLLY. It is not the will of the majority that ultimately prevails. That which ultimately prevails is the ideal of the noblest of each general.

PEARSE. A wave of cynicism will bury Ireland forever if we don't fight now.

NARRATOR. It's suicide!

CONNOLLY. Deep in the heart of Ireland has sunk the sense of degradation wrought on its people – so deep and so humiliating that no agency less powerful than the red tide of war on Irish soil will ever be able to enable the Irish race to recover its self-respect.

CEANNT. What number of men can we count on?

MACDERMOTT. As many as will follow.

CONNOLLY. Without the trace of irreverence but in all due humility and awe, we recognise that of us, as of mankind before Calvary, it may be truly said 'without the shedding of blood there is no redemption'.

NARRATOR. Christ-was-wrong!

They continue to ignore her.

CONNOLLY. We're going out to be slaughtered, do we need a vote?

They don't need a vote.

PEARSE. We may make mistakes in the beginning and shoot the wrong people, but bloodshed is a cleansing and sanctifying thing and the nation which regards it as the final horror has lost its manhood. There are many things more horrible than bloodshed and slavery is one of them.

CEANNT. Well, it's too late today now.

PLUNKETT. What about tomorrow?

CLARKE. Tell any of them ye're unsure of, it's manoeuvres. (*Directly to* NARRATOR.) England should not be here. (*And leaves following the others.*)

NARRATOR. I hate nationalism! (*To herself.*) England has no right to be here. I hate the English. No. I am honest and in control. I hate nationalism. It doesn't exist. I love life. Heigh-ho! And I'm not getting involved. (*Coming out of reverie.*) What? – Yes – Howandever. What the English were doing that Easter Sunday morning.

Scene Nineteen

The UNDER-SECRETARY, *the* LORD LIEUTENANT, *the* ACTING-COMMANDER-IN-CHIEF *of the troops – he has a copy of the 'Sunday Independent' – and the* COMMISSIONER OF POLICE.

ACTING-C-IN-C. 'Owing to the very critical position all orders given to Irish Volunteers hereby rescinded.'

UNDER-SECRETARY. (*dismisses it*). Yes, I read it.

ACTING-C-IN-C. 'No parades, marches, movements will take place.' Why not, who's stopping them?

UNDER-SECRETARY. Oh, one of those perverse attempts at publicity to give themselves some importance. Now, the matter to hand that we met to discuss.

ACTING-C-IN-C. 'Owing to the very critical position': What critical position? What does Intelligence say?

UNDER-SECRETARY. Trouble in their own little camp, thieves fall out.

LORD LIEUTENANT. They're probably sitting in that den, Liberty Hall, right now, cooking up more sedition.

UNDER-SECRETARY. Oh, come, a parcel of pro-German cranks. We're not here to discuss a notice in a newspaper. Now, this 250 pounds of gelignite that was stolen this morning.

CHIEF-OF-POLICE. I've traced it to Liberty Hall.

UNDER-SECRETARY. Yes. Well. That's good.

CHIEF-OF-POLICE. What d'you want me to do, Under-Secretary?

LORD LIEUTENANT. Recover it before it's distributed.

UNDER-SECRETARY. Let's not be hasty.

LORD LIEUTENANT. Maybe get the ring-leaders as well.

UNDER-SECRETARY. It's Easter Sunday morning, gentlemen!

ACTING-C-IN-C. There's a bigger smell then gelignite in this whole business.

UNDER-SECRETARY. Yes, and Westminster knows exactly what is going on –

LORD LIEUTANANT. The German boat thing during the week –

ACTING-C-IN-C. That Casement fella –

LORD LIEUTENANT. That German boat can be considered as an invasion.

ACTING-C-IN-C. The messages that were intercepted –

LORD LIEUTENANT. The Volunteers Association with the King's enemies –

UNDER-SECRETARY. *All* a very delicate matter, *all* a matter for the Home Secretary and Westminster. And remember what the Chief-Secretary said? America: Still neutral. So now, this business of the gelignite.

CHIEF-OF-POLICE. I've traced it to Liberty Hall . . . What d'you want me to do, Under-Secretary?

LORD LIEUTENANT. I urge that you take action.

ACTING-C-IN-C. I agree.

UNDER-SECRETARY. What d'you mean?

LORD LIEUTENANT. Swoop.

UNDER-SECRETARY. When?

ACTING-C-IN-C. Now.

UNDER-SECRETARY. We have no authority to do anything of the kind. The Chief-Secretary is away for the weekend, the Commander-in-Chief is away for the weekend.

LORD LIEUTENANT. I'd take the responsibility.

UNDER-SECRETARY. I've no authority to let you take the responsibility.

Scene Twenty

NARRATOR. Easter Monday, noon. While the main detachment was marching on the GPO and while other detachments were marching on St Stephen's Green, Bolands Mills, the Four Courts, Jacob's Factory, the Mendicity Institute, the South Dublin Union, Phoenix Park Magazine Fort, to take as many places as they could as far as the men – and the women – went round, there was an attack on the gates of Dublin Castle.

As in Scene Six – only now it's daylight – a party of rebels are approaching the gates of Dublin Castle. The SENTRY *(played by* NARRATOR*), as before, is amused:*

SENTRY. Are ye back, lads?

This time they keep coming forward:

SENTRY. Halt! Halt! Stop, let ye! Stop!

The SENTRY *is killed.*

NARRATOR. The first stroke of the Angelus, the first shot was fired and one man was dead outside Dublin Castle – Yeh?

While the main detachment was arriving at the GPO, Volunteers, IRB, Citizen Army – whatever you call them – the Rebels – were now one, the new army, the Irish Republican Army: the IRA – Yeh?

Halt, left turn, the GPO, charge.

CONNOLLY. Halt! Left turn! The GPO. Charge!

They charge. The rapid fire of the dialogue, shouted, conveys the confusion and frenzy of the scene.

CLARKE. Get your hands in the air! – File out! –

MACDERMOTT. Everybody out! Come on! – Get out! – Fast! –

CONNOLLY. Smash the windows, fortify them! – Up with the barricades before we're attacked! –

PEARSE. Man the roof! – Take the telephones! – Evacuate anyone there! –

PLUNKETT. Hack a hole through that wall into the next building! –

WOMAN. (*customer*). I will not leave! –

YOUNG REBEL. Go out, go out, Ma'am! –

WOMAN. I came in for a stamp –

YOUNG REBEL. Go out, go out, ma'am! –

WOMAN. How dare you! I shall inform the –

YOUNG REBEL. Or I'll blow your head off!

CONNOLLY. Get the food and water in and over there! –

LATECOMER. Why wasn't I mobilised?! –

1ST REBEL. Come in – come in – come in – come in – come in! –

LATECOMER. (*cut by window glass*). Jesus, that glass! –

WOUNDED REBEL. (*wounded by a bomb that goes off accidentally*). Sweet Jesus!

2ND REBEL. Sweet Jesus! – But if that's all the damage our bombs will do! –

PEARSE. Nurse! Take care of this man! – Go for a priest! –

CLARKE. Have the telephones and the guards up there been secured?! –

MACDERMOTT. Hands in the air! – Put down your guns! –

PRISONER. We surrender, we surrender! – We've no ammunition! –

PLUNKETT. Take charge of these prisoners! –

YOUNG REBEL. (*confused and frightened, is crying*). I – I – I – I!

CONNOLLY. (*angrily*). What is the matter, man?!

YOUNG REBEL. I – I – I – I! I wasn't at confession, I want a priest!

CONNOLLY. (*gently*). And your hands are cut.

YOUNG REBEL. (*crying*). I – I – I – I!

CONNOLLY. And you have no uniform. Would you like to go home for a while and come back later when you feel better? Good man.

YOUNG REBEL *goes. The others too would like to leave. The lull lasts only for a moment, the quick fire shouting resumes.*

CONNOLLY. What kind of barricade is that?! – A charge of schoolgirls would knock it over! – Get it up properly before we're attacked! –

WOMAN REBEL. Rotten English! – Sassanach! – Dirty rotten English Protestants! (*As in abusing prisoners.*) –

PLUNKETT. Report to the hospital for work there! –

PEARSE. Willie, take charge of those prisoners! – Lock them up!

2ND REBEL. What did Commandant Connolly mean when he said our chances were a thousand to one?

1ST REBEL. What d'you think he meant?

2ND REBEL. What about our work tomorrow? (*The others laugh.*)

LOOKOUT. The Tommies are coming!

Several guns go off.

1ST REBEL. False alarm! False alarm!

CLARKE. Stop firing! Stop firing!

A REBEL emerges — as from a tunnel he has been digging — carrying an effigy or some object — or it can be nothing. (Throughout, the more restricted the use of props of any kind, the better).

REBEL. I've just captured Lord Kitchener!

They find the remark funny and thus ends the first phase of the Rising.

NARRATOR. 'We strike at noon with as many men as will follow.' Not the ten or twenty thousand they'd been talking about. A handful: (*Shrugs.*) fifteen hundred? With more hammers than guns.

Look at that.

Scene Twenty-One

The populace watches the spectacle.

JIM. Looka tha'! Looka tha'!

MOLLY. Wha're they a'?

BIDDY. Looka the damage!

MICK. Look what they're doing to the windows!

MOLLY. Wha're they a'?

JIM. Wha'ever they're a' they won't be a'it long!

MICK. Weren't we lucky we hadn't the money to go to the races: There'll be fun here yet.

MOLLY. The dirty bowsies! Wait'll the Tommies come – Where's the police?

JIM. Oh the rozzers scarpered!

BIDDY. Yiz'll never find the rozzers when they're wanted!

MOLLY. An' did no one call them back?

MICK. Why would anyone call them back, isn't it only a bit of fun, sure?

MOLLY. Are yous contradicting me? Yeh scabby-headed ape of a thick-nosed coilltie! – Go back down the country where yeh belong!

BIDDY. He isn't contradictin' yeh, but I am! Yous and all your poxy relations – Go back to the Southside where you belong!

MOLLY. Poxy relations?! – Stand back or I'll paste yiz down there to your tribe in the Monto!

JIM. Looka tha'! Look-a'-tha'!

BIDDY }
MOLLY } Wha're they a'?!

MICK. What next?!

JIM. Look up!

BIDDY }
MOLLY } (*pleased*). Flags!

FARMER. Whist on ye, he's going making a speech!

JIM. Jasus, an' I hope 'tisn't as long as his last one!

CONNOLLY *holds a flag, as at half-mast.* PEARSE *reads the proclamation.*

PEARSE. The Provisional Government of the Irish Republic to the People of Ireland.

Irishmen and Irishwomen: In the name of God and of the dead generations from which she receives her old tradition of nationhood, Ireland, through us, summons her children to her flag and strikes for her freedom.

Having organised and trained her manhood through her secret revolutionary organisation, the Irish Republican brotherhood, and through her open military organisations, the Irish Volunteers and the Irish Citizen Army, having patiently perfected her discipline, having resolutely waited for the right moment to reveal itself, she now seizes that moment, and supported by her exiled children in America and by gallant allies in Europe, but relying in the first on her own strength, she strikes in full confidence of victory.

We declare the right of the people of Ireland to the ownership of Ireland, and to the unfettered control of Irish destinies, to be sovereign and indefeasible. The long usurpation of that right by a foreign people and government has not extinguished the right, nor can it ever be extinguished except by the destruction of the Irish people. In every generation the Irish people have asserted their right to national freedom and sovereignty; six times during the past three hundred years they have asserted it in arms. Standing on that fundamental right and again asserting it in arms in the face of the world, we hereby proclaim the Irish Republic as a Sovereign Independent State, and we pledge our lives and the lives of our comrades-in-arms to the cause of its freedom, of its welfare and of its exaltation among the nations.

The Irish Republic is entitled to, and hereby claims, the allegiance of every Irishman and Irishwoman. The Republic guarantees religious and civil liberty, equal rights and equal opportunities to all its citizens, and declares its resolve to pursue the happiness and prosperity of the whole nation and of all its parts, cherishing all the children of the nation equally, and oblivious of the differences carefully fostered by an alien government, which have divided a minority from the majority in the past.

Until our arms have brought the opportune moment for the establishment of a permanent National Government, representative of the whole people of Ireland and elected by the suffrages of all her men and women, the Provisional Government, hereby constituted, will administer the civil and military affairs of the Republic in trust for the people.

We place the cause of the Irish Republic under the protection of the Most High God, Whose blessing we invoke upon our arms, and we pray that no one who serves that cause will dishonour it by cowardice, inhumanity, or rapine. In this supreme hour the Irish nation must by its value and discipline and by the readiness of its children to sacrifice themselves for the common good, prove itself worthy of the august destiny to which it is called.

Signed on behalf of the Provisional Government –

CLARKE. Thomas J Clarke.

MACDERMOTT. Seán MacDiarmada.

PEARSE. P H Pearse.

CONNOLLY. James Connolly.

MACDONAGH. Thomas MacDonagh.

CEANNT. Eamonn Ceannt.

PLUNKETT. Joseph Plunkett.

CONNOLLY. Thank God, Pearse, that we have lived to see this day. (*He raises the flag.*) Isn't it grand?

Scene Twenty-Two

NARRATOR. Clip-clop, clip-clop, clip-clop, clip-clop.

LOOKOUT. (*a voice*). An attack, an attack, the cavalry!

SECOND VOICE. An attack, the cavalry! –

1ST REBEL. The cavalry! –

2ND REBEL. The Lancers are coming down the street, sir!

CLARKE. Good.

PLUNKETT. Take positions!

CONNOLLY. Don't fire till I give the order!

MACDERMOTT. Don't fire until ye receive the order!

CONNOLLY. D'ye hear – D'ye hear?!

CLARKE. Wait for the signal.

NARRATOR. The first British attack on the Rebels' headquarters. Mounted Lancers on horseback, pompous in their saddles – Yeh? – looking left or right, no, coming down Sackville Street as if only on a march-past. Clip-clop, clip-clop. Shhh: the Rebels waiting. Clip-clop, clip-clop. Shhh, wait for the signal.

A sombre FIGURE wearing a bass drum – single beats of the drum as in a dead march – is entering. (Or some such stylising device to effect these scenes of death.)

NARRATOR. (*shouts a warning*). They're waiting for yiz!

The Rebels open fire.

NARRATOR. The Rebels open fire, too soon. But. Four Lancers dead and a horse. Charging defended buildings with horses – Yeh? Which side is committing the suicide? . . . (*Sings softly.*) 'Oh we're off to Dublin in the green, in the green, where the bayonets glisten in the sun . . .' Let's go up to St Stephen's Green.

The sombre FIGURE with the drum continues his slow, impassive, inexorable circling.

Gunfire, as appropriate through the following.

(*Quietly.*) 'Where the bayonets glisten . . .' in the rain . . . The Countess de Markievicz and Michael Mallin and their detachment were well hemmed-in in St Stephen's Green. They hadn't enough men to man the roof-tops on that side of the Green and, so, made sitting ducks of themselves. Machine-guns up there. And see: four dead already there. And he's dying. Maybe they'd wait for the darkness and get to the rebel-held buildings on that side. Or maybe help would come. From where? Be-cause, be-cause all Ireland did not rise up once the fighting started: The fools, the fools, the fools, they did not wish to become Fenian dead! (*Quietly again.*) 'Bayonets glisten in the sun, in the rain . . .' (*Sing-songing, trying to shake off mood.*) So we're off t'join th' IRA, he's the boy I do adore an' the bayonets flash an' lal-la la la to th'echo of a Thompson gun!' – Let's go somewhere else.

She becomes still.

FIGURE *with drum still circling.*

A NURSE is coming in – as to attend to someone.

NURSE. I'm coming, I'm coming. There-there, I'm here, there-there.

Burst of gunfire: the NURSE is dead.

NARRATOR. Weren't we all right the way we were? And we don't *really* hate the English, do we? Wasn't Home Rule on the way? Whatever that is. Wouldn't we be free sometime? Whatever that is. But, Jesus Christ, let there be conqueror or no conqueror and if it be yes, then let him – or her – rule so hard that there can be no questions, no rebels, no – faithful? – no coercion, no concessions, no *nurses*! There's freedom in fascism – Yeh? . . . But hark, soft – or is it shush? – it is night.

FIGURE with drum continues inexorably.

Three British SOLDIERS are moving cautiously along a street, trying to watch every door, window, rooftop, singing their fear in undertones, 'Down at the old Bull and Bush'. Report of a rifle: one of them is dead. 'Down at the old Bull and Bush.' Report of a rifle: the second one is dead. The third one, terrified, can't find the enemy, 'Down at the old Bull and Bush', kicks down a door, goes into a house, reappears with a BOY or an OLD MAN, makes BOY/OLD MAN to kneel in the street and shoots him. 'Down at the old Bull and Bush.' Report of a rifle: third soldier is dead.

NARRATOR. Anyways, 'what's the news, what's the news, O me bold Shelmalier' – Yeh? Oh, it was getting inconvenient, and more inconvenient as the days went on. No trams, no milk, fires breaking out, no trains. Civilians getting shot be-the-dozen be the British and be the Irish alike. Food getting scarcer – and even if it was in plenty, no banks or post-offices to get a penny out itself to buy it. Not a place itself to cash a separation allowance. No news at all, at all, me bould Shelmaliers, rumours only – yeh?

The FIGURE with the drum has come to a standstill and suspends drumbeat temporarily for the following.

MOLLY, BIDDY, JIM *and* MICK *are huddled together, waiting, trying to get into a pub.*

MOLLY. An' did yiz hear the Pope is gone?

JIM. Gone? – Aa no! –

MICK. His Holiness, now, the crayture –

BIDDY. Gone?! –

JIM. He – sufferin' Jasus! – musta lost heart – Aa, come on, Barney, let us in!

MICK. An' Jim Larkin – Did ye hear?

JIM. Oh Jem, Jem, Jem Larkin an' meself.

MICK. Well, they tell me he's marching from my side in the West with a million even American soldiers.

BIDDY. Barney, let us in out of the curfew.

JIM. But did yous hear this: the Irish Volunteers Reserves has taken London, wha'?

MICK. Stop!

JIM. Oh now! – Jasus, Barney, sure there's no risin' out this way!

MOLLY. Sure it's only us an' Jim an' Mick the Culchie.

BIDDY. An' did yiz hear the English has artillery on the way to level Dublin?

MICK. Wouldn't it break your heart?

JIM. An' that Pearse an' Connolly both is dead?

MOLLY }
BIDDY } Fought a duel on topa the GPO – we heard.

MICK. Whist!

JIM. Wha'?

MICK. There's someone comin'.

VOICE. (NARRATOR). Who's there?

JIM. Two ladies and gents with a serious thirst.

VOICE. The password.

BIDDY. Keep off the streets.

They get into the pub (they leave).

NARRATOR. (*to herself*). Keep off the streets? . . . But, a fact:
British reinforcements in their thousands were pouring into
Dublin after Dublin Castle got a telephone wire connected.

The FIGURE *with the drum has started up again, the drumbeat,
the slow, regular, circular movement.*

Not that they were getting things their own way, no indeed.
(*Spreads her hands as if indicating the carnage.*) Mount Street
Bridge.

(*Historically, Mount Street Bridge was the scene of greatest
death. Seven Rebels manned the windows commanding the small
bridge: British soldiers fell in waves trying to cross the bridge.
British casualties were put at 234.*)

Ten dead! Twenty, forty British soldiers! (*She is becoming
abandoned.*) 'Too long a sacrifice can make a stone of the heart.
O when may it suffice? That is heaven's part!' Fifty – yeh? 'Now
are we resurrected, now are we who lay so long beneath an icy
hand, new risen into life and liberty because the spring – ' – the
spring! – 'has come into our land!' Oh, seventy, eighty of them
at this stage. (*She casts it at the* FIGURE *with the drum.*) The
British would need their artillery.

FIGURE *with drum goes off; but there is a resoluteness about
him: he will be back.*

(*Gently, eyes cast down.*) Yeh.

*She goes to the gramophone: a distorted Irish tenor in party
piece.*

Keep off the streets!

*Looting in Sackville Street (now O'Connell Street) outside the
GPO. JIM, MICK, MOLLY, BIDDY are the looters. They are
drunk, raucous, singing; they are trying to sell their loot; they
steal from one another; a fight breaks out. Revelry. (Apportion
the lines and improvise.)*

LOOTERS. 'Soldiers are we, whose lives are pledged to Ireland . . .' (*Drunken rendering of the National Anthem – the Rebels' anthem.*)

Up the Republic! – It's a great day for the poor!

Ninepence each the watches!

Who'll give me four bob for a fur coat?!

Half-a-crown a bottle of whiskey!

Tuppence each the packets of tea!

Oh Jasus, yeh robber yeh, stealing a poor old woman's bita china! I'll swing for yiz! (*Etc.*)

NARRATOR. Keep off the streets said Dublin Castle.

LOOTERS. Up the Republic!

NARRATOR. Keep off the streets said the Rebels.

LOOTERS. Up the Crown, up the King!

PEARSE *and* CONNOLLY *watch the scene in horror.*

PEARSE. Don't disgrace us! Don't disgrace yourselves! Don't disgrace the Rising! Don't dishonour what we're fighting for!

LOOTERS. It's a free country!

Up the Republic!

Up the Crown, up the King!

'Soldiers are we . . .'

CONNOLLY. Disperse them!

PEARSE. Send out the Special Squad!

CONNOLLY. Fire on them! Fire a volley over their heads!

PEARSE. Rapine. Rapine. (*And turns his back on the scene.*)

CONNOLLY. Rapine. (*And leaves.*)

The tenor and the party music on the gramophone is winding down, tailing off. The last of the looters staggers off drunkenly.

LOOTER. Sure Jasus, I only wanted to enlist.

NARRATOR. Yeh? . . . But hark, soft – or is it shush again? It is the small hours.

A tired young SENTRY, looking out at the night, at nothing. PEARSE, nearby, turns and he too is looking out at nothing. Then, absently, as if to himself.

PEARSE. It was the right thing to do . . . was it not?

SENTRY. Wha'? . . . Yes.

PEARSE. After a few years they will see the meaning of what we tried to do . . . But it was the right thing to do . . . was it not? . . . Oíche mhaith. (*Good night.*)

Young SENTRY has been privately surprised by PEARSE's self-questioning, but is now reverting to tiredness again.

VOICE. How are we doing, sir?

CONNOLLY. (*entering, without stopping*). We've won.

ANOTHER VOICE. Sir, sir, the English are stealing up on us along the roofs of Henry Street.

CONNOLLY. They're not.

CONNOLLY comes to a stop behind tired young SENTRY – where PEARSE stood a moment ago – and he too is now looking out at the night. (He was a married man with five children.)

. . . Are you married?

Tired young SENTRY shakes his/her head . . . CONNOLLY is about to move on.

SENTRY. Ah, Mr Connolly – Commandant.

CONNOLLY. Yes?

SENTRY. I mean – sometimes I forget: what are we fighting for?

CONNOLLY. The sovereign right of every race and nation to . . . Ireland. For a start. Did yeh hear the one about the British officer saying to the rebel, 'You Irish are an ungrateful lot: we have a good mind to leave you to your barren little potato patch.' 'That's all we want,' said the rebel. Good night.

Scene Twenty-Three

NARRATOR. Boom. The artillery and General Sir John Maxwell were brought in to have the final word.

(MAXWELL *may be represented by the figure with the bass drum: if so he does not have to move about or beat the drum, the directness and volume of his voice tells the unequivocation of his resolve.*)

MAXWELL. I, General, Sir John Maxwell, have been appointed GOC of the forces in Ireland from the 26th instant inclusive. His Majesty's Government desire that in this capacity I will take all such measures as may in my opinion be necessary for the suppression of insurrection here and I am accorded a free hand in regard to the movement of all troops now in Ireland or which may be placed under my command hereafter and also in regard to such measures as may seem to me advisable under the Proclamation dated 26th April under the Defence of the Realm Act. If necessary I shall not hesitate to destroy all buildings within any area occupied by the rebels. (*An aside, as he walks off.*) Dig a grave for a hundred men.

NARRATOR. It is now Thursday and the British cordon around the city is tightening in, and any of the rebels that can are falling back on their headquarters, the GPO. And Patrick Pearse, the poet sure, is taking the opportunity to pay a final tribute to his men.

PEARSE. Headquarters, Army of the Irish Republic, General Post Office, Dublin, 28th April, 1916. 9.30 am.

The forces of the Irish Republic which was proclaimed in Dublin on Easter Monday, 24th April, have been in possession of the centre of the capital since twelve noon on that day. Our positions are still being held, and commandants in charge are confident of their ability to hold them for a long time.

NARRATOR. It is now Friday, the city is burning.

PEARSE. The enemy has burned down whole blocks of houses,
apparently with the object of giving themselves a clear field for
the play of artillery and field guns against us. We have been
bombarded during the evening and night by shrapnel and
machine-gun fire, but without material damage to our position,
which is of great strength.

NARRATOR. The city is burning, the end is near.

MOTHER. (*as before, she may find these sentiments questionable*).
I do not grudge them, Lord,
I do not grudge my two strong sons . . .
But I will speak their names to my own heart
In the long nights;
The little names that were familiar once
Round my dead hearth.
Lord, thou art hard on mothers:
We suffer in their coming and their going;
And though I grudge them not, I weary,
Weary of the long sorrow – And yet I have my joy:
My sons were faithful, and they fought.

NARRATOR. The GPO is on fire.

PEARSE. We deserve to win this fight and win it we will! –
Though it be in death! Already we have done a great thing:
Dublin is redeemed from many shames and her name made
splendid among the names of cities!

NARRATOR. They'll finish us off with a bayonet charge.

CLARKE. (*quietly*). They'll finish us off with a bayonet charge.

PEARSE. Let me who have led the soldiers of Irish freedom into
this, speak in my own name and in my fellow-commandants'
names, and in the name of Ireland present and to come, their
praise.

NARRATOR. James Connolly lies wounded but is still the guiding
light of our resistance.

CONNOLLY *is shot, twice, by a sniper.*

PEARSE. James Connolly lies wounded but is still the guiding light
of our resistance!

CONNOLLY. To Soldiers: This is the fifth day of the Irish
Republic. For the first time in 700 years the flag of a free Ireland
floats triumphantly over Dublin city. Courage, boys, we are
winning, and in the hour of our victory let us not forget the
splendid women who have stood by us and cheered us on. Never
had a man or woman a grander cause, never was a cause more
grandly served.

NARRATOR. The Soldiers' Song.

SINGER. 'Soldiers are we, whose lives are pledged to Ireland . . .'
(*Others joining in.*)

NARRATOR. Evacuate.

MACDERMOTT. Evacuate!

REBELS. No!

MACDERMOTT. We're not surrendering! – We'll get through,
northwards, and continue the fight there!

They evacuate, leave wearily, all joining in 'The Soldiers' Song'.

PEARSE. If we accomplish no more than we have accomplished, I
am satisfied. I am satisfied that we have saved Ireland's honour. I
am satisfied that we should have accomplished more, that we
should have accomplished the task of enthroning, as well as
proclaiming the Irish Republic as a Sovereign State, had our
arrangements for a simultaneous rising of the whole country
been allowed to go through on Easter Sunday. Of the fatal
countermanding order which prevented those plans being carried
out, I shall not speak further. Both Eoin MacNeill and we have
acted in the best interests of Ireland. For my part as to anything I
have done in this, I am not afraid to face the judgement of God,
or the judgement of posterity.

*He leaves, following the others who are now off. 'The Soldiers'
Song' concluding.*

REBELS. '. . . we will chant a soldiers' song.'

NARRATOR. Will yiz? The British will soon redden your arses.

She does a little dance in celebration of their defeat, her victory.

Scene Twenty-Four

NARRATOR. Escape to the North and continue the fight there? They got a few yards. (*Points.*) In there. They spent the night in there, No. 16, Moore Street, talking. What are they to do? There is no bargaining to be done. What *can* they do? (*Laughs.*) 'In order to prevent the slaughter of Dublin citizens, and – ' Yeh?

PEARSE'S VOICE. In order to prevent the further slaughter of Dublin citizens, and in the hope of saving the lives of our followers now surrounded and hopelessly out-numbered, the members of the Provisional Government present at headquarters have agreed to an unconditional surrender and the commanders of the various districts in the city and country will order their commands to lay down arms.

NARRATOR. PHP, quarter-to-four, twenty-ninth April, nineteen sixteen, AD. Five days, three hours, forty-five minutes. Five hundred dead, three hundred of them civilians; two-and-a-half thousand wounded, two thousand of them civilians.

The REBELS *are filing in,* PEARSE *bringing up the rear with a white handkerchief of surrender.*

The struggle was over, the boys had had their 'nough, and where was the redemption they were talking about? The sacrifice musenta (*Must not have*) been great enough. So, yer risin' was a failure: I knew all along and I was right not to play. (*Confident sweep, takes the white handkerchief.*) Take them away! Ends: The Disgraceful Story of 1916.

They do not move. PEARSE *smiles.*

Go, the play is ended! . . . What?

ALL. Ready! Take aim!

PEARSE. Goodbye, dear mother. I have not words to tell my love of you, and how my heart yearns to you all. I will call to you in my heart at the last moment.

ALL. Fire!

NARRATOR. No-no-no – Go! – it's all over now. (*She is resolved not to yield.*)

ALL. Ready! Take aim!

MACDONAGH. I, Thomas MacDonagh, declare that in all my acts I have been actuated by one motive only, the love of my country, the desire to make her a sovereign independent state. I am ready to die and I thank God that I die in so holy a cause.

ALL. Fire!

NARRATOR. . . . What?

ALL. Ready! Take aim!

CLARKE. I, Thomas J Clarke, and my fellow-signatories believe we have struck the first successful blow for freedom. The next blow, which we have no doubt Ireland will strike, will win through. In this belief we die happy.

ALL. Fire! – Ready! Take aim!

PLUNKETT. Father, I am very happy. I am dying for the glory of God and the honour of Ireland.

ALL. Fire! – (*All whispering.*) Patrick Pearse, MacDonagh, Clarke, Plunkett, Patrick Pearse, MacDonagh, Clarke, Plunkett – (*They shout.*) Willie Pearse, Fire! MacBride – Fire!

NARRATOR. No! – Go! – *We* are in control!

ALL. Ready! Take aim!

CONNOLLY. The Socialists will never understand why I am here. They will forget I am an Irishman.

ALL. Fire!

(*Whispering.*) Patrick Pearse, MacDonagh, Clarke, Plunkett, Willie Pearse, Seán MacBride, James Connolly. Patrick Pearse, MacDonagh, Clarke, Plunkett, Willie Pearse, Seán MacBride, James Connolly . . .

NARRATOR. (*speaking over the above*). No, no, *we* are in control. We do – not – *hate* anyone – We *hate* nationalism! Look at the destruction, the damage was caused – Look at the windows, the burnt buildings! – Five-hundred people *dead*, two-thousand five-hundred people maimed – hurt – wounded –

three-hundred civilians dead! . . . (*She realises that they have stopped whispering. She whispers.*) What?

ALL. Ready! Take aim!

CEANNT. I, Eamonn Ceannt, leave all I have in the world to my wife to do with what she wills. Ireland has shown she is a nation. Áine, mo bhean, tóig do cheann agus bíodh foighde agat go bhfeicimid a chéile arís i bhFlaithis Dé. (*Áine, my wife, raise your spirits and be patient until we meet in heaven.*)

ALL. Fire!

NARRATOR. (*will not yield; quietly*). No. That's all finished and done with now.

MACDERMOTT. I, Seán MacDiarmada, before paying the penalty of death for my love of Ireland and abhorrence of slavery, desire to make known to all my fellow-countrymen that I die as I have lived, bearing no malice to any man and in perfect peace with Almighty God.

ALL. Fire!

NARRATOR. No.

ALL. (*whispering*). Patrick Pearse, MacDonagh, Clarke, Plunkett, Willie Pearse, Seán MacBride, James Connolly, Eamonn Ceannt, Seán MacDermott. (*Now building to a crescendo.*) Michael Mallin: Fire! Edward Daly: Fire! O'Hanrahan – Fire – Heuston – FIRE – Colbert – Kent – Casement – FIRE!

NARRATOR. UP THE REPUBLIC!

PEARSE. . . . . And you were only playing the narrator.

The REBELS *move off.* PEARSE *waits by the exit for the* NARRATOR.

NARRATOR.
Oh! If we had guns and trumpets, if we had
Aught of heroic pitch or accent glad
To honour you as bids tradition old,
With banners flung or draped in mournful fold
And pacing cortege: these would we not bring
For your last journeying.

PEARSE. Come on. Come on home.

The Blue Macushla

for Jane

The Blue Macushla was first performed at the Abbey Theatre, Dublin, on 6 March 1980.

EDDIE O'HARA	Donal McCann
PETE	Barry McGovern
ROSCOMMON	Deirdre Donnelly
MIKE	Emmet Bergin
NO. 1	Pat Leavy
VIC CAMDEN	Paddy Long
NO. 2	Pat Laffan
HOODED FIGURE	Marcus O'Higgins
DANNY MOUNTJOY	Stephen Rea
COUNTESS	Fedelma Cullen
BRITISH AGENT	Paul Brennan
MULLARKY	Paul Brennan
O'MALLEY	Pat Laffan

Director Jim Sheridan
Settings Brian Collins
Lighting Richard Caswell
Costumes Ib Jorgensen
Fight Scenes and Stunts Pat Whelan
Music Peter O'Brien

ACT ONE

Scene One

A desklamp is switched on (By EDDIE) and the light falls on a figure slumped in a chair. The figure is hooded and appears to be loosely bound, a whitish cloth is draped indifferently over the shoulders obscuring a dark costume. EDDIE comes around the desk into the light to stand behind the hooded figure. He wears a white tuxedo. There is an air of crazy detachment about him, he could be almost talking to himself. He produces a gun during the following, holds it absently.

EDDIE. We become quite int'mates you'n'me, kid-priest, an' lot in common. Yous is from big fam'ly too: I was readin'. Can't remember 'xactly how many o' us they was, but you wasn't born in Lady O' Perpetual Succour Mansions. Why, with 'n address like that, even before unemployment become unemployment, an' you 'proached a place lookin' for work you was 'rested for all sorts o' intentions. So none o' us workin' 'cept Mom. Yeah. Most my family's, I would say, mainliners now: some's inside, some has even had their legs sawed off. Two them comes along oh sometime back: Sure, I get rid o' them fast: 'Go get rehabil'tated.' For what they says an' was grinnin' kinda foolish. But understood what they meant. The only sane brother I got left is crazy. Washes his hair six times a day in every day 'n' draws the dole, Fridays. Then has comp'titions with my ole man, I'm told, at relievin' theirselves through the broken pane to the winda-box was left behind by Mom. Oh but got a older sister. Now Susie was a looker an', so, married this guy in reg'lar work an' she helped out Mom a lot. Only her husband — husband? Understand that word? — Only her husband's then got no job an' starts a-burglin', right? Only he's su'prised one night, see? an', so, stabs this guy to death an', so, he's in for life. Now Susie's

pregnant – pregnant? – with two twins while this comedy's goin'
on an' has two other young uns too as well, an' one o' yours, a
coonic (*Priest.*), comes runnin' to her rescue with his ros'ry
beads. Offer it up he tells her. Needn't tell yeh what our Susie
says to him, cause in Lady O' Perpetual Succour Mansions the
rats had took a fancy to her babies bottles. But now she's makin'
out, ole Susie is. I tell her once, 'pack the pushin' game', but
she's doin' fine she says an' the christian guys she's workin' for
'll kill her if she does, an' fort'nately she don't want out. 'Out
where,' she says. I 'gree. Bishopspricks. (*Takes out a silencer and
fits it to the gun.*) Oh yeah: like we wasn't all zombies: some was
nat'ral retarded, like Mom's own favourite, Tim. He was blessin'
in disguise she said. But O'Hara's quite a name up there, cops in
all hours hide-n-seek about the place, maybe that's what made
him do it. Tim. A overdose o' somethin'. Rat poison? Could be.
An' I figure that's the straw at last broke our Mom's back.
Naaw, never went to see her. What for? Yeh, bishopspricks. But
only part o' one family's history an' I'm feelin' kinda tired.
(*Sighs at the gun.*) Always knew somhow'd hafta use one o'
these. Thought has held fas'nation for me alright. Sorry, kid-
priest, it had to be you but Jesus went out with the fairies. (*He
shoots the figure in the chair.*) An' then o' course they was me. I
just wantedta, yeah, forget. I just wantedta become a person . . .
But where did this story begin?

Special lighting effect for flashback.

Scene Two

*Spotlight on paino-player dressed-up as Santa Claus finishing a
tune and finishing a drink. Applause. EDDIE, now the confident
and proud proprietor, steps into the spot, takes up the mike.*

EDDIE. Thank you, thank you! An' thankin' you, ole Santa Claus
for that bagful o' tunes! Sips a bit much, don't he? An' don't be
fooled by those ancient whiskers, ladies, dips a bit much too.
(*Laughter.*) An' now, folks, prepare to be transported, star of
our li'l show, star of the galaxy, is gonna sing li'l number has
kinda special meanin' for us here at The Blue Macushla! Take it
away, Santy!

More applause as the sexy and sexy-sounding ROSCOMMON enters the spot. Santa Claus tinkling the introduction, EDDIE hands the mike to ROSCOMMON and stands just outside the spot to listen to her singing.

ROSCOMMON. 'Macushla, Macushla, your sweet voice is calling/ Calling me softly, again and again / Macushla, Macushla, I hear its dear pleading / My blue-eyed Macushla I hear it in vain.

'Macushla, Macushla, your white arms are reaching / I feel them enfolding, caressing me still / Fling them out in the darkness, my lost love Macushla / Let them find me and bind me again if they will . . .'

Instrumentation continues.

MIKE, the giant-sized doorman/bouncer has arrived to whisper something into EDDIE's ear. As they move off together:

EDDIE. What!

MIKE. Three guys, Boss.

EDDIE. You left them downstairs!

MIKE. They said they was 'sociates.

EDDIE. You let them into my office!

A new spot: as in Scene One, it is the desk-lamp: focussed on an empty chair – the same chair that the hooded figure sat in. We are in EDDIE's office. Two figures in overcoats are standing on the periphery of the light. The short one is VIC CAMDEN, No.3; the taller one, carrying a brown-paper parcel and wearing thick-lensed spectacles is NO.2. The glow of a cigar tells us that a third figure is seated behind the desk: this is NO.1. NO.1 wears a broad-brimmed hat: the face is constantly in shadow: indeed the face is not properly distinguishable until Act Two, Scene One.

EDDIE. Okay, the house is full, you gotta book at least two weeks in advance . . . Hey, what's goin' on here? Mike, get these guys –

VIC has moved up behind EDDIE, his gun in EDDIE's back.

VIC. We don't need Mike, okay? Be a good doorman, Mike, an' get back out there on duty.

MIKE. Huh? Boss?

EDDIE. Yeh, Mike, you get back on duty.

MIKE *leaves.*

I sure am sorry, boys, but I can't do a thing 'less you got a reservation.

VIC. We just come from there, the reservation, Chief, for a pow-wow.

EDDIE. Would one o' yiz mind tellin' me what this's about?

NO.1. Please be seated, Mr O'Hara.

EDDIE. Now yous hold on, this is my office, that's my chair yous is sittin' in.

VIC. Sit, Chief.

NO.1. . . . You must forgive us for intruding on your privacy, Mr O'Hara.

EDDIE. Not at all.

NO.1. How good of you! How little kindness is left in the world!

A gesture from NO.1's *cigar and* NO.2 *places his parcel on the desk.*

EDDIE. . . . What's that? Whatcha got there?

NO.1. Show Mr O'Hara what the package contains.

NO.2 *unwraps the parcel.* EDDIE *is frightened by the ordinariness of the contents.*

EDDIE. Yeh? . . . What is that?

NO.1. Tell Mr O'Hara what it is.

VIC. That there, Chief, is a pure 9 x 4 x 18 inch carat concrete block.

NO.1. Now, would you be so good as to tell us where you bank?

EDDIE. Bank? – I don't bank. This is a fun place, sure, but I been havin' to borrow here, there'n'everywhere just to help it all along, see?

NO.1. Yes, quite, we know that you *borrow*, particularly from the Anderson Ryan Banking Company.

EDDIE. Can't rec'llect I been in that one.

NO.1. Really?

NO.1 passes a slip of paper to NO.2 who passes it to VIC who passes it to EDDIE.

It is a facsimile of a note left at the Anderson Ryan Bank after business hours six weeks ago.

EDDIE. Yeh? What d'yeh know, how 'bout that!

NO.1. Yes, how about it?

EDDIE. You gonna let me in (*on*) what this is all 'bout now?

He returns the slip of paper to VIC, who passes it to NO.2, who passes it to NO.1. NO.1 has produced a small black book, hands it to NO.2, who hands it to VIC.

NO.1. Debtors' section, under O.

VIC. (*finds page*). Yeh. O'Hara. Thirty-five thousand.

NO.1. Thirty-five thousand pounds.

VIC passes the book to NO.2 who, instead of returning it to NO.1, keeps it.

EDDIE. Thirty-five Gs, that's lotta lettuce.

NO.1. We want the money you stole in our name, Mr O'Hara.

EDDIE. This is a joke! . . . On my mother's grave, I don't know what yous is on about!

NO.1. I do not think your mother would be proud of your avowal. Show Mr O'Hara how the concrete block works.

NO.2 lifts the concrete block delicately to a height, then drops it on EDDIE's desk: EDDIE withdraws his hands just in time.

NO.1. You see, a simple but effective invention. Next time you
   may not be able to remove your fingers in time. But, I am not a
   violent person, Mr O'Hara, I abhor violence. But what am I to
   do in the face of your blatant dishonesty. (*Gestures to* NO.2 *to
   repeat the action.*)

EDDIE. As God's my judge! —

   NO.2 *with concret block raised,* VIC *now pressed up behind*
   EDDIE *so that* EDDIE'*s hands are on the desk.*

   Okay-okay, yeh! But I haven't got it! I'd some bad debts here,
   see, an' every last sprazzy'n'dime was left after that, also went
   into here — You gotta believe me!

NO.1. We believe you. (*Gestures to others to relax.*) But, oh dear,
   what are we to do? We could inform the police, but the police
   do not look kindly on our work so why should we assist them?

EDDIE. Gimme time, I'll get it together, the club's beginnin' to
   really swing an' — Huh?

NO.1. (*has silenced him with a gesture*). But we are not an
   unreasonable order and, where possible, we try to find a
   constructive solution for those who can find within themselves a
   sympathy for our work and a wish to further our ideals. And
   yes, come to think of it, your premises is conveniently situated
   on the river and if you would be so kind as to allow us the
   facilities it has to offer from time to time, we may have the
   solution to our problem. Don't just sit there, Mr O'Hara, please
   tell us if you agree?

EDDIE. Yeh, sure, yeh, I agree.

NO.1. How good of you! Now, let us introduce a little formality,
   the ceremonial of which will help you to keep in mind your
   obligation and the consequences of any default thereof. Please
   rise.

EDDIE. Just one thing, how'd you figure *me* for that bank job?

NO.1. Rise, Mr O'Hara.

EDDIE. A *solo* job! — No one could've known but me!

VIC. Stand, Chief.

NO.1. Please take the oath.

EDDIE. (*reads from a card*). 'My brothers and sisters, I, number – ' number?

NO.1. Your number is 19, your division is Dublin North-Central.

EDDIE. 'I, number 19, division Dublin North-Central, do solemnly swear that while life is left me I will actively seek to establish and defend a united Ireland. That I will execute all orders coming from the proper authority to the best of my ability. That I will foster a spirit of unity, nationality and brotherly love among the entire people of Ireland. I swear that I take this obligation without reservation and that any violation thereof merits the severest punishment.' Yeh.

NO.1. So help you God.

EDDIE. So help me God.

NO.1. Brothers, it affords me pleasure to introduce you to your new brother. (*Clicks his fingers at* NO.2.)

NO.2. Ay?

NO.1. The book!

NO.2 *returns the small black book to* NO.1 *and leaves with his concrete block.* NO.1 *follows.*

VIC. Erin go brath, Chief, we'll be in touch. (*And follows.*)

Simultaneous with their leaving, light going down on EDDIE *and up on* ROSCOMMON *concluding her song.*

ROSCOMMON. 'Macushla, Macushla, your red lips are saying / That death is a dream and that love is for aye / Then awaken, Macushla, awake from thy dreaming / My blue-eyed Macushla, awaken to stay.'

Scene Three

Three months later, St Patrick's Day. There is a brass band in the distance, growing louder as it approaches.

The theoretical lay-out of the set is as follows. Back centre, a stairs leads to a landing (which the script assumes to be visible): turning left on the landing will lead to the club proper, turning

*right will lead to the 'Hospitality Room'. But we are in a basement
or semi-basement, an adjunct space in the belly of the club: the
decor is informal with pipework showing: a temporary storage
place, a place in which to rehearse a song — it has a piano — as well
as suggesting a place where hospitality might be extended to
favoured guests, to sport and drink with the proprietor. The
kitchens/cellars are assumed to be off on one side but there is a
small bar showing — and, perhaps there is a dumb-waiter; on the
other side is EDDIE's office.*

*It always feels like night down here. And, because of the gloom,
nothing is defined as yet, but the place is in its usual state of
disarray — the debris from last night and the cargo it contains for
tonight's party upstairs.*

*The door to the street is a staff door (not the main door to the
premises). It opens: PETE letting himself in with his key. The
surprise of daylight from outside. PETE is the piano-player but,
like everyone else, he mucks-in with other work. His habitual
attitude is to look and act camp; at the moment, though, he
appears edgy, like a man who was being pursued or like someone
who has beaten another to a destination and is now unsure about
what to do next. It's difficult to tell about people in this place. The
brass band is growing louder and he closes the door.*

*The brass band growing still louder and MIKE comes hurrying
from rear of premises (registers PETE but does not stop), to crouch
at a window, look up and out at the band passing by. He is
carrying something — a new commissionaire's topcoat.*

MIKE. Huh, Pete, brass band, goin' up to join the main parade.
Wow! Wow! Look (*at*) them girls! Look them — Wow! Look at
them 'Merican . . . (*His voice is lost in the brass band.*)

> PETE *leaves a small bag somewhere, gets out of his topcoat, a
> newspaper from his pocket. The band is receding, diminishing in
> the other direction. PETE switches on a light.*

Wow! Them 'Merican girls — Whatcha call them, Pete? Pete?

PETE. Majorettes, Mike.

MIKE. Major — yeh. Must watch out for them again when they
come back this way with the whole parade this evenin'. Thighs
on them girls nearly bigger'n mine! (*He remembers he is carrying*

his new commissionaire's coat; he is very proud of it.) Huh?
Pete? New coat, huh?

PETE. Yeh, neat – The Boss in?

MIKE. Yeh. Snazzy, huh?

PETE. Yeh. (*He is registering a car pulling up outside.*)

MIKE. Yous is in early, Pete?

PETE. Yeh, thought I'd run a few numbers over with Roscommon.
(*Sits with his newspaper.*)

MIKE. Neat, yeh – (*And is about to hang up the coat.*)

There is a knocking on the door.

Place is shut!

More knocking, violent, continuous.

I said the place don't open till six-thirty! What they bangin' the
staff door for? Don't yiz got ears out there an' don't yiz wanta
keep them?! (*He has opened the door.*) Oh, Mr – Mr! didn't
know was you.

*A hooded whimpering figure, hands tied, is pushed in the door
followed by NO.1, followed by VIC. NO.1 and his prisoner
continue up the stairs, turn right to the Hospitality Room off.*

VIC. Who's he?

MIKE. New piano player, Vic. Come in early to rehearse for the
party tonight.

VIC. Do yous like playin' the piano, Fingers? (PETE *nods.*) That's
good. Start rehearsin'. (*Gives car-keys to* MIKE.) Take care o'
the pony, (*To* PETE.) Hey! Where yiz goin'?

PETE, *on the stairs, gestures 'to the club'; that there is a piano
up there.*

VIC. (*points at the piano in this space*). What's that? Down here.

PETE *obeys.* VIC *follows* NO.1 *and prisoner to the Hospitality
Room.* MIKE *is about to hang his new coat up again,
remembers:*

MIKE. Oh! I'm meant to tell the Boss.

He buzzes the office on the house phone. EDDIE, in shirt-sleeves, enters from an inner room to answer the phone.

EDDIE. Yeah?

MIKE. (*whispering*). Boss?

EDDIE. Yeh?

MIKE. That you, Boss?

EDDIE. Yeh-yeh, Mike, what is it?

MIKE. They're back. They've a beat-up guy with a hood round his head.

EDDIE. (*to himself*). J.C., Jesu Christu, St Patrick's Day?!

MIKE. Boss?

EDDIE. So they're back, so what! (*Puts down phone.*)

MIKE. You said I was meant to tell yiz every time they . . . (*Puts phone down.*) Dopey! How come the Boss don't know nothin' no more?

PETE. I wonder who's going to win the big game on Saturday?

MIKE. Like he's pretendin' things is like they always used to was, Pete?

PETE. I thought we just discussed that just now.

MIKE. Huh? Oh yeh! – (*And laughs as if understanding a joke. Then remembers his coat and hangs it up.*) But I mustn't get it dirty. (*Remembers the car.*) Oh yeh. (*Going out.*) Aw gee, wish it was tonight.

Absently, MIKE has left the door ajar.

PETE is playing the piano.

There is a cry or groan of pain from upstairs.

Since the phone-call with MIKE, EDDIE has been sighing to himself in his office. But he's restless, comes out of his office, perhaps a glance up the stairs.

EDDIE. Hi, Pete, that's cute. You waitin' for Ros? Big parade. First one I missed in a while. How many guests we got in all?

PETE. Three.

EDDIE. (*sharply, pushing reservation book aside*). How many guests we got comin' tonight, I said! (*Picks up newspaper.*) 'Cabinet Cabal Calls Secret Session.' (*To himself.*) Cab'net Caballs, huh? 'Heinous Crimes To Cause Feelings of Indignation And Rage.' Listen to that rage'n'indignation out there. (*The bands in the distance.*)

EDDIE *reading further. There is a cry or groan from the Hospitality Room. EDDIE wondering could there be a link between what he is now reading and what is going on upstairs.*

PETE. (*quietly*). St Patrick's Day, it must be something important.

EDDIE *nods absently.*

Are you planning something to stop these choir-boys coming here?

EDDIE. Give her coupla minutes an' she'll be out. (*And returns to his office with the newspaper. Calls to an inner room.*) Pete's outside, Baby! (*Reads paper.*) 'British Intelligence Defector Disappears Without Trace. Search Now Concentrated On Dublin Area.'

And he goes off to inner room. PETE continues his piano-playing. DANNY comes in carrying a cheap suitcase. He has a pronounced Dublin accent. PETE gets a start when DANNY taps on the inside of the door.

PETE. Who the!

DANNY. Sorry, sorry – how yiz – But I tried the main door up there! (*Moves about proprietorially.*) So this is The Blue Macushla! So this is The Blue Macushla! Tell us, is this The Blue Macushla?!

PETE. If that's what the sign says.

DANNY. (*in celebration*). Janey Sufferin' Macalice Jasus!

PETE. Did you want to talk to someone?

DANNY. (*laughs*). Did I wha'?! Oh sweet holy livin' mother of the divine Jasus!

Cry of pain from Hospitality Room.

What was that?

MIKE. (*coming in*). Hey, how'd you get — Place is shut till six-thirty —

Another cry of pain.

DANNY. What's happenin' up there? —

MIKE ⎫ Where'd d'yiz think yiz're —
DANNY ⎭ Is Eddie up there? —
PETE ⎫ Take it easy, Mike —
MIKE ⎭ Fella like you got his head busted in here last night.

DANNY. For what? —

MIKE. For nothin' —

PETE ⎫ Easy —
MIKE ⎭ So, you leavin' or lookin' for trouble? —

PETE. He's not —

DANNY. He is — D'yiz want some?

MIKE. Outside, buster —

DANNY. Why not here? —

MIKE. Boss's 'structions: Like the police we deal with trouble *outside* the station, then if we like them we send for an ambulance.

PETE. Take it easy! Are you a friend of Mr O'Hara's?

DANNY. You might say that.

PETE. Tell the boss someone's here.

MIKE. *Whom* shall I say?

DANNY. Danny Mountjoy, *buster*. Just say Danny's here.

MIKE *goes to office and off to inner room.*

(*To himself.*) Sufferin' . . . .

PETE. (*offering a cigarette*). Here, these can damage your health too. You up from the country? On vacation?

DANNY. I've been on one.

PETE. (*puzzled*). Haven't we met before, handsome?

DANNY. No, we haven't – an' I enjoyed every moment of it. (*To himself.*) Sufferin' Jasus!

PETE. You're Kid Mountjoy. You used to drive those hot-rods – I saw you race in the Park. Sorry about the reception, Kid, but yeh know the way things are.

DANNY. I don't know. I mean to find out.

EDDIE *comes in followed by* MIKE.

EDDIE. Well-well, well-well, am I seein' straight? This is some surprise!

DANNY. How yeh, head.

EDDIE. Lemme take a look at yeh, yeh look just great!

DANNY. Discipline, Eddie. How yeh doin'?

EDDIE. Well-well!

MIKE. Everythin' okay, Boss?

EDDIE. Yeah! – You get them crates in from the yard, barrels hooked up, all that stuff up to the club? – Come in to my office, Kid – Give Mike a hand, Pete.

PETE. They said – (VIC *told him to play the piano.*)

EDDIE. *I* said! – Come in, come in, Kid! (*Calls back.*) And-lock-that-door!

MIKE *and* PETE *go off about various business.*

Well-well, well-well! I reckon y'could do with one o' these (*a drink.*) – Whydn't yeh call me?

DANNY. No small change.

EDDIE. Yeh?

DANNY. Good luck!

EDDIE. Boopsie'n'Aisling!

DANNY. An' how's your ma?

EDDIE. Who? Oh, mom, mom, why, mom's gettin' 'long just fine.

DANNY. An' Bill an' Jer an' Joe an' –

EDDIE. 'N' Bill – 'n' – Jer – 'n' – Joe – 'n' – Yeh!

DANNY. Susie?

EDDIE. Now Susie's really doin' swell.

DANNY. God! (*They were good days.*)

EDDIE. 'N' Frank – 'n' – Sheila – 'n' – Tim.

DANNY. An' your da?

EDDIE. Yeh! (*Toasts again.*) Boopsie'n'Aisling'n'Ciara! You been up (*to*) the 'Mansions'?

DANNY. Ma passed on.

EDDIE. Oh! – Disremembered – Yeh – Rest her.

DANNY. What's goin' on, Eddie?

EDDIE. What's goin' on where, Kid?

DANNY. Buster and the fairy tinklin' the haspicall out there.

EDDIE. Colour, that's colour 'n' good for business.

DANNY. An' sounds like someone's heatin' the poker for some mush upstairs.

EDDIE. Oh that! Bunch o' hot-head card-playin bums I rent my Hospitality Room to. (*Putting on a tie, a jacket.*) But I'm gonna sling 'em to hell outa here one o' these days.

DANNY. I like the threads.

EDDIE. This clawber, Kid? – Naaw –

DANNY. No, yeh do! – Sharp!

EDDIE. Well, suppose I always did.

DANNY. (*remembering the old days, smiling*). Yeh.

EDDIE. (*remembering with him*). Yeh.

DANNY. Remember that time we . . . (*They start laughing.*) God! (*They were good days.*) I've been hearin' stories about yiz inside.

EDDIE. What stories, Kid?

DANNY. Oh, how yous are doin' fine, how they're callin' yiz an important person, how yiz're movin' in big circles.

EDDIE. What circles, Kid?

DANNY. The best. It sort of was a help to me.

EDDIE. Oh, you mean the parties I throw? – But with the point'n'purpose o' buildin' up the contacts, right?

DANNY. Right.

EDDIE. Right?!

DANNY. Right!

EDDIE. (*to himself*). An important person. Goddamit, I should've written you, Dan, I should've a card, a goddamn food-parcel – But I been busy.

DANNY. I can see.

EDDIE. (*getting carried away with himself*). Right! It's a lip-smackin' lib'ral age an' you make love'n'lolly in the hay while the sun's shinin'n'blindin' their eyes, an' don't nobody tell yeh diff'rent. People come in my front door up there, Kid, the classiest: that's the boss they say an' he just smiled my way. They know who's runnin' things. An' those guys I got workin' out there – Okay, so I'm vain, so what? – but it's 'Sure, Boss, yeah, Boss, you're the boss, Boss' – Yeh, I insist it but (*I*) kinda like it.

DANNY. Right! –

EDDIE. 'N' politicians –

DANNY. Pol?!

EDDIE. The biggest! They come cruisin' up t'my door in their armour-plated Mercs, takin' the country for a ride. An' the broads, Kid – them tiara-tessies we useta gawp at through the railin's round the big houses? – why, you own a place like this an yeh gotta carry an' axe to keep choppin' their arms off from hangin' round your neck.

DANNY. Yeh, I can feel things stirrin' – first time in a long time.

EDDIE. All the things welfare mask-wearin' faces said you'd never have.

A cry of pain from upstairs.

DANNY. Stakes must be high up there.

EDDIE. An important person. (*Then, hearing the cry in retrospect.*) Yeh, I'm slingin' 'em out to hell one o' the days. 'Nother drink, Kid?

DANNY. Maybe in a while. Let's take a look at the place, show us around. Yous sure did things with our roll, head.

EDDIE. (*the last stopping him*). Your share was – huh?

DANNY. Right! Same as yours Eddie. It's good to be home, partner.

EDDIE. (*then laughs*). Ain't seen each other in – two years? – an' –

DANNY. Five –

EDDIE. Five – we's (*al*)ready on to greenbacks. Today'n'tonight *you* cel'brate. It's not just ole St Patrick's birthday, it's yours too. Anythin' you want, name it. Champagne'n'caviare for starters, an' for the main course –

DANNY'*s attention now on the alluring figure of* ROSCOMMON, *who stands languorously in the doorway of the inner room.*

. . . for dinner, Kid – I'd like for you to meet Roscommon.

DANNY. (*to* EDDIE). Ros?

EDDIE. Ros, this is Danny Mountjoy, my best an' oldest buddy.

ROSCOMMON. Hallo, Mr Mountjoy.

DANNY. How – how d'you do.

He can't take his eyes off her and she, accustomed to being looked at, looks back – and, privately, she too finds him attractive.

EDDIE. Roscommon's our main attraction an' – Well, I'll be! (*He sees that they are attracted.*) Hey! break it up, you guys. Pete seems t'have come in early, Baby, to run over a few numbers.

ROSCOMMON. See you around, Mr Mountjoy.

DANNY *watches her leave;* EDDIE *watches* DANNY.

DANNY. Who is *that*?

EDDIE. You like?

He grins, gestures DANNY to stay put and leaves the office. DANNY unlocks and opens the window and enjoys a deep breath of fresh air. Outside the office, EDDIE has caught up on ROSCOMMON. MIKE is working behind the bar and PETE enters later, in response to EDDIE's call. And, in a few moments, VIC comes down the stairs.

It's not 'see you around Mr Mountjoy': This guy may look it but he ain't that big a cake an' he's askin' lotta questions.

ROSCOMMON. You're hurting my arm, Eddie.

EDDIE. Gee, sorry, Baby, but this guy wasn't meant to be out for – I don't know when! You pump him, get close to him – yeh, yeh, take him up to your room.

ROSCOMMON. What d'ya take me for?

EDDIE. (*calls*). Pete! What d'ja say, Baby?

ROSCOMMON. You got another star attraction over there. (VIC *coming downstairs*.)

EDDIE. (*to* ROSCOMMON). You're makin' waves. (*Following* VIC.) Hey, you, Camden!

VIC. No.3 to you, O'Hara, Erin go brath! –

EDDIE. Yeah – yeah –

VIC. (*to* PETE *who has come in*). You're not rehearsin'.

PETE *looks at* EDDIE, EDDIE *gestures him out of his way and continues to* VIC.

(*To* MIKE.) Brandy, big boy. Our guest up there needs revivin'.

EDDIE. I'm meant t'have a party happenin' here tonight.

VIC. Yeh? Remember No.2, four-eyes, our concrete-block-layin' friend, remember him? Well, he got his hands on that little black book of ours an' sold it to the guy up there. We're askin' him where he hid it.

EDDIE. I don't wanta know! You're stinkin' the place out, customers got noses – D'yeh know how many bookin's I got tonight?

VIC. We don't find that little book they's goin' to be a lotta bookin's. It contains some very classified information.

EDDIE. I said I don't wanta know!

VIC. Yeh? As far as I recollect it contains a little item on you too. (*He's going back upstairs with brandy.*)

EDDIE. Listen, Camden, you get outa –

NO.1 *is standing on the landing.* PETE *has been playing 'I Dreamt I Dwelt in Marble Halls' (Bohemian Girl),* ROSCOMMON *half-heartedly singing bits of it. (First verse.)*

(*Hisses.*) Yous all get outa here!

But EDDIE *sounds weak.*

In the office, DANNY *reacts mildly to the interrupted music outside and to* EDDIE's *hissing – though he can't quite hear what is being said.*

On the landing, NO.1 *brushes aside the brandy which* VIC *is timidly proffering, says something to* VIC *which we do not hear, plus –*

NO.1. Car!

VIC *comes hurrying down the stairs, to the bar, to* MIKE.

VIC. Keys! (*Car keys.*)

NO.1 *has come down the stairs,* VIC *hurrying to the door to open it for him.*

What yiz mean we got the wrong guy?

They leave.

PETE *resumes playing.*

ROSCOMMON. (*dismissing music*). 'That you loved me still the same – ' The number's fine, Pete's fine, everythin's fine – It's the way you introduce it's what needs workin'!

DANNY *has come in from the office.*

EDDIE. (*smiling, public image*). Yeah, come in, come on over, join us, Kid – Whatcha say, Pete, Baby?

ROSCOMMON. The number's fine, it's you that's cock-eyed: Pete had to play the intro three times last night!

EDDIE. (*to* DANNY). See the way they treat the Boss – (*To* ROSCOMMON.) Pleeese – (*To* DANNY.) the hired help? I'll do the intro with yiz later – Promise! – but how bout you'n'Pete – *now* – li'l teaser-trailer for the Kid. Play, Pete.

EDDIE *has a word in* MIKE's *ear and goes to his office: once in his office his hands to his head like a man with a bad headache. He goes off to inner room.*

MIKE – *acting on the word from* EDDIE – *sets glasses and champagne in front of* DANNY. DANNY *listens in rapt attention to* ROSCOMMON.

ROSCOMMON. 'I dreamt that suitors sought my hand . . . you loved me, you loved me still, the same.'

DANNY. That was – that was – God! Yiz know how to put a song over.

ROSCOMMON. You learn lots of things in my business.

DANNY. Champagne, wha'! Will yiz? Have a drop?

She shrugs, sighs okay, but remains standing.

Champagne, Jasus! twelve o'clock in the day, what a place!

ROSCOMMON. Yeh, it's one helluva place.

DANNY. Good luck! – I mean, to Boopsie an' – Skol – Bottoms up – Sorry.

ROSCOMMON. Good luck'll do.

DANNY. I mean, people are talkin' funny here: where did the Malones move to, Molly an' her little brother Pa'?

ROSCOMMON. Oh, Eddie likes it this way.

DANNY. Yeh? Likes yiz to talk like?

ROSCOMMON. He likes his staff to *perform* all sorts o' ways.

DANNY. Colour, I get yiz now!

ROSCOMMON. You're a nice guy, Mr Mountjoy, stay that way. Thanks for the drink. (*She is moving away, stops, a deep breath at the prospect of going into the office.*)

DANNY. What's up? (*Joking, showing her that he can do the lingo too.*) Say, you're a real busted valentine.

(*She smiles.*) Won't yiz join us?

(*She hesitates.*) I haven't talked to a lady in five years.

She sits with him.

Is there somethin' on your mind? Put it on your other boss's shoulder. Yeh, me an' Eddie's partners now.

ROSCOMMON. Yeh don't say.

DANNY. How 'bout tellin' me the story of your life, maybe I can provide a happy endin'.

ROSCOMMON. (*sharply*). By doin' what?

DANNY. No, no! (*Meaning she has misinterpreted him.*) Tell us, tell us about your family, your ma, your da.

ROSCOMMON. Mom played the harp while dad played his organ.

DANNY. Yeh?

ROSCOMMON. Are you for real, are you on the level?

DANNY. The bubble's right in the middle, kitten. (*They laugh.*) More? (*Champagne.*)

ROSCOMMON. (*no*). I'm workin'.

DANNY. It's good stuff? No, but seriously, I'd like to get to know yiz, all about yiz.

ROSCOMMON. What's there to know? (*Rueful smile, looking at him.*) There's always been a guy with slow-movin' eyes for me to end the night with, learnin' a new trick on the tamborine.

DANNY. Tell us, Ros, do yous really come from –

ROSCOMMON. Let's swap, Mr Mountjoy –

DANNY. Danny.

ROSCOMMON. How was it with you, Danny?

DANNY. Just another chiselur in the 'Mansions'.

ROSCOMMON. Eddie told me you were quite a guy.

DANNY. Did he say that? (*She nods.*) Well, yeh, that's friendship. But – can I tell yiz somethin'? – I wasn't anything an' I feel I've been nowhere till I . . . till today. (*And till he met her.*)

ROSCOMMON. How'd yeh get in trouble with the cops?

DANNY. I'll tell yiz. I was a wild kid, yeh? Specially about cars. King Ace o' the joyriders? – that was me. That was bad. Then, bita racin' in the Park? (*For*) Guy who'd broke his legs? but he recovers, so I've lost my wheels. Then Eddie finds a beat-up truck. Come in with him? I do a job on it an' we're in the furniture-removin' game. Truck will do, oh, sweet hundred miles an hour, yeh? – no problem, only the furniture doesn't like its looks – Sure? ('*More Champagne?*' '*No*'.) Okay – so it's goodbye Murteen Durkin' we're sick'n'tired o' workin' – D'yiz know that one? (*She doesn't.*) So, Eddie has a skill at makin' contacts? – An' Irish butter made down here is cheap up North an' if we can get it out an' back down here an' sell it, we're importers, yeh?

ROSCOMMON. Butter?

DANNY. An' pigs. We're expandin'. An' other things. Simple: Depended on the supply o' labels an' ear-tags was available. (*She doesn't understand; neither does he but he feels that he is impressing her.*) Now we're importin' Irish dairy'n'farm produce. But now we start exportin' it back out again. (*She doesn't understand.*) Now we're playin' the subsidy game. Okay, I'm concentratin' on the drivin': We do a trip up North an' get a load was made or grown down here across the Border in the dark, importin' it back down here, yeh? Followin' day, it's daylight, yeh? we pick the same load up again an' take it back up North again, exportin', yeh? only the pigs are wearin' different ear-rings this time.

ROSCOMMON. But –

DANNY. Ask Eddie. An' maybe up again that self-same night for that self-same cargo once again for maybe once again to go re-exportin it back next daylight. To-in', fro-in' – Why that last run, I'd almost got to know them individually, regular commutin' buncha pigs, ears punched oftener'n railway tickets. Simple.

ROSCOMMON. Yeh?

DANNY. The last run? Okay. By Eddie's accountin' we'd got eighteen hundred stashed, nine hundred for Eddie, nine for me. But I've been thinkin', maybe Eddie's contacts were short-changin' us on the lats. But I'm not complainin' – it was okay money? (*She nods.*) So we're on our last run. After this, we were thinkin', maybe a run-down pub, maybe a – maybe a million things, maybe – wha'? Jasus! a Blue Macushla! Sure? (*'More Champagne?' 'No.'*) But maybe one of us got careless, not mappin', not changin' the route, but I'm at the wheel – Chewwwshhh! (*Travelling fast.*) Suddenly up ahead there's this ramp – the rozzers, yeh? Cops – I can't go back. Chewwwshhhwheeee!

ROSCOMMON. What?

DANNY. I'm air-liftin' my pips! Sufferin' Jasus – chewwwwheeee! Now I'm up so high the terrain below me's remindin' me o' crazy-pavin'! (*He's laughing, caught up in the memory; pulls himself together.*) But that was wrong.

ROSCOMMON. Whatcha do then?

DANNY. I touch down. I'm tellin' myself you've done it, Kid, but now the rozzers are givin' chase, yeh? – I'm runnin' outa petrol – gas, yeh? – I calculate I've ripped my tank flyin' the ramp but I still think I can make it, but Eddie thinks no. 'Slow, slow, slow it down, Kid, next bend', an' before he jumped he promised, me an' him are partners, fifty-fifty, straight down the middle.

ROSCOMMON. An' the cops?

DANNY. Yeh.

ROSCOMMON. An' you took the rap.

DANNY. I made a gen'ral confession an' asked for all my other sins to be taken to account. They gave me a seven-to-nine, remission on two for GB but I did a five stretch. D'yiz know what I'm goin' to tell yiz now? That hydrogen's (*Champagne.*) every bit as good for yiz as Guinness. Now, yous goin' to show me my half o' here?

They go upstairs, turn left on the landing to the club. He is drunk, laughing and playing with her hand. And she is inclined to laugh with him.

PETE has been around the place during the above. EDDIE arrives to watch ROSCOMMON and DANNY disappear upstairs. He too is considering going upstairs – to the Hospitality Room – But someone is knocking at the door.

MIKE has appeared behind the bar-counter with a glass of green Guinness.

MIKE. Place is shut! The mix on this Guinness okay, Boss?

EDDIE. P'lite, Christ's sakes, answer it polite! (*And has gone off, to hide behind the bar.*)

MIKE. (*opens door*). Yeah, please?

COUNTESS. Et's only me.

Chic COUNTESS has come in, dark top and dark slacks under her topcoat. Slight foreign-sounding accent.

Hello, darlinks.

PETE. Not watching the parade, Countess?

COUNTESS. You see one of thems you see two of thems. Es Eddie around?

PETE. Yeh, and Roscommon's around too.

MIKE. Yeh, and Ros –

Phone is ringing and he answers it.

COUNTESS. But I only come to gev you boys a hand.

MIKE. (*has answered phone: 'Blue Macushla, yeah?'*). It's for the Boss.

EDDIE. (*immediately to hand*). Put it through to my office –

COUNTESS. Oh Eddie –

EDDIE. Thought I told you two t'get that work done in there –

COUNTESS. Oh Eddie –

EDDIE. Not now. (*And goes into his office without stopping.*)

MIKE *and* PETE *to bar and off behind bar area.* COUNTESS *putting away her coat, up the stairs to peep into the club, returning, appears to hesitate on the landing – could she be thinking of the Hospitality Room? – but comes back down the stairs, perhaps because* PETE *has come in briefly for his bag. A glance at the office – she is interested in* EDDIE *– then follows* PETE *off as if to see what's happening in that quarter.* EDDIE's *action from coming into the office to taking the phone call is continuous.*

(*Note: A light may or may not come up on* VIC *for the phone call: He is in another location: A kiosk perhaps, or is in* NO.1's *apartment. Or we may simply hear his voice.*)

EDDIE. Blue Macushla.

VIC. That you, 19?

EDDIE. (*takes a deep breath*). O'Hara's the name.

VIC. This is No.3 –

EDDIE. Yeah-Yeah, Erin go brath – okay, mouseface, say whatever you gotta say, I'm in a hurry.

VIC. Yous listen good to this. We left a parcel of meat, dead meat in your Hospitality Room: No.1 says you dump it in the hills. Have you got that?

EDDIE. . . . Now *yous* listen good. You tell No.1, I ain't in the undertakin' business: That ain't part o' our deal.

VIC. Deal, what deal? Yous'd better do like yous's told to.

EDDIE. An if I don't?

VIC. Try usin' your imagination.

EDDIE. Hey, Camden, come on! I was never asked nothin' like this before.

VIC. So, you're graduatin'.

EDDIE. Why couldn't yous've done it?

VIC. We were in a hurry: We got the wrong guy but now we've got the right guy an' we're goin' to be busy with him.

EDDIE. Lemme talk to No.1.

VIC. Get rid of the stiff.

EDDIE. Lemme talk to . . . Hey, Camden, Camden!

VIC *has hung up.* EDDIE *puts down the phone. He needs a drink but resists his need.*

You get rid o' the stiff. (*Then considering the feasibility of this; then.*) Jesu Christu, what'm I thinkin'? (*Takes up drink, but resists it again. Considering. Then, impulsively, dials 999.*) Hello, Police?

COUNTESS *comes into the office, sexy attitude.*

COUNTESS. Remember me?

VOICE ON PHONE. Hello, Police? (*or 'Garda Siochana'.*)

EDDIE. Whatcha want, Countess?

VOICE ON PHONE. Hello, Police, hello!

COUNTESS. (*speaks into the phone*). Hello. (*And replaces it on the receiver.*)

EDDIE. You've two things to say, sister, you've said one of them.

COUNTESS. What es the other?

EDDIE. Goodbye.

COUNTESS. Your singer friend es engaged upstairs with a handsome –

EDDIE. I said beat it, not now.

COUNTESS. (*Looking into inner room*). That couch en there looks ver invitink-

EDDIE. (*going to the door as if to open it for her*). Okay, I got work to do.

COUNTESS. You look like a man with a beg (*big*) problem. Maybe I can help you forget? Or maybe you need – money? (*Ringed hands held up before her breasts.*) Look, my beg – jewels? I vell maybe show you more, come. (*She has gone in to inner room.*)

EDDIE. (*swallows the drink*). . . . You got thirty-five Grand I could borrow?

COUNTESS. Try me.

EDDIE *follows to inner room.*

ROSCOMMON *and* DANNY *returning from club. He is looking behind him, he likes what he has seen. They pause on the landing.*

(ROSCOMMON *is genuinely unaware of the drama that has been going on in the Hospitality Room.*)

DANNY. What's over here? (*Direction of Hospitality Room.*)

ROSCOMMON. (*shrugs*). Just some rooms. I have to go now, try on a new costume.

DANNY. Roscommon . . . (*He takes her hand.*)

ROSCOMMON. (*whispers*). Don't.

He embraces her for a moment; she succumbs helplessly, limply, for a moment.

Why me, why always me?

DANNY. Thanks.

ROSCOMMON. For what? (*About to go, turns to him again; she would like to warn him.*) Things aren't always what they seem. (*He doesn't understand.*) Watch where yeh go.

DANNY. (*calls after her*). See yeh round, Kitten! (*And returns to have another look at the club, eagerly.*)

ROSCOMMON *goes into the office, lights a cigarette, drags on it deeply. She is unhappy in her situation and her attraction to men with slow-moving eyes is once again adding further confusion to her life. She goes off to the inner room and returns angrily, almost immediately.*

EDDIE. (*off*). Baby! Baby!

ROSCOMMON. (*under her breath*). Baby, baby!

EDDIE. We was just, we was just talkin'!

ROSCOMMON. Sure, Eddie.

EDDIE. Just me an' the ole Countess! (*Coming in, followed by* COUNTESS.) Baby! We was just sayin' hello! Go powder your nose, Countess.

COUNTESS. Okay – (*Whispers.*) darlink. (*And leaves.*)

EDDIE. Hey, I love *you*.

ROSCOMMON. Listen – *mister*, – you're not talkin' to one of your – chumps – now, you're talkin' to me – Roscommon – who knows you, mister, green, white'n'orange!

EDDIE. (*laughing*). Baby! –

ROSCOMMON. You don't love no one – you never have. You're even suspicious of that guy up there, your best'n'oldest buddy. You only love this – club – of yours, only it don't appear to be yours no longer – does it?

EDDIE. (*deadly earnest*). Right, you got it, an' that's 'xactly what I'm gonna settle today. It can't wait no longer. I love this place, I love it more'n anythin' an' I'll do anythin' for it!

ROSCOMMON. Anything?

EDDIE. (*not listening*). This was my hope, now it's my dream an' *I* made it.

ROSCOMMON. Yeh sure did.

EDDIE. (*he has picked up the house phone and is buzzing it*). An' ain't sharin' it with no splinter-boys organisation no longer or with no new-come ole buddy neither! Hey, Mike.

MIKE. (*has come in and taken up phone*). Yeah?

EDDIE. Boss! – Boss! Take some refuse sacks up to the Hospitality Room: There's a parcel there, wrap it in 'em. Then get my jammer outa the shed 'n' put the parcel in the boot. You got that?

MIKE. Boss, what kinda parcel, Boss?

EDDIE. A parcel's a parcel.

MIKE. A big parcel, Boss?

EDDIE. Yeh, yeh, a big stiff piece o' meat – Do it.

He puts down the phone. He unlocks a safe, or produces money from somewhere. Counts some of it and when replacing the remainder, he finds a coin, considers it, spins it in the air, pockets it: closes the safe.

ROSCOMMON. (*through the above*). What's goin on, Eddie, what gives?

EDDIE. That li'l job I gave yeh.

ROSCOMMON. What's goin' on?

EDDIE. What'd yeh find out?

ROSCOMMON. About what, about whom?!

EDDIE. 'Bout Danny – Whom, Baby, that's what!

ROSCOMMON. He's okay.

EDDIE. What's that mean?

ROSCOMMON. What's it usually mean?

EDDIE. How come he's out so soon?

ROSCOMMON. He got remission on two for GB.

EDDIE. Good behaviour, figures. An' they got no room for them in there – What else?

ROSCOMMON. He's nobody's plant or stoolie if that what you're –

EDDIE. How d'yeh know that?

ROSCOMMON. He just thinks he's in for half.

EDDIE. Yeah, gonna settle that matter too (*in*) a minute.

ROSCOMMON. What do you mean you're goin' to 'settle' it?

EDDIE. Aaa! an' she likes. (*He is smiling but his eyes are cold, frightening.*) You still my girl?

ROSCOMMON. Yeh.

EDDIE. Yeh love me Baby?

ROSCOMMON. Yeh. Yeh.

EDDIE. Come 'ere. Tell me.

ROSCOMMON. I love you, Eddie.

EDDIE. Yeh know ain't no one in the world like you – What else?

ROSCOMMON. (*is frightened and near tears*). I don't know, Eddie, somethin' bout some guy or contact –

EDDIE. Huh?

ROSCOMMON. Goodboy Murteen Someone – I don't know.

EDDIE. (*silently*). Oh! (*Succumbs to memory.*) Goodbye Murteen Durkin, I'm sick'n'tired o' workin' (*Then hard again.*) Bishopspricks! – What else?

ROSCOMMON. I can't think, he's okay, nothin' else.

EDDIE. You get close to him? You-get-close to him?

ROSCOMMON. Y'told me be nice.

EDDIE. (*pulls her to him*). This close? Uh-huh. Then y'must know if he's packin' hardware.

ROSCOMMON. No, he don't have a gun.

EDDIE. Yeah? – What then?

ROSCOMMON. (*tearfully*). Just lotta old-fashioned friendship for you, that's all.

She is weeping.

MIKE *has returned and is buzzing the office.*

EDDIE. Yeah?

MIKE. Boss?

EDDIE. Yeah?

MIKE. That you, Boss?

EDDIE. Yeah-yeah, you done what I told yeh, you got my car out?

MIKE. Yeah, but that parcel –

EDDIE. Gimme ten minutes. (*Puts down the phone.*)

MIKE. But that parcel, Boss, that stiff . . . Boss?

MIKE, *confused and agitated, goes upstairs to take up an uneasy position near the Hospitality Room.*

EDDIE. Baby, baby.

ROSCOMMON. Don't ask me no more, Eddie, I'm all mixed up. I only came here to sing.

EDDIE. (*continues, quiet soothing sound, but perhaps he is going crazy*). Sure, Baby, you stepped in that door an' you knew what you come here for: Heat. Big shots, booze, bangs 'n' a good time. (*She starts to rise but he holds her there, almost unconsciously.*) 'Lax. (*Relax.*) I say things I don't mean to sometimes. I been under pressure. Know what I mean, Baby? 'N' I don't like sharin'. An' don't think I don't feel deep 'bout bein' only kinda half-boss here this while back.

ROSCOMMON. Can I go get changed now, Eddie?

EDDIE. An' the kinda feelin' lately that I'm being' set up by someone or some party, an' I ain't talkin' 'bout them choirboys. (*Coming out of reverie.*) Huh? (*Did she say somethin'? Grins.*) But I got it figured: tomorrow everythin's gonna be okay again.

ROSCOMMON. Whatcha goin' to do, Eddie?

EDDIE. Simple. A, I'm gonna pay-off your A-okay guy, my old buddy –

ROSCOMMON. He don't want no pay-off –

EDDIE. Sure he does! B, then I look after the goons.

ROSCOMMON. What they don't want lookin' after?

EDDIE. Sure they do, they gotta! I do li'l run to the hills for them now while the town's busy on parade. C, tomorrow I got certain sum o' money comin' from a certain quarter an' – see? – that's goin' to be 'nough for them.

ROSCOMMON. Eddie –

EDDIE. Then's so long, s'been good to know yiz, I'm out, period.

ROSCOMMON. You're goin' crazy in the head –

EDDIE. I'm talkin' no more! –

ROSCOMMON. You're puttin' your neck further in the loop –

EDDIE. Sure I am an' that's my token to them I'm gonna keep my trap shut. (*Turns her to face him.*) That's the way to figure it, ain't that so, Baby? (*Her face refuses to agree. He's dejected again.*) Can't think no other tokens I can give 'em.

ROSCOMMON. . . . . Seems like someone's been helpin' yeh with this new figurin'. That dumb rich dame!

EDDIE. Okay, so you know.

ROSCOMMON. How d'yeh know she ain't on the blower right now to the cops?

EDDIE. Baby! I know dames.

ROSCOMMON. Did your mother drop you on your head?

EDDIE. Same with all these foreign dames – She's been tryin' to get her hands on me for months.

ROSCOMMON. There's something funny about the 'Countess'.

EDDIE. She's stacked!

ROSCOMMON. An' how!

EDDIE. With chips – I got her in slips – I'm levellin' with yiz! She's comin' 'cross with the cabbage I need. Then I play like I'm nice to her for coupla weeks.

ROSCOMMON. Nice?

EDDIE. Goddamn coupla weeks she becomes member o' my staff, that's all I'm talkin' 'bout! – Whatcha' doin'?

ROSCOMMON. (*making for the door with her coat.*) I'm quittin'.

EDDIE. No you're not.

ROSCOMMON. No?

EDDIE. Because I won't let yeh.

ROSCOMMON. How yeh goin' to stop me?

He is looking at her as if he could kill her.

Yeh?

He kisses her fiercely. She remains unresponsive in his arms.

ROSCOMMON. Let me go now, Eddie, I'm so tired.

EDDIE. Yeh don't just stop lovin' someone.

ROSCOMMON. Now I don't know if I ever did.

EDDIE. I *need* yeh – Please – I gotta get out from under again!

ROSCOMMON. This (*Club.*) is all yeh need. Now, let me go.

He slaps her, hard. She recoils from him, hurt, crying.

What'd yeh do? What's happenin'? To everyone? To life, to love, to friendship?

EDDIE. Get changed!

ROSCOMMON *goes to inner room.*

(*To himself.*) Okay, so what I got presently ain't sufficient to buy me out, but I feel it: somethin' else's comin' my way. I feel it. An' tomorrow is a beautiful day.

He goes out of his office with his smiling, public image. MIKE, uneasy on the landing, is hurrying down to meet him. DANNY, drunk as before, during the following, enters from club and strolls across the landing to the Hospitality Room.

EDDIE. (*coming out of office*). Pete! – Where's Pete? –

MIKE. (*coming down the stairs, urgently*). Boss! –

EDDIE. Pete!

PETE, *as usual, is almost immediately to hand.*

MIKE. Boss! –

EDDIE. (*having a private word in* PETE's *ear, aside to* MIKE). Gimme ten minutes more –

MIKE. (*whispering*). But that parcel, Boss –

EDDIE. Get lost! – Where's the Kid?

PETE *has started to play 'Murteen Durkin' on the piano. DANNY is coming down the stairs at this point. He has been briefly in the Hospitality Room – opened the door, saw or heard something and retreated from it to shake his drunken head on the landing. He is coming down the stairs. MIKE goes upstairs during the following to take up his confused and uneasy position again outside the Hospitality Room.*

EDDIE. Kid! (*Sings.*) 'Goodbye Murteen Durkin, I'm sick'n'tired o' workin, no more I'll – ' How 'bout that?! – 'No longer I'll be fooled, sure's my name is Carney I'll be off – ' Ta? – 'Cal'forny, an' 'stead o' diggin' praties I'll be diggin' lump o' gold!' – (*Puts a drink in* DANNY's *hand.*) T' old times! To freedom, Kid! – To *your* freedom! (*Sings.*) 'No more I'll dig the praties, no longer . . .' (*He is tossing the coin that he found in the safe earlier.*) Call.

DANNY. Boopsie'n'Aisling! (*Drinks; confused.*)

EDDIE. (*laughs; tosses coin again*). No, call!

DANNY. Harps.

EDDIE. 'N' harps – tails it is. Yous's always the winner. Remember this? My lucky coin, Kid. You gave it me, why, must be twenty years ago. No, ole Eddie forgets nothin', he don't forget friendship an' he don't forget a debt. (*He gives a roll of money to* DANNY.)

DANNY. What's this?

EDDIE. That's yours, count it.

DANNY. Wha'?

EDDIE. Count it, a Grand, the nine hundred smackers, Kid, remember? plus hundred interest extra: Sorta comin'-out present was waitin', yeh.

DANNY. Naaw –

EDDIE. Yeah! – Your cut, straight down the middle like I said.

DANNY. Naaw! – Eddie, we have some talkin' to do but, first – (*Returns the money.*)

EDDIE. 'S' yours, Kid –

DANNY. Naaw! – That's capital. I amn't goin' to be some silent partner that comes along an' takes –

EDDIE. Kid –

DANNY. That has to be pumped back into the business –

EDDIE. Kid, that's yours –

DANNY. I read every single book there was inside about business an' –

EDDIE. I reckon that's too much readin'. That's capital, Kid, but you take it.

DANNY. Naaw –

EDDIE. Look – ! Look, I just don't have the time, plus I just took on a extra staff member, plus well, I got no time right now for economic discussions –

DANNY. No, Eddie – Somethin's goin' on. I've a few questions to ask yiz.

EDDIE. Okay, I tried it one way. That's yours, an an'thin' else you'd like is on me, it's on the house, *today*. Then, you ever need a handout, gimme call. Now I gotta go out somewhere.

DANNY. (*catches him*). Wait a minute, what kind of shuffle is this?

EDDIE. (*shakes off DANNY's hand*). Where yeh been, Kid?

DANNY. Where I – ?! I been in one of them – sing-sing? – places! or had yous forgotten that?

EDDIE. How much you think nine hundred smackers's worth?

DANNY. Thousand eight-hundred an' twenty-five days, not countin' th' extra one for the leap year!

EDDIE. I made all the moves, I made all the contacts, I took all the –

DANNY. Yous made-made took-took all-all sittin' in the truck I was drivin'! –

EDDIE. I been wheelin', dealin', organisin', financin' –

DANNY. Romancin' an' partyin' an' dancin' an' –

EDDIE. Sure! – Sure! An' I been spillin' my guts 'n' my brains 'n' – You know what I had to do to keep this place floatin'? – Look, I don't have to do no explainin' to no one, I gotta go now.

DANNY. (*catching his coat*). Not so fast.

EDDIE. You're bendin' the threads, Kid.

DANNY. Alright, unless yous start talkin' I'm goin' out that door an' comin' –

EDDIE. Back with bunch creeps o' tuppenny ex-cons! You think it's still a game o' fox'n'goose 'n' butter'n'pigs, you belong on a farm. You should try *beef*. This is what I got for you. (*Roll of money.*) Take it while I'm still feelin' gen'rous. (*He is walking away.*)

DANNY. Hey, head – (*Taps EDDIE on the shoulder and as EDDIE turns.*) – I've somethin' for yous too. (*And hits him.*)

EDDIE *goes sprawling in the open doorway of the office,* DANNY *following and* PETE *following* DANNY *and* MIKE *coming down the stairs.*

The world has passed *who* by?!

PETE. (*has produced a gun; he appears peculiarly concerned about passers-by outside*). Mountjoy!

MIKE. Boss? –

PETE. I've got it, Mike!

EDDIE. (*picking himself up*). Still pretty nifty with the mits – I think we may have a prize-fighter wants to meet yeh, Mike.

PETE. There's people passing up and down outside, Mr O'Hara.

ROSCOMMON. How d'yeh like my new costume, Eddie?

ROSCOMMON *has come in wearing a hat, topcoat and carrying a suitcase.* DANNY *takes advantage of the distraction and disarms* PETE.

DANNY. Let yiz – No one does nothin' till – till I think.

MIKE. Boss?

DANNY. (*to EDDIE*). Yeh? (*Meaning that he had better warn* MIKE.)

EDDIE. Do as he says, Mike.

DANNY. What's goin' on in our club?

EDDIE. Okay, but you're un'customed to drink, Kid, 'n' mixin' 'em, an' that thing in your hand can kiss eagerer'n a young wida (*Widow.*) comin' outa black.

And, indeed, DANNY *looks excited and confused and he reacts jumpily to the next:*

COUNTESS. (*coming from bar area*). Oh Eddie!

EDDIE. (*gesturing that he will deal with it*). Good work, Countess, (*I*) like your class. Do some nice floral 'rangements for me – 'preciate it – then you'n'me'll have li'l drink together.

COUNTESS *goes off.*

DANNY. Okay, talk.

EDDIE. Yeh see, what's goin' on here's patriotism. Guys?

MIKE. Erin go brath.

EDDIE. Us all is banded together to create united li'l ole Emerald Isle. Ireland, Kid, that's what's goin' on.

DANNY. Yeh?

EDDIE. You've heard o' the Organisation?

DANNY. I've heard of a lot of organisations, like the boy scouts an' girl guides.

EDDIE. Well, this ain't quite no scout troup tyin' up Brownies in slip-knots. What we got here is a splinter o' a splinter group, an' they consider jack-knives is old-fashioned. Guns.

The phone rings. An uneasy pause. EDDIE *asking does* DANNY *want him to answer it.* DANNY *nods unsurely.*

EDDIE. (*on the phone*). Blue Macushla . . . It's for him. (PETE.) Wife keeps callin' him up durin' workin' hours.

PETE. Hello? . . . Actually, a little inconvenient to talk right now, Michael . . . The shopping list has been mislaid? . . . Yes, I'm – I'll search.

DANNY. That's enough –

PETE. I marked that item on the O'Malley and Mullarky catalogue —

DANNY. Goodbye.

PETE. Bye-bye. (*Replaces phone. Nervously.*) That was Michael.

DANNY. Guns: Are yous tellin' us that The Blue Macushla is used as a droppin'-off place?

PETE. Yes, sometimes.

A glance from EDDIE and the nervous PETE looks sheepish.

EDDIE. Yeah, kinda depot y'might say. First, it was just one (*or*) two toys, like what yeh got in your hand, to be picked up later, take-'ways, by passin' trade. Then, like, the ole Liffey just keeps rollin' 'long out there, which means the docks is only up the way, right? — an some li'l shipments o', oh, spec'lised nite-club 'quipment began to 'rive, also for take-'way consumption. An' there was th' occasion o' the Christmas crackers — Yeh get me?

DANNY. Jelly?

EDDIE. An' custard, Kid, lots o' custard. 'N' that's it.

DANNY. 'N' that's it.

EDDIE. Huh?

DANNY. The room up there.

EDDIE. Forgot, yeh, Hospitality Room. Yeh see, they're kinda social animals an' now'n'again they like to show an individual their 'preciation, or, a other kinda individual their un'preciation. Why today, for instance, they gone a step further an' left — can I whisper? — (*Whispers so that only DANNY can hear.*) they left a stiff up there for me to take care of. You still want half o' here?

DANNY. An' yous're goin' to dump this *stiff* for them? D'yiz think I'm a gomey? Nanty up on the pipin' us the fanny geeze. (*Stop giving me false information.*) Okay, Eddie, try again, take it from the top, just give us the facts.

EDDIE. That's what I'm doin', schmuck!

DANNY. Yiz're not – schmuck! There's somethin' – someone in a corner in that room up there, only it ain't dead, it's alive, see?!

EDDIE. Huh? (*This is big news to* EDDIE.)

MIKE. That's what I've been tryin' to tell yeh, Boss.

EDDIE. Huh?

MIKE. He ain't in good shape, but he ain't dead.

ROSCOMMON. So what're yeh goin' to do now, Eddie?

EDDIE. But *they* think he's dead.

ROSCOMMON. Finish him off? You figure that'd be sufficient token to buy yeh out?

EDDIE. (*smiling; absently*). Whatcha say again, Baby?

DANNY. Yiz're thinkin' so hard, Eddie, yiz're goin' give yourself a hernia in the loaf.

EDDIE. (*now eager to have done with the interview*). Yeah, what else you wanta know, let's get it over with. (*He has taken the lucky coin out of his pocket, starts tossing it up and down through the following.*)

DANNY. How did this – organisation – threw the loop over yiz in the first place?

EDDIE. Yeh.

DANNY. When yiz spent our money they were pickin' up the tabs yiz were leavin' all over town after your big-shot parties.

EDDIE. Not quite, Kid. These days – look 'round yeh! – Yeh wanta be big y'act big 'n' forget th' ole proverbs 'bout mickles'n'muckles. Guys like me is goin' places, why, that nine hundred o' yours, was somethin' for instance I'd put on a plate at a charity do, just to impress a good-lookin' nun. To keep movin' with the times, yeh need a higher octane ratin' in your tank. So what'd I do?

He has gestured, drawn DANNY *away from the others to impart the following confidential material.*

I done me a bank job. Yeh. Only I leave a callin' card at the bank, sayin' 'Thanks. Yours sincerely, Erin Go Brath'. Well, the Erin Go Braths don't like that, but they still don't know who done it. Nobody does, only me. But someone – I don't know who, how, why: it don't make sense – but someone, somehow figures me for it an' fingers me, an' I get a call from the splinter boys who ask me for the dough. I ain't got it. (*Indicates that it went into the club.*) So they start to heat the poker: that, or would I like to become member o' their brotherly band o' patriots. Membership fee: use of one club. Yeh see, Kid, everyone wants part o' this place.

He has tossed the coin in the air yet again, only this time he does not catch it. DANNY's eyes follow the coin to the floor and EDDIE hits him and disarms him.

How 'bout that! You taught me that trick yourself: no one can keep his eyes off the deck when money falls.

DANNY is starting to get up and EDDIE hits him again, stunning him and is about to hit him again –

ROSCOMMON. Eddie!

EDDIE. (*to her, without looking at her*). Get changed! This time in your correct costume.

She goes to inner room.

You got one o' these toys too, Pete? (*The gun.*)

PETE. I work late for you, Mr O'Hara. Going home late, we boys have to protect ourselves from other boys.

EDDIE. (*I'd*) Like to borrow it for a little. Now, this live guy in our Hospitality Room, who is he, what is he?

PETE. I know nothing about it.

MIKE. He don't look like no bad boy to me.

EDDIE. Whatcha got there?

MIKE. (*hands EDDIE a crucifix and chain*). One of them crosses. Like they tore it from round his neck.

EDDIE. A goddamn crucifix! (*Superstitiously throws it across the room.*) Them things is a jinx! (*Then, remembering headline from newspaper.*) 'British Intelligence Agent Disappears Without Trace.'

PETE. Is that who you think we've got up there, Mr O'Hara?

EDDIE. Naaw. I figure that's who they was after but they said it themselves, they was a slip-up, they got the wrong guy. (*Then to himself.*) Huh? (*Finds the newspaper and reads.*) 'Riddle of Missing Priest in City Drama!' (*And smiles.*)

MIKE. Priest!

EDDIE. I got a better deal for them now an' riddle-o'-missin'-priest's my black ace in the hole. You got something up your nose?

PETE. I don't like it. (*He picks up the crucifix.*)

EDDIE. *You* don't like it? So call the cops, huh?

PETE *dumps the crucifix and chain on the desk.*

MIKE. He's only a kid, Boss.

EDDIE. Whatcha all talkin' 'bout, whatcha all – ! (*Conscious of the gun in his hand: Puts it away.*) I'm handin' him back to them – for a price. That's all I'm gonna do! Ain't it?

ROSCOMMON. (*enters in a new costume, a cloth-cap 'Paddy' costume*). How do I look, Eddie?

DANNY *has been groggily coming-to.*

EDDIE. Okay, Kid, I got business to attend to, so let's have done with you first.

ROSCOMMON. Costume feels good, Eddie.

EDDIE. (*continuing to DANNY*). You got your liberty an' a grand in your pocket an' all yeh gotta do is be on your way, so what d'yeh say?

DANNY. Yiz're all twisted up inside.

EDDIE. I don't think you're sayin' thanks.

ROSCOMMON. Eddie, what d'yeh think? (*About the costume.*)

EDDIE. Okay, me'n'Mike's takin' care o' the Kid, you'n'Pete go do that other number.

ROSCOMMON. You comin' to introduce it?

EDDIE. I said I'm kinda keen for yous to do that number *now*, I'll do the intros later.

PETE *and* ROSCOMMON *go.*

DANNY. Yous aren't Eddie O'Hara from Lady O' Perpetual Succour Mansions –

EDDIE. You bet I ain't –

DANNY. Half of here's mine an' I'm goin' to –

EDDIE. So it's gonna be the hard way. (*To* MIKE.) Take him out back an' tell him what he owns, then, Mike, you come back, join me up there. (*Hospitality Room.*)

(*We now, perhaps, return to the lighting convention used in the opening scenes of the play: A series of spots.*)

PETE *has played the introduction to 'Off to Philadelphia' and* ROSCOMMON *sings: Her concerned eyes follow the figures on the periphery of the spot* (MIKE *hustling* DANNY *out to the yard*) *but she cannot interfere.*

ROSCOMMON. 'O me name is Paddy Leary from a spot in Tipperary / The hearts of all the girls I'm a thorn in / But before the break of morn, faith, 'tis they'll be all forlorn / For I'm off to Philadelphia in the morning. With me bundle on me shoulder. . . .' (*Etc. Other verses if required.*)

EDDIE *comes into spot briefly to whisper something to* PETE *and to give him the roll of money (for* DANNY). *Then* EDDIE *goes (to Hospitality Room). Song and accompaniment do not stop for the above.*

Spot up on yard, DANNY *and* MIKE.

MIKE. Okay, here'll do.

DANNY. Yiz're workin' for me now as much as for Eddie . . . Eddie's gone out of his skull, Mike.

MIKE. No one says an'thin' bad about the Boss.

He has swung at DANNY *and missed; swings again, misses.*
DANNY *has pulled himself together somewhat and now
counters, landing a few to* MIKE's *head.*

(*Yeh.*) Shouldn'ta done that.

DANNY's *dextrous, but* MIKE *keeps coming forward: He is
unstoppable.* DANNY *is sent reeling, and again.* DANNY *is
down, is getting up: He's flattened again: Trying to get up,*
MIKE *is waiting.*

ROSCOMMON. Mike!

ROSCOMMON, *song over, has arrived with* PETE. *She hangs
back;* PETE *coming forward to the crumpled heap of* DANNY.
MIKE *returning to the club.*

PETE. I think we've had enough, Mr Mountjoy, let's get you on
your feet.

DANNY *attempts a swing at* PETE.

Easy, Mr Mountjoy. I'm genuinely sorry.

DANNY. Sorry for what?

PETE. I'm sorry you're so stupid. Here – (*Putting roll of money
into* DANNY's *pocket.*) Like Mr O'Hara says, you're free, you
have money in your pocket, what else can anyone need? The
wind is favourable, bend with it.

DANNY. (*proffering the money*). It's yours – for your gun.

PETE. You're-not-registering-me! (*Points.*) That's your gate.

He is walking away. DANNY, *about to follow, collapses.*

ROSCOMMON. Danny! (*Hurries to him, tries to lift him up.*)
Pete! Help me get him up to my room.

PETE *shakes his head and is continuing back to the club.*

Hey, you bent rainbow! You owe me. You were starving three
months back an' came crawling to me to help get you that job in
there!

PETE. (*returns, assists her, but with the proviso/warning*). But no one starts bringin' this party to an untimely climax? (*Does she understand.*)

Momentarily, she is puzzled by PETE — *the new authoritative note in his voice, the campness temporarily dropped — but her concern is for* DANNY. *Together, they get* DANNY *on his feet and are helping him back inside.*

Simultaneous with ROSCOMMON, DANNY *and* PETE *going out,* EDDIE *and* MIKE *supporting hooded figure of young* PRIEST *coming into a new spot — the office.* PRIEST *is put in the chair. He continues silent throughout, in Christian fortitude.*

MIKE *leaves.*

MIKE. Priest.

EDDIE. (*alone with* PRIEST, *removes the hood and a gag*). . . . Smoke? . . . How come nice kid like you gets involved in all this? . . . (*Working it out for himself.*) I get the picture. Yeh. Remember ole four eyes, our concrete-block-layin' friend, remember him? Yeh, steals No.1's li'l house-accounts book an' sells to our British Disappearin' Intelligence Agent. Only our disappearin' Intelligence Agent figures he ain't bein' paid sufficient for his intelligence: yeh, an' goes into the retail business an' the book's up to the highest bidder. Li'l drink? Then you happen along. Coincidence? Who cares? You stumble onto where our retailin' Intelligence Agent is holed up, only now, the Erin Go Braths is closin' in, yeh. So, you bein' a professional Christian, right? you swap your dog-collar for this guy's dog-tag an' they's temporarily confused. Some piece o' hoodwinkin', yeh. I said whatcha lookin' at me like that for?! (*Picks up the phone.*) Me now, I'm a pro too, a pro-party-goin' successful son o' a lib'ral-lovin' age, that's me. 'S all a ball, I love a ball, how 'bout you? An' ain't no-one, nothin' gonna stop me meetin' young Cind'rella tonight. (*He is dialling a number.*)

A second spot comes up on COUNTESS: *she is on the phone; she has a Northern Ireland accent.*

COUNTESS. No.13 here, put me on to No.1, urgent. Somethin's come up.

EDDIE, *in his spot, puts down the phone.*

EDDIE. 'S engaged. (*The newspaper is in front of him.*)
Nationwide searches, cabinet cabals, secret sessions – What's
everyone so het-up about? 'Part from li'l detail on me, debtor's
section, what's this li'l black book contain makes everyone want
it so bad? (*Dialling number again.*)

COUNTESS, *in her spot, has been talking in dumb show or just
nodding to the instructions she is receiving. Now:*

COUNTESS. Erin go Brath!

Puts phone down. Blackout on her.

EDDIE. 'S' ringin', don't go 'way, kid, my number's ringin'.

ACT TWO

Scene One

NO.1's *apartment. A telephone is ringing. Spot on a figure slumped in a chair: the* BRITISH INTELLIGENCE AGENT. *Perhaps there is a goldfish bowl. Glow of a cigar from the shadows:* NO.1 *is waiting.* VIC *arrives and holds up the little black book.* BRITISH AGENT – *now that the book has been recovered – hopeful that his troubles might be over, is straightening himself in the chair.* NO.1, *minus hat and topcoat and carrying a tie, comes into the light. Privately,* VIC *is congratulating himself that he is on* NO.1's *side:* NO.1, *reciting/sing-songing 'A Battle Hymn' (by Countess de Markievicz) is strangling the* AGENT, *sinking behind the* AGENT *as the* AGENT *slumps out of the chair on to the floor.*

NO.1.
> 'Armed for the battle, kneel we before thee,
> Bless thou our banner, God of the brave;
> Ahland (*Ireland*) is living, shout we exultant,
> Ahland is waking, hand grasp the sword . . .'
> (*Etc., as/if required.*)

The phone has stopped ringing. The AGENT *is dead,* NO.1 *breathing heavily and sweating after the exertion. We are beginning to see* NO.1's *face for the first time: A butch, feminine face, framed in chopped hair.* NO.1 *is removing jacket and waistcoat.*

(*Chuckles phlegmatically, humourlessly.*) Oh dear! A British Intelligence Agent, an English Officer and a Gentleman, Victor. I know every jot and tittle of his background as I know my own. Public school, boring summer hols, mother's stupid social calendar, father's tantrums, oh dear! Yes, tantrums at table – one parent outdoing in intolerance the other – if the cuisine did not come of the correct dimension or consistency. The consomme not to the exact hue, the souffle a centimetre too high, oh dear! And I, a child – I was a child, Victor – with a passion for ketchup. How they both hated me! How I hated them both!

The phone has started to ring again. Slight move – perhaps only of the eyes – from VIC to answer it. NO.1 warns VIC to ignore it. It stops during the following.

We know who it is. (*They know it is* EDDIE.) The unhappiness that attends privilege. And no relief at my elitist schools, those nasty English girls.

Now, minus waistcoat, we notice the heavy breasts under the shirt: NO.1 *is a woman.*

(*Irrationally, to the corpse.*) No material motives prompt me in what I do! And though I too am English, I am proud of Ahland, my chosen native land, and I have no desire to do aught but frustrate the schemes of my chosen country's enemy – *England!* I must shower. (*Sing-songing, going off:*) 'England is breaking! shout we triumphant, England is beaten! Ahland is free . . .'

The phone has started up again. NO.1 *changes her mind about leaving, laughs phlegmatically:*

Oh dear! Answer Mr O'Hara, Victor.

Spot up on EDDIE. EDDIE *on the phone, young* PRIEST *in the chair as before.*

EDDIE. Goddammit, they playin' me up or somethin'?

VIC. (*on phone*). Sackville residence.

EDDIE. Okay, mouseface, put me on to No.1.

VIC. Yiz talk to me, 19.

EDDIE. What I hafta say I say to No.1. Tell him I got a surprise for him.

VIC. (*to* NO.1). He wants to surprise yeh.

They share a chuckle. NO.1 *takes the phone.*

NO.1. Ah No. 19, how good of you to call!

EDDIE. Not at all. Yeh see, I –

NO.1. Indeed, I was going to call you! –

EDDIE. Yeh, sure, but –

NO.1. Because I have decided on a change of plan.

EDDIE. But wait'll yeh hear my –

NO.1. You see we were tricked this morning into apprehending the wrong gentleman. However, that error has now been entirely corrected and we should be most grateful if you would despatch a *second* large parcel together with the one you have got there already.

EDDIE. But that's what I'm tryin' to tell yeh: This *dead* parcel I got here is kinda su'prise package.

NO.1. I now consider that it would be more to our advantage to think of a destination further afield than our lovely local countryside.

EDDIE. But you're not listenin' –

NO.1. Please –

EDDIE. But –

NO.1. Please! Business first.

EDDIE. Okay, proceed.

NO.1. How good of you! What a pretty indictment it would make if our two parcels were to be unearthed up North near a certain British Army Intelligence Barracks! One, a defecting British Agent who, sickened and conscience-stricken by the indiscipline, violence and murder perpetrated by his comrades, was refusing to hand over a little black book that had come into his possession.

EDDIE. Li'l black book that – sounds swell – you finished?

NO.1. The second, a man of the cloth, an innocent at large, who, endeavouring to do God's work on earth, had gone North to befriend the unhappy defecting agent.

EDDIE. Befriend the unhappy defecting – one-two-three-ten parcels, destination few miles, hundred miles away! – Nice job – even though nationwide searches – but why not? – nice job.

NO.1. Then you approve?

EDDIE. 'Prove?! – Why I just remembered I even got the very guy for that spec'lised kinda drivin' if –

NO.1. Splendid! –

EDDIE. Sure! –

NO.1. We have no problem then.

EDDIE. *I* got no problem, but, yeh see, I don't know if this one's for me. Let me tell yeh the surprise.

NO.1. Before you surprise me, one further thing.

EDDIE. Oh, I see, you're *not* finished?

NO.1. Of course the parcel we left with you will first have to be converted from live weight to dead. It is still alive, I take it . . . No. 19 are you still there? Oh dear, we seem to have a bad line.

NO.1 *sharing a private chuckle with* VIC.

EDDIE *is dumbfounded that* NO.1 *should know that the* PRIEST *is still alive.*

EDDIE. (*privately*). They got a plant in the place!

NO.1. No. 19?

EDDIE. Yeah, still here, still 'live I take it.

NO.1. Then Victor shall call and look after that detail. And now for your little surprise . . . Oh dear, you have not forgotten it! How little surprise is left in the world!

EDDIE. Hold on! I just remembered it. Nobody touches this guy here unless we talk turkey.

NO.1. What did you say?

EDDIE. We seem to have a bad line. I said this parcel, this guy here is mine. He's one helluva conversation'list an' he's been tellin' me – Yeah – how when he befriended the unhappy disappearin' agent how they was 'mazed together lookin' at the contents o' that li'l black book o' yours. This guy here's loaded, No. 1.

NO.1. That is the worry and the urgency of the matter. We must protect the names of our most generous and loyal supporters.

EDDIE. (*pleased at eliciting this information*). Creditors section.

NO.1. Prominent and public citizens, both from home and abroad.

EDDIE. Well, that's what I'm sayin', I 'gree, this guy's loaded, but my position: how can I hand him over unless we got a deal?

NO.1. A deal?

EDDIE. Yeah, or let the goose loose, fly, to preach one helluva spiel 'bout all those prom'nent cit'zens, from both home and abroad.

NO.1. I do not make deals –

EDDIE. I want out –

NO.1. I do not accept conditions –

EDDIE. I want to be a person again –

NO.1. I only do things one way, my way –

EDDIE. Then we got nothing further to discuss –

NO.1. Mr O'Hara! You are playing a very dangerous game.

EDDIE. I sure as hell know I am, Mr Sackville.

NO.1. I do not permit brothers to use my name.

EDDIE. 'Nother surprise: I know you don't permit no one to use your *real* name *Mister* Sackville.

NO.1. You're beginning to sound desperate, No. 19.

EDDIE. You'd better believe it. (*About to hang up.*)

NO.1. Mr O'Hara!

EDDIE. Yeh?

NO.1. (*quietly*). We are not an unreasonable order, I am not an unreasonable person. There is *one* condition, and if you are willing to comply with it, I might consider your request.

The condition being that EDDIE *should shoot the* PRIEST. EDDIE *looking at his gun, holding his breath.*

. . . The thought holds peculiar fascination for us all, does it not?

EDDIE. You got 'xactly thirty minutes to consider my proposition. (*He hangs up.*)

VIC. Do I get the pony round front, Boss?

NO.1. Boss! Boss! You use such vulgar term of address to me?! So, Mr O'Hara wants a deal. Then let us leave him to perspire and ponder the deal I have proposed to him for thirty minutes, then we shall visit him.

Blackout NO.1's apartment.

EDDIE. My God, kid, what we gonna do? . . . Thought holds fas'nation for us all does it not . . . Have li'l drink with me, kid, will yeh? . . . They's askin' us for the big token together . . . Here, kid, this is yours.

About to put crucifix and chain around PRIEST's *neck. Slight movement from* PRIEST – *the first he has made* – *withdrawing his head.*

Huh?

Movement again to give PRIEST *the chain and crucifix.* PRIEST, *slow shake of his head, his hand rising slowly in a gesture of absolution.*

PRIEST. (*whispers*). For you. (*Meaning that the crucifix is for* EDDIE.)

EDDIE. Huh?

PRIEST. It's for you.

EDDIE. Whatcha sayin'? – I ain't decided nothin' yet! – Whatcha?! (*Angrily buzzing house phone for* MIKE.) Yeh don't drink, yeh don't smoke, yeh don't take sugar! – sugar, honey, dames – dames spell the big C, huh? – Capit'l C for chastity – so what's

the odds? (*Into phone.*) Mike, get in here! (*To* PRIEST.)
Women'n'kids is gettin' it, ain't they, an' it don't matter – an' it
don't matter who's givin' it to them! – so what's with a snotty-
nosed kid of a priest! Put that in his mouth – He talks too much
– An' put his bonnet back on, 'n' tie him up.

MIKE *has come in and is carrying out the instructions.*

MIKE. Barrels is all hooked up, Boss, crates in from the yard, place
swept up, so can I put on my new coat now?

EDDIE. (*to himself*). An' they got a plant in the place. (*Now
listening to* PETE, *off, playing piano.*) . . . Yeah, hi Pete, that's
real cute. (*He has misread the situation, thinking* PETE *to be
NO.1's plant.*)

MIKE. Boss? An' my cap?

EDDIE. That Mountjoy guy still around?

MIKE. He's with Roscommon.

EDDIE. That's good. See he don't leave – polite. (*Dismissing
MIKE.*) Yeh.

MIKE. You okay, Boss?

EDDIE. Yeah, I'm just thinkin', Mike, I'm just thinkin'.

MIKE. Oh. (*And goes out.*)

EDDIE *produces an envelope and a sheet of paper: He starts to
write.*

Scene Two

A bedroom. DANNY, *divested of jacket and, perhaps, shirt, being
nursed, patched-up by* ROSCOMMON. PETE's *piano-playing off
('Molly Brown'). DANNY attempts to stand but his ribs hurt.*

ROSCOMMON. Easy. Talk, Danny, I like to hear you talk.

DANNY. (*grimly*). What about?

ROSCOMMON. Anything. What were you thinking just now?

DANNY. I was t'inking how I used lie on my bunk in the chokey. Night after night. I could see the stars through the bars of my window high up on the wall. T'inkin'. Every last one o' them stars a beckonin'-home signal, but a million miles away. But I didn't care cause I kept t'inkin' your welcome-home light's no astral pie in the sky: There's real world waitin' for yiz called The Blue Macushla.

ROSCOMMON. Y'don't have t'do time to think.

DANNY. T'inkin'.

ROSCOMMON. They don't have to lock you up to dream. Hold still.

DANNY. (*has tried to get up again and failed*). Hafta get up.

ROSCOMMON. Shhhhh! This (*Iodine.*) is goin' to hurt.

DANNY. I'm alright I tell yiz – Ouch!

ROSCOMMON. There. I think you'll hold together. Just rest up a little longer, then you're goin' to blow, yeh? Okay?

DANNY. Everybody wants me in Connemara.

ROSCOMMON. ('*No*'). Well, maybe that ain't such a bad idea. No. Just walk out that door down there an' don't once look back. Danny?

DANNY. No.

ROSCOMMON. Yes. Don't get mixed up in here –

DANNY. I am mixed up in here – Half this place is mine.

ROSCOMMON. Shhh, listen –

DANNY. Half –

ROSCOMMON. Forget it –

DANNY. Forget it?

ROSCOMMON. You wanta go straight? – That's what yeh told me.

DANNY. A coupla – bends – have come up. Hafta – hafta get up. (*He gets up, dresses, etc.*)

ROSCOMMON. You're goin' to take on the world? – Fat Man too, Vic Camden an' – Yeh? Well, you're goin' to find they're mean, you don't know how mean.

DANNY. They sound like somethin' we used to step on in the 'Mansions'. An' I hafta get a gun.

ROSCOMMON. No! Once you take a gun in your hand you –

DANNY. Do yeh know where I can get a gun?

ROSCOMMON. Great! Another gun –

DANNY. D'yous have a gun?

ROSCOMMON. Sure, I know where you can lay your hands on a gun – Listen to me! –

DANNY. I've listened –

ROSCOMMON. You want those goons on your back? –

DANNY. (*empties out the contents of her handbag*). D'yous have a gun, a rod, a piece, a gat, a shooter in here? –

ROSCOMMON. Well, you're goin' to find they're heavy, same as Eddie an' others found –

DANNY. Stop it, stop it! –

ROSCOMMON. Why d'yeh think, no one has feelin's anymore? –

DANNY. Stop it! –

ROSCOMMON. Why d'yeh think no one knows no one, no one knows who anyone is? –

DANNY. Stop it, stop it! –

ROSCOMMON. Why d'yeh think everyone's suspicious of everyone else? I took one look at you an' I thought maybe here's someone who's different, maybe –

DANNY. An' I took one look at yous an' – Stop it!

His hand raised to hit her. He is shocked by what he was about to do.

ROSCOMMON. . . . (*quietly*). Go ahead, Mr Mountjoy, it don't
hurt no more. Just part o' that social disease I've been tellin' yeh
about that's goin' round.

DANNY. . . . Ros –

ROSCOMMON. The Countess, that rich dame that's been hangin'
round the club carries a gun in her purse. I saw it once when we
were in the powder room together. Pete's waitin' for me.

*He doesn't leave so she begins to undress out of her 'Paddy'
costume.*

DANNY. . . . I'm sorry . . . I need the gun to even matters up . . .
An' there's a kid – I t'ink he's a priest – down there.

She looks at him: 'Who is he?'

Danny Mountjoy: I'm nobody. Will yiz help me with a few
things?

Scene Three

MIKE *emerges from bar/kitchen/yard cautiously: There is no one
else around and he starts to dress in his new commissionaire's
overcoat, having a sneak try-on of it. There's someone coming and
he stands back in the shadows, afraid of being caught. But it is
only the* COUNTESS.

The COUNTESS *comes in, ostensibly on some chore – a vase of
flowers for the bar – watchful of everything, except* MIKE.

MIKE. Countess, huh?

COUNTESS. (*startled; NI accent*). Jesus Christ!

MIKE. (*showing off his coat*). While the Boss ain't watchin'.

COUNTESS. That's yeh – es enchantink.

MIKE. Yeah.

COUNTESS. But you haf must keep it clean.

MIKE. Oh yeah, I hafta must keep it clean. (*He is about to take off the coat when he sees* DANNY *coming down the stairs.*) Hey, where you — ('goin'. *Remembers that* EDDIE *said 'polite'.*) Would yous like a drink, please?

DANNY. Gimme a double.

MIKE. A double what?

DANNY. A double anythin'. An' whatever the lady's havin'.

COUNTESS. (*has been rooting in her handbag for a light.* DANNY *lights her cigarette.*) Thanks. We haf met before?

DANNY. Before what?

MIKE. Aw my God! Aw my God! (*He has got a stain on his new coat and goes off to do something about it.*)

COUNTESS. You are the good-looking man I see with the singer earlier.

DANNY. (*raises his glass*). Boopsie'n'Lisabeth'n'Aisling.

COUNTESS. But I haf not see you in here another time.

DANNY. I've been away.

COUNTESS. How far es away?

DANNY. Too far. (*He moves up close to her. His purpose is to get the gun from her handbag which is somewhere behind her.*)

COUNTESS. I seem to haf misplaced your name.

DANNY. People are always droppin' it.

COUNTESS. What business are you in?

DANNY. I used to drive cars an' things, I'm good at a lotta things.

COUNTESS. How are you on the roads leading North?

DANNY. South's a good direction too. (*One hand to her thigh, the other around her back.*)

COUNTESS. (*removing his southward hand*). Maybe you drive too fast.

DANNY. Only when I get the signal.

COUNTESS. En case you don't know et you're doin' okay, but how about you take the rest of the driving test en shorthand, Mr – ?

DANNY. Frenchies always like the name: Mountjoy.

COUNTESS. What a pity I am from Hungary.

DANNY. Hung'ry? Bratislava or d'yiz come from the capital, Prague?

COUNTESS. Oh, et – et es ver' beg place.

DANNY. So they tell me.

COUNTESS. Here they call me the hungry Countess.

DANNY. Let me keep it in mind. (*He has got the gun.*)

MIKE. (*returning*). Yeah, think it's just a water-mark. I hope.

Half-way out of his new coat, he freezes: EDDIE has come out of his office. EDDIE is locking the office door: MIKE fears a reprimand. But when EDDIE turns he is wearing his public image, smile matching his (now) white tuxedo:

EDDIE. Yeah, Mike, put on the clawber now, looks swell! – Good work, Countess! – I like it! (*He likes the flowers, etc.*) – All 'cept'n' that every kind o' creep an' ex-con's bein' served drink in here – Thought I told yeh, Mike, to serve no punk in a liberty-suit!

DANNY *is moving to punch EDDIE but EDDIE is grinning, his chin thrust out.*

Go ahead, Kid, sock me another one, right on the button, I got it comin'.

DANNY. What's the new play?

ROSCOMMON *is coming down the stairs.*

EDDIE. I'm a dumb son of a dodo, that's what is! – I'm a jealous skunk of a junk-head punk! I see this baby (ROSCOMMON.) makin' with the peepers at yeh an' I'm riled, see? Ladies, this guy, the old days, an' I'd pick me the dishiest chick in town an' suddenly she's dumbcluckin', 'Who's yer friend, bub, who's the guy with the eyes?' I was riled, an' I was stupid. But now I got me a Countess – right, baby? – What (*do*) I want with a deuce o' tome feeks (*Two beauties*)? Put it there, Kid, let's set the clock back, what d'yeh say, we start the beginning, buddy?

DANNY. Partner?

A car has pulled up outside.

EDDIE. With what's about to come in that door, would I pipe yeh? Okay, partner, you wanta be a friend then first you gotta be one: Answer the door – Make like you was packin' some hardware.

DANNY. I'll try.

EDDIE. Mike.

DANNY *going to answer the door,* EDDIE *having a private word with* MIKE, *placing him on guard outside the office door* (PRIEST *is tied and hooded in the office*), *and* PETE *has arrived quietly on the scene following the arrival of the car and the knocking on the door.* PETE *has cleaned himself up and changed into his evening clothes.*

VIC *and* NO.1 *come in.*

VIC. (*to* MIKE). Take care o' the pony.

EDDIE. (*to* VIC). You take care of it.

A tense moment.

PETE. It's on a double-yellow out there, I'll take care of it.

EDDIE. You just remain 'xactly where y'are, *Uncle* Pete, okay?

COUNTESS. I'll take care of et, Eddie?

EDDIE. Yeh.

COUNTESS *takes keys and goes out.*

How good of you to call, Mr Sackville, how little genuine social intercourse is left in the world!

NO.1. How good of you to say so!

EDDIE. Pleasure. 'S all genuine social screwin' these days.
(*Gestures* ROSCOMMON *to leave, the others to move back.*)

NO.1. But you are not abandoning your friends – your lovely lady-friend – on my account, Mr O'Hara? Victor, invite the lady to our table.

VIC. (*to* ROSCOMMON). Okay, you're invited to sit over there.

NO.1. And this tall gentleman is?

EDDIE. Mr Mountjoy works for me.

DANNY. Mr O'Hara an' me is partners.

NO.1. (*to* ROSCOMMON). How d'you do, my dear! Such a pretty hand, such a soft warm hand – you must sit next to me.

EDDIE. Why not, I'm in no hurry either.

NO.1. To be surrounded by such beauty! My lonely hours, my dear, are spent with my goldfish. Lovely creatures, colourful innocents, but they do not have soft warm limbs, do they?

EDDIE. (*I*) Got all the time in the world too.

NO.1. An' you sing so sweetly. Dare I presume to think that you might sing for me?

EDDIE. Presume? – Naaw! Sing (*a*) few – six – songs – 'n' cupa tea!

NO.1. But I cannot decide which is more delightful, having you sit beside me or hearing you sing.

DANNY. Well, since yiz can't decide –

EDDIE. Yeh, let's shovel the horse-manure and you'n'me go upstairs for our li'l chat.

COUNTESS. (*returning*). There are two policemen come strolling up the street!

NO.1. Then perhaps it *is* time for a song. Something patriotic, my dear, something of Ahland.

ROSCOMMON *and* PETE *conferring, going to the piano.*

EDDIE. Useful fella that Pete of ours, can turn his hand to most anythin'.

NO.1. Please! (*For silence.*)

ROSCOMMON, *accompanied by* PETE, *sings in her husky, sexy or whatever style 'The Dear Little Shamrock'.*

ROSCOMMON. 'There's a dear little plant that grows in our isle / 'Twas St Patrick himself sure that set it / And the sun on his labour with pleasure did smile / And the dew from his eye often set it.'

EDDIE. (*his nerve beginning to crack*). An' the dew from his fly often wet it! — Let's face it —

NO.1 *silences him with a gesture.*

COUNTESS. (*peeping out the window*). Shhh! they're passing by. (*The policemen.*)

ROSCOMMON. 'It shines through the bog, through the brake and the mireland / And they call it the dear little shamrock of Ireland.'

NO.1. (*singing last line with her*). '. . . little shamrock of Ahland'.

EDDIE $\left.\vphantom{\begin{matrix}a\\b\end{matrix}}\right\}$ Let's face it, I got the cards now. You got guns an' muscle but now I got the same —

ROSCOMMON (*continues*). 'The dear little shamrock, the sweet little shamrock' —

EDDIE. An' I got the ace in the hole —

ROSCOMMON. 'The dear little, sweet little shamrock of — '

Song is terminated by a violent action of EDDIE's — He kicks a chair across the room. He gestures the others back so that he is now isolated with NO.1.

EDDIE. You finished harmonisin' or you wanta sing business, which?

NO.1. You are not behaving patriotically, No. 19, and the remarks you have been making about the cleric we left with you are stupid.

EDDIE. Okay, let me repeat my first stupid remark. I got the cleric, see, an' I can decide to let him go right now, (*to*) preach the biggest spiel since Sermon on the Mount: is that stupidly clear enough for yeh?

NO.1. The cleric belongs to us.

EDDIE. Okay, I'm reasonable man too, so let's settle with the common opinion an' say that he belongs to God.

NO.1. Then allow us to send him post-haste to his Maker.

EDDIE. Not yet –

NO.1. Victor is experienced in such matters.

EDDIE. Victor! The slip-up you been makin'! an' you're talkin' confidence in that little torpedo!

NO.1. You are saying that we keep Victor out of it?

EDDIE. I'm sayin' – I'm sayin' – Yeh. This business is between you'n'me.

NO.1. Thank you for the clarification, No. 19. Continue.

EDDIE. I'm sayin' I'll do what yeh want, make the delivery up North, etcetera.

NO.1. Deliveries.

EDDIE. Deliveries.

NO.1. The second large parcel will be deposited in your car before we leave.

EDDIE. My fee is thirty-five grand – (NO.1 *raises his hand*.) – which I'll have took to have been paid to me some months ago in advance. Second, my name is Mr O'Hara, No. 19 don't even belong in a crap game. Third, I don't wanta play in your yard an' I don't wanta see you nor none o' your numbered gorillas in my yard ever again. Stupidly clear?

NO.1. And, No.19, what if –

EDDIE. Ah! Number?

NO.1. Mr O'Hara. What if I should not agree?

EDDIE. I told yeh: I let this guy go. I'm blowin' the whistle.

NO.1. On yourself also?

EDDIE. On me too, an' cops an' special branch guy'll be round here so fast we'll all think Jack Robinson's some guy's pet tortoise.

NO.1. Anything further?

EDDIE. Yeh. An' in case you got any bright ideas, like supposin' I was to be hit sudden, like by fork-lightnin', well, I got this li'l envelope mailed to my broker to be opened in case o' such emergencies.

NO.1. Mailed *already*.

EDDIE. Well, if yeh wanta gamble on it. An' among the details it contains it makes special mention o' where the cops has got it wrong, lookin' for this famous division leader, callin' him Mister this an' Mister that an' English Jack – yeh got me? So we don't have to worry 'bout fork-lightnin'. So, I'll deliver your parcels etcetera, an' by doin' so, I'm implicatin' myself like I never done before an' that means, sure as hell, that my oath of secrecy will be my total silence, period. Sufficient clear?

NO.1. Not quite. You will make the deliveries, etcetera: that is your part of the bargain?

EDDIE. Continue.

NO.1. 'Etcetera' is a vague clause: Can we clarify that?

EDDIE. Yeh, sure, yeh.

NO.1. On your insistence we are keeping Victor out of this, therefore I must conclude that by 'etcetera' you mean that, prior to setting off to deliver the two parcels, you will first *seal* the one in your possession. That is your meaning, is it not?

EDDIE *hesitates, then nods.*

Because, to be certain of your silence, that is how it must be, Mr O'Hara?

EDDIE. Yeh.

NO.1. Yes?

EDDIE. Yeh – yes – I said so, didn't I?

NO.1. That you will shoot the cleric?

EDDIE. How it must be, thought holds fa'nation for me, yes.

NO.1. You really love this vulgar little place of yours: Real estate is indeed the order of the day.

EDDIE. It sure ain't people. So, we got a deal or ain't we?

NO.1. I do not fear your threats, Mr O'Hara, but it is expedient that the matter be completed without further delay, error or mishap. I have never liked you –

EDDIE. Aw gee –

NO.1. Your ostentation and vulgarity revolt me, but I believe what you say. Each one of us will go so far, then, reckless of the consequences, even the worm turns. (*He gives a paper to* EDDIE.) Here is the map and your instructions. Let me see your gun.

EDDIE *opens his coat for* NO.1 *to glance at the gun* (PETE's). NO.1 *beckons to* VIC *to join them.* VIC *produces a silencer surreptitiously and is offering it to* EDDIE. EDDIE *holds up his hand, refusing it as yet.*

EDDIE. Your little black book, debtors' section under O, scrub O'Hara, thirty-five Gs.

NO.1 *produces the black book, tears a page from it and gives it to* EDDIE. EDDIE *now accepts the silencer.*

NO.1. You have got your *deal*. See that you carry it out impeccably and I shall be glad to consign to oblivion all thoughts of your existence.

EDDIE. Just see yeh forget me. (*Calls to* ROSCOMMON.) Sing all yeh want, Baby! – 'Dear li'l shamrock, sweet li'l – ' Car, Countess, our guests is leavin'!

COUNTESS *goes out.*

ROSCOMMON. (*end of song*). 'The dear little shamrock, the sweet little shamrock, the dear little, sweet little shamrock of Ireland.'

NO.1. (*applauds and, perhaps, brushes away a tear*). What victims we are of a little patriotic emotion! Come to my side again, my dear, till I say goodbye to you.

ROSCOMMON *rejects* NO.1's *request and goes to* DANNY.

(*Goes to her.*) Then let me simply congratulate you on your rendition of a true Irish song. (*Takes her hand.*) But your hand, so soft, has become quite cold. Oh, how clumsy of me!

ROSCOMMON *screams:* NO.1 *has burned her hand with a cigar.* DANNY *is going for* NO.1. ROSCOMMON *intervenes, throwing her arms around him.*

ROSCOMMON. No, Danny, it was nothin', it was an accident!

NO.1, *in self-pitying pique, has gone to the door,* VIC *joins* NO.1.

NO.1. Why does everyone dislike me, Victor?

VIC. Hold it right there, No.1, not *everyone* dislikes yiz!

NO.1. Be warned, O'Hara, should any betrayal ensue, should you slip up in any way, I shall know within seconds.

EDDIE. Yeh – (*With a glance at* PETE.)

NO.1. And your whistle, your police, the contents of your envelope shall not stop me from getting to you. Your deadline is ten minutes from now.

NO.1 *and* VIC *leave.*

EDDIE. Set 'em up for me'n'my partner over here, Mike – You okay, Uncle Pete? – Ros, Pete looks kinda outa place here, take his hand, check the spots an' your mikes up there – li'l job to discuss with yeh, Dan: one final li'l number to show your further good faith an' – Hey-hey-hey, yous all standin' round! – Big parade's goin' passin' on the homestretch out there in a little, then shortly my door's to be opened an' nothin's done! – Good work, Countess!

COUNTESS. (*has come in, locked the door*). Everything okay, Eddie?

EDDIE. The club, Countess –

COUNTESS. Et's all prepared –

EDDIE. Check it again – I want everythin' right'n'double right! We's makin' new start, partner, you'n'me! Just leave the bottle, Mike – (*Toast.*) Stella'n'Lisabeth!

EDDIE *and* DANNY *are now alone. Off, in the club proper,*
ROSCOMMON *and* PETE *rehearsing.* EDDIE, *by turns,*
cunning, abandoned, morose.

DANNY. This little job, Eddie?

EDDIE. You in love with my gal?

DANNY. I thought yous had somethin' goin with the Countess?

EDDIE. (*laughs*). Sure I have, but – sure I have! Yous always is the
winner, Kid. My gal: But what the hell, why, you'n'me's more'n
friends, why, we's almost kin an' when you do one li'l trip up
North for me – one-one-one-one-one, Dan – special li'l ole
Roscommon's goin' be pretty'n'waitin' – 'n' – soft'n'ready – 'n'
– perfumed'n'slow – 'n'movin'n'eager when y'get back.

DANNY. Stella an' – ?

EDDIE. Yeh, Lisabeth! Remember that guy in our Hospitality
Room, remember him?

DANNY. Yeh.

EDDIE. Well, could be kinda serious for us if someone was to
come along an' find him on our prem'ses.

DANNY. (*nods. And toasts again*). Stella an' Elisabeth.

EDDIE. Yeh can see that, can yeh, yeh can see that, partner?

DANNY. I can see that.

EDDIE. Well, all our work, all this, all – both our lives work –
Pffff! (*Up in smoke.*) – if someone was to, huh?

DANNY. Unless we get him safely outa here.

EDDIE. Unless we 'xactly! Safe, clean, out'n'away from here
because . . . You're fillin' my glass again, Kid. That's three times
y'done it . . . (*Then he smiles.*) How 'bout doin' it fourth time?
'N' have one yourself.

DANNY. Eddie'n'Dan!

EDDIE. (*laughs, toasts*). You got it! Oh! Detail. Disremembered to tell yeh. The guy was in our Hospitality Room – huh? (*Remember him?* DANNY *nods.*) Well, he passed on.

DANNY. He?

EDDIE. Yeh. Rest him. So what's the odds?

DANNY. He?!

EDDIE. 'N', o' course, when you got back, the contract –

DANNY. Sufferin' –

EDDIE. Hasta be proper contract –

DANNY. Eddie –

EDDIE. For this whole shebang 'tween you'n'me, legit.

DANNY. No.

EDDIE. Huh?

DANNY. There's another way.

EDDIE. You're beginnin' to look real earnest, Kid.

DANNY. There's another way, the right way.

EDDIE. You in opposition-somethin'? Like the guy we got in opposition in government? He's already wearin' spectacles on tel'vision!

DANNY. I'm levelin' with yiz – I wasn't goin' to – But we *are* more than friends an' we can start fresh. Listen to me, head, I'll stand by yiz –

EDDIE. Yous'll stand by *me*?! With *me – inside*?!

DANNY. Eddie –

EDDIE. Yous's – yous's – yous's been livin' on a other island! Don'tcha – don'tcha – don'tcha know where y'are, Kid? This is haha-heehee-hoho-land yous's livin' in now! An' I'm all for it, I'm all for it! –

DANNY. Listen to –

EDDIE. Cause in haha-heehee-hoho-land yeh know where yeh stand, y'expect the worst an' yous's prepared, see, an yous have nice time!

DANNY. The way to start 'fresh –

EDDIE. (*to himself*). He still don't follow: some guys is so good they don't count. 'S all 'bout survival! From Noah'n'Adam, th' Ark – th' Beginnin', baboons to bananas to bread! Only some folks want all o' the bread!

DANNY. Eddie, I've learned a lot an' the first thing for startin' fresh is to discontinue all bad practices.

EDDIE. Yeh?

DANNY. Crime-Don't-Pay!

EDDIE. Krect! (*Correct.*) Leads to *better* corruption!

DANNY. There's a thing call morality –

EDDIE. Morality? –

DANNY. Listen to me! –

EDDIE. Bishopspricks! Shh-shh-shh! (*Allow.*) 'Low me, el-low me. Let me tell yeh somethin' bout morality. Was at this big-shot shindig few months back an' there's a guy there called John who decides to do a maudlin turn an' confess a murder to all present. He's big in development an' the buildin'-game, see, an' he's got this well an trusted 'sociate-friend called Martin, only they just wasn't gettin' along. So, one day, John climbs up on his crane an' drops forty ton o' steel on Martin's head. An' yeh know what the party says to our murderer? They was bankers, professors, guys from government an' big business – the guys is changin' the world to the right way like you? Know what they says to our murderer? They says 'Don't let people see yeh cryin', John'. Huh? They was 'barrassed. They was em-barrassed for our murderer. Don't let people see yeh cryin' John, ain't that somethin'. (DANNY's *head is bowed.*) He don't think that's somethin'.

DANNY. The kid, the priest, is he okay?

EDDIE. He passed on, he passed on! Even if he hadn't, so what, he passed on, that's all y'hafta know, what's the odds?! People ain't just shootin' people out there nowadays, they're eatin' one another, all walks life 'n' 'joyin' the taste! This's one great big canine cannibal do an' the chump is the guy with lockjaw. *Please* understand'n'believe me, Kid. The chump is the guy ain't got the stomach. Well, I got the stomach, just gimme coupla minutes more. (*He drinks. He feels he may have gone too far, he grins/laughs/whatever to cover it.*) Why, these days, partner, you got a ugly granny you'll hang her yourself with her own cotton nightie! So, yous gonna drive that car for me or not?

DANNY. . . . Game ball, rasher.

EDDIE. 'Preciate it, buddy. We come long ways. Goddamn doughnut parties, huh? An' my mom an' your mom an' Susie an Tim, an' . . . yeh. Kinda feel lonely this evenin'. Li'l deadline paperwork to do in here.

ROSCOMMON *is coming down the stairs followed by* PETE *a few seconds later.* EDDIE, *en route to his office, stops drunkenly to admire her.*

Ain't she a picture?

DANNY *gestures/nods secretly to* ROSCOMMON.

ROSCOMMON. Eddie, everything's set up, Eddie, song's fine, Pete's playin's fine, everything 'cept your intro, Eddie.

EDDIE. Complaints from the hired help, huh? (*Then continuing to the office.*)

PETE *finds the remark funny and laughs.*

ROSCOMMON. Please – Eddie! – let's get it right, it'll only take a minute.

EDDIE. (*has stopped*). Somethin' funny, Pete? (PETE *shakes his head.*) Come 'ere. How 'bout this one then: Finish the gig here this evenin', then you're fired. Drop by for your wages an' the toy – (*Taps his breast-pocket, the gun.*) yeh lent me. Now, let's ask Pete: do I have (*a*) minute t'do that intro?

PETE, *naturally, has been puzzled by* EDDIE's *new attitude towards him: he shrugs, nods.*

Perfectionist's our Uncle Pete an' he says we got our minute.

EDDIE *goes upstairs followed by* ROSCOMMON *and* PETE *to the club. Through the following we hear them rehearsing off.* DANNY *into action: he tries the office door only to find it locked: he hurries out, rear of premises.*

He is no sooner gone than COUNTESS, *looking worried, comes down the stairs from the club. She dials a number on the phone.*

COUNTESS. No. 13. Get back, the deadline's up, I can smell the double-x . . . Yeh.

She puts down the phone, unlocks front door, tries the office door – it's locked – searches a drawer or shelves behind the bar – for spare keys.

Simultaneous with the above, DANNY *climbing in the office window from the yard. (He unlocked it in Act One. Scene Three.) He switches on the desk-lamp: The beam of light hitting the hooded figure of the young* PRIEST *tied in the chair. He is removing the hood, the gag and trying to untie the* PRIEST *while, at the same time, dialling a number.*

DANNY. *(on the phone).* Wheels Kelly – Oh, that you, Wheels? aw good. Danny . . . Danny Mountjoy – *Danny* . . . Yeh, got out today – Can't tell yiz now. But can yiz – it's important, Wheels – can yiz drive over to The Blue Macushla? . . . I mean now, I mean right away . . . Wha'? . . . I have the lats – I'll give yiz a brick – a deuce o' bricks – I'll make it a ton. Wheels, I'm beggin'! Wha? . . . Back *(Sighs.)* entrance, do the best yeh can.

He has heard the COUNTESS *at the office door: she has found a bunch of keys or a key. He produces the gun he stole from her handbag earlier and moves to stand behind the door.*

(Whispers.) One peep outa yous, padre, an yous become a cardinal.

COUNTESS *comes in. She sees the* PRIEST *in the chair and is searching her handbag.*

This what you're lookin' for – Countess? (*The gun. He shuts the door.*) Now yous – yous just stand there. (*He resumes untying the* PRIEST.)

COUNTESS. Are you a cop?

DANNY. No – Yous stand there!

COUNTESS. Then what es this to you?

DANNY. An' I'm no Hungarian Count neither. Yiz failed a little geography test I gave yiz earlier. (*To* PRIEST.) Try to stand up – Try, try, get up on your feet.

COUNTESS. There's money in it for yeh, mister –

DANNY. Yiz hafta get up, kid – Try, try –

COUNTESS. Don't let him go –

DANNY. (*to* COUNTESS). Yous don't! (*move.*) That's good, kid –

COUNTESS. What is he? He's a nothin', a mumbo-jumbo man, a parasite, collaboratin' with the high an' mighty hypocrites that care nothin' for Ireland –

DANNY. That's good, try a step, kid – That's good – Now another –

COUNTESS. Be meek, turn th'other cheek to the foreign an' native exploiters of our land –

DANNY. See the window? – That's where we hafta get to –

COUNTESS. Don't let him go! –

DANNY. Yiz're goin' to have to make it on your own –

COUNTESS. (*has found some kind of club*). See him Jesus-creepin', back to betray the cause, to corrupt imperialist establishments, for his crumbs of praise, his holy consolation an' his pay! –

DANNY. One step more, lady – Go on, kid, go on! –

COUNTESS. Yeh won't shoot me –

DANNY. No? – Get outa that winda will yiz, hide out there till –

COUNTESS. Mister, please. Together we can be the loudspeakers of a passive society –

DANNY. Get out that winda –

COUNTESS. Mister, we can have a nice time together, we can go –

DANNY. (*pointing the gun*). I'm warnin' yiz!

COUNTESS. You won't shoot me.

She is going for the young PRIEST, DANNY whacks her on the chin with his fist. He catches her as she falls and dumps her in the chair. DANNY helps the young PRIEST to get out the window.

DANNY. (*whispering out the window*). Wheels, wheels! (*Wheels would appear not to have arrived.*)

The rehearsal above in the club has ended and DANNY is aware of it. What does he do now? He puts the hood on the COUNTESS, drapes/ties the rope around her, switches off the light and gets out the window and closes it behind him.

EDDIE unlocks the door and comes into the office. He has a soiled tablecloth (or tablecloths) which he throws over the shoulders and body of the figure in the chair. He switches on the desk-lamp.

During the last above – EDDIE's coming into the office – the special lighting used at the end of Act One, Scene One, has been coming up: The flashback is nearly over.

EDDIE. (*as in Scene One, fixing silencer to his gun*). . . . Always knew somehow'd hafta use one o' these. Thought has held fas'nation for me alright. Sorry, kid-priest it had to be you but Jesus went out with the fairies.

He shoots the figure in the chair.

An' then o' course they was me. I just wantedta, yeah, forget. I just wanted to become a person . . .

Scene Four

Simultaneous with the special lighting effects, our return from flashback to present time, brass bands in the distance — they increase in volume through the following at they approach and pass by outside — and, closer at hand, a car pulling up outside. MIKE has come hurrying in.

MIKE. They're back, Boss!

EDDIE. (*continues in a daze*). Yeh, sorry, kid-priest, but (*I*) knew I'd hafta (*kill*) someone.

MIKE. Whatcha do, Boss?

> NO.1 *and* VIC *come hurrying in.* NO.1, *seeing that the figure in the chair is shot, is comparatively relieved.*

NO.1. Ah! You had us worried.

MIKE. Boss?

NO.1. (*to the dazed* EDDIE). Get a grip on yourself, O'Hara, the job is unfinished — (*To* VIC.) Give him the car-keys. (*Meaning give them to* MIKE.)

MIKE. Boss, whatcha want me to do?

NO.1. Get our car to the yard, then . . .

> VIC *has been eyeing the figure in the chair suspiciously, now delicately drawing back the tablecloth covering, removing the hood, revealing the figure to be* NO. 13, *the* COUNTESS. *The back of* NO.1'*s hand/fist into* EDDIE'*s face.* VIC, *following the example, a cosh — a length of wavin-piping from his pocket — beating* EDDIE *to the floor with it.*

MIKE. (*astonished to see* EDDIE *thus treated.*) Boss!

> 'St Patrick's Day', 'It's a great day for the Irish', etc: The brass bands are beginning to blare past ouside. MIKE lets out a bellow — its volume, as with the following, is drowned by the bands — objects in his way knocked aside, including NO.1, as he goes for VIC. VIC's cosh is useless against MIKE and he retreats, terrified. He draws his gun.

VIC. Yous keep back! . . . Keep back, d'yiz hear? . . . Yous keep
   away from me! . . . Keep —

   VIC shoots, hitting MIKE.
   MIKE stops and looks astonished at the bloodstain appearing on
   his new coat.

MIKE. My coat! (*And continues his pursuit of* VIC.)

   DANNY *is coming in from rear of premises, drawing his gun*
   coming into office, but NO.1, *with her gun, is behind him and*
   takes DANNY's *gun.*

NO.1. I'll take that, Mr Mountjoy.

VIC. (*has shot* MIKE *a second time and, now, a third*). Keep back,
   keep back, d'yiz hear!

   EDDIE *stunned on the floor, comes to for a moment to call*
   weakly, groggily —

EDDIE. Do as he says, Mike! —

   And faints off again. But he could be feigning the faint,
   collapsing with an arm outstretched towards the gun which he
   dropped earlier, presently just out of reach of his hand. MIKE *is*
   beyond the stage of hearing EDDIE's *call or anybody's call and*
   continues his stumbling pursuit, taking three more bullets from
   VIC; VIC *now throwing the gun at* MIKE, (*breaking a chair*
   over him?). VIC *is huddled, helpless, in a corner.*

   But now, MIKE, *blind as well as being beyond hearing, has*
   stumbled up to NO.1, *his hands on* NO.1's *lapels.* NO.1 *shoots*
   and the giant, heroic MIKE *goes down at last.*

   EDDIE, *meanwhile, has taken the opportunity to retrieve his gun*
   and, while still pretending to be in a stupor, is concealing it.

   DANNY, *taking the same opportunity, has retreated out of the*
   office. And, a moment later, VIC, *availing himself of the same*
   chance, bolts for it. But, out of the office, he can only take to the
   stairs, (DANNY *being in his way if he wanted to get out the*
   front door).

But meanwhile, ROSCOMMON, with PETE a few steps behind her, is coming down the stairs. VIC grabs her, holds her hostage, using her as a shield, a knife to her throat.

DANNY moves to resuce ROSCOMMON.

VIC. One step more an' she gets it.

The same warning in dumb show to PETE who is above him. PETE's hands are in the air, demonstrating his willingness to comply with VIC's instructions, his ineffectiveness and timidity, that he just wants to get out of it, inching down the stairs, sliding past VIC and hostage-ROSCOMMON, then to scurry for it, but not out the front door but off to bar/kitchen area. At PETE's sudden burst of activity – his scurrying – VIC loses his nerve, thrusts ROSCOMMON down the stairs at DANNY and runs for it – upstairs.

DANNY sets ROSCOMMON aside –

DANNY. Phone the police! –

Before pursuing VIC.

ROSCOMMON retreats in a petrified way, only half-comprehending DANNY's command, then stands there, transfixed in fear and concern.

Meanwhile, in the office, NO.1 has been searching EDDIE's desk (for EDDIE's 'Insurance Policy'). NO.1 now leaving down her gun to search a drawer more thoroughly.

EDDIE is now sitting up, holding his gun, and holding up an envelope which he produces from his pocket –

EDDIE. This what you're lookin' for, *Mister* Sackville?

EDDIE fires – but with a none too steady hand – and misses and, before he can aim again, NO.1 shoots EDDIE. EDDIE's gun goes off in the air. Now NO.1 is taking the envelope out of EDDIE's hand.

Meanwhile, DANNY has caught up with VIC in the club because he and VIC come tumbling from the club on to the landing. VIC has the advantage: he's armed with the knife and he's desperate.

Meanwhile, PETE has returned: he is (perhaps) behind the bar counter, has produced a walkie-talkie from the bag he entered with and is speaking calmly but earnestly into it. In a moment, done with the walkie-talkie, he will produce a gun – more sophisticated-looking than the one he gave to EDDIE earlier – with a silencer attached (or he fits one to it) from the bag.

The loud music of the brass bands – now passed by – is receding. (We can hear the dialogue again.) NO.1 is coming out of the office. DANNY, engaged in the life-and-death struggle with VIC on the landing, appears to be at NO.1's mercy.

NO.1. Mr Mountjoy!

PETE. Over here, Sackville!

PETE shoots, getting NO.1 in the head. NO.1's broad-brimmed hat falls off as she collapses and dies with a venomous death-rattle –

NO.1. England . . . is beaten!

ROSCOMMON now remembers herself and takes up the phone. PETE restrains her.

ROSCOMMON. Danny said to call the cops.

PETE shoots again, this time at the landing – a questionable rather than a daring shot because he could hit either man up there – and VIC is hit and (preferably over the bannister rails) falls to his death.

PETE. The cops is here, sweetheart. (*Flashing his badge.*)

ROSCOMMON. Special Branch Agent, Tom O' –

Two men have come in, in overcoats, one from the rear of the premises, one through the front door. They could be anyone but they are, in fact, Special Branch men, MULLARKY and O'MALLEY. They look frightening to ROSCOMMON and she retreats from them, to the office. PETE finds car-keys on VIC's body and tosses them to MULLARKY.

PETE. There's a car on a double-yellow out front, get it out of there. This one's for us, we don't want the boys in blue in on it.

MULLARKY *goes out.*
DANNY *coming down the stairs.*

(*Perfunctorily to* DANNY.) Wait in there.

O'MALLEY. (*seeing that* NO.1 *is a woman*). I'll be hung for a witch!

PETE *and* O'MALLEY *commence a thorough search of* NO.1's *and* VIC's *bodies.*
DANNY, *obeying* PETE, *has come into the office.*
ROSCOMMON *is crying: she has discovered the dying* EDDIE *and is cradling his head in her lap.*

ROSCOMMON. Oh Eddie.

DANNY *checks* EDDIE's *pulse: there appears to be no hope: he lights a cigarette and puts it between* EDDIE's *lips.*

EDDIE. Can't hear the music, can't hear Pete so good.

ROSCOMMON. Oh Eddie.

EDDIE. Play, Pete, play 'Macushla'.

DANNY. You're alright, head, we're with yiz.

EDDIE. Who threw (*the*) biggest parties at the Shelbourne?

ROSCOMMON. You did, Eddie.

EDDIE. Why-why'd they shoot me?

DANNY. Take it easy, head.

EDDIE. Oh yeah, now I remember. 'S all a ball, canine cannibal do. (*To* ROSCOMMON.) Don't let people see yeh cryin' – John. (*Laughs, sing-songing.*) 'Goodbye Murteen Durkin . . . sick'n'tired o' . . . (*It turns into a bout of coughing.*)

DANNY. Easy, head.

ROSCOMMON. Oh Eddie.

EDDIE. My pocket, Kid, my pocket!

DANNY. (*finds the crucifix and chain in* EDDIE's *pocket*). This what yiz want, Eddie?

EDDIE. Pray for me, Baby, pray for me, Kid.

ROSCOMMON. You have to pray too, Eddie.

EDDIE. (*clutching crucifix*). Oh God, don't let me die, I got a few more parties to throw.

And he's dead.
PETE *and* O'MALLEY *have found the envelope and – trumps! – the little black book on* NO.1's *body.* MULLARKY *has returned. They come into the office.* PETE *nods to* MULLARKY *and* O'MALLEY *to search the office and* EDDIE's *body.*

O'MALLEY. (*to* DANNY *and* ROSCOMMON). Okay, we'll take care of him (EDDIE.) now.

PETE. (*speaking dispassionately and as if to no one in particular*). Okay. Roscommon knows the score. She's been around, an' how. No one's lookin' for headlines on this one. She understands that. (?)

Slight inflexion on the last: she can go if she agrees to what he has said. She bows her acquiescence, she will remain silent.

So she can clean up and go.

She leaves. DANNY, *too, would like to leave but there is something about* PETE's *manner which tells him he is not allowed to do so.* PETE *has opened the envelope which he found on* NO.1.

. . . O'Hara's life insurance policy to his broker. Useless things, life insurance, these days. (*Now looks to* DANNY.) Yeh wanted the cops, yeh got special ones: Depending, I'll maybe take that into account. Yeh just got out today, I don't know if yeh want back in. Yeh got the message I gave Roscommon, I don't know if yeh got her eloquent reply to all my meaning. So, tell us, what's your interest in this place?

DANNY. I just dropped in for a drink.

PETE. The place is shut. But yeh can use the toilet to wash your hands, then on your way.

DANNY *leaves*.

O'MALLEY. Nice one, Tommo. But how'd yeh figure O'Hara for the Anderson Ryan Bank job in the first place?

PETE. That didn't appear like a political job to me or the chief. Then I noticed a few guys round town spendin' free an' payin' off bad debts. O'Hara was one of them. It was only a hunch but I decided to play it an' anonymously fingered O'Hara to the Erin Go Braths. If the hunch paid off I knew they'd muscle-in here. They did, an' I had the place observed an' bugged an' could monitor every move they made from here.

O'MALLEY. But what if O'Hara *hadn't* done that bank job?

PETE. So what? O'Hara was born to lose.

*He has the little black book in his hand and is dialling a number. (*PETE, MULLARKY *and* O'MALLEY *are reminiscent of* NO.1, VIC, *and* NO.2 *in Scene Two*.)

(*On the phone*.) I'd like to speak to the Minister. Sure, he's not at home, he's at dinner, he's tired-out after the parade, but tell him it's O'Bannion an' I've found the shoppin' list.

He holds on, flicking through the little black book. Then talking to the Minister.

Sir . . . Yeh . . . The crazy Englishwoman, the one they called the Countess an' the little joker, Camden . . . The patsy too, O'Hara . . . *They* got the defector . . . No, he's okay: Mullarky intercepted him in the yard: *very* idealistic I'd say: foreign missions'd appreciate a guy like him . . . I've got it right in front of me. Names, dates, creditors an' debtors. Donations received, favours expected . . . Abroad? Yeh . . . An' the congressman an' his crew. CIA guy an' some stuff about NATO . . . At home? Yeh, he's here . . . The developer too. Very generous man . . . Army? The Commmandant . . . Coupla showbiz stars . . . An' the businessman from his constituency . . . (*Tears a page out of the book*.) No, sir, your name's not here. (*Sets fire to the page*.) Everyone's already been told, right, to be contained: Just another

piece of St Patrick's Day fireworks . . . Me? Your place? I'd be –
thank you, sir – I'd be glad to.

*Puts the phone down and lights a cigarette with the last flickers
of the page.*

Scene Five

ROSCOMMON *is standing outside The Blue Macushla: Topcoat,
hat, suitcase beside her, car keys in her hand.* DANNY, *cleaned up,
comes out of the club, carrying the suitcase he arrived with. He
sees her and approaches her.*

DANNY. Where yiz goin'?

ROSCOMMON. Dunno.

DANNY. Will yiz give us a lift?

ROSCOMMON. Where to?

He looks up and down.

We have no place to go.

DANNY. Let's go there.